Ernest Seyd

The Bank of England note issue and its error

An address to the holders of Bank of England stock

Ernest Seyd

The Bank of England note issue and its error
An address to the holders of Bank of England stock

ISBN/EAN: 9783337123987

Printed in Europe, USA, Canada, Australia, Japan

Cover: Foto ©Suzi / pixelio.de

More available books at **www.hansebooks.com**

Monsieur L. Wolowski.

With the Author's Compliments,

THE

BANK OF ENGLAND

NOTE ISSUE

AND

ITS ERROR.

AN ADDRESS TO THE HOLDERS OF BANK OF ENGLAND STOCK, AND TO
BANKERS AND ECONOMISTS GENERALLY.

BY ERNEST SEYD, F.S.S.,

AUTHOR OF "BULLION AND FOREIGN EXCHANGES," "THE LONDON BANKING AND CLEARING HOUSE SYSTEM,"
&c., &c.

CASSELL, PETTER & GALPIN,
LONDON, PARIS, AND NEW YORK.
1874.

LONDON:
W. W. MORGAN, PRINTER,
67, BARBICAN, CITY.

PREFACE.

NEXT to the painful task of writing a book on the Controversy of the Bank of England, comes the task of reading it. This is one of the difficulties of which the swarm of authors seem aware, who, ever since 1844, have inundated us with hundreds of short pamphlets and press articles, forming, in the aggregate, a mass of literature of the most extraordinary kind. The differences of opinions expressed in these short, firm-toned, and authoritative pamphlets, range from "unlimited right of issue of Bank-notes, to be given, not only to all Banks and merchants, but to everybody," to the total abolition of all Bank-notes, "including those of the Bank of England." Within these extremes come classes of opinions advocating the issue of notes by Banks and Bankers only, some without, others with restrictions, and requirements of capital—"say, one million cash "—are laid down, which shall entitle a Bank or Banker to issue notes. Occasionally the proposal is made : "let Banks and Bankers issue notes only in times of crises and panics." Others boldly recommend the American Bank-note system. More reasonable authors seek to reform the Bank of England system itself, and call for an extension of its issue, or advocate the issue of a kind of Exchequer Bill to help us over a " crisis." In each of the many sub-divisions of opinions on the Bank of England system there are again many dissentients on points of detail, which happen to turn uppermost for the moment. The whole mass of suggestions, not to speak of the heavy parliamentary blue-books on Royal Commissions Enquiries, has hitherto had no result—it leaves us as we were. The want of success of all these pamphleteers is due, perhaps, to the fact that they make their pamphlets too short and concise, not so much for the sake of the reader, but because the authors themselves are unable to grasp the subject in all its bearings.

By one who has closely followed all this,—from the insufficient declarations of Adam Smith to the dogmas of later economists, from the history of John Law to that of Mr. Lowe's proposal for reform in 1873 ; from the occasional attempts of publications, akin to the *Family Herald*, to that of the daily and weekly articles of the leading modern press,— all these unlucky endeavours are easily understood. *The cause of their failure lies in their one-sidedness.* In the first place, the majority appears to have regard only to one thing, *more Bank-notes !* The minority recognises that the mere printing of Bank-notes does not solve the problem, and it endeavours to deal more reasonably with what may be called the *elements* of monetary science, or the factors to which regard must be had in a system of Bank-note issue. In their turn the writers of the latter class make this great mistake : in the inventions which they submit to the public they fix their minds upon one principal factor, and manipulate it so as to suit one of the others ; when, having done so, they are contented. They entirely ignore, or are not aware of the fact, that there are a number of factors to be considered, that each of them has its characteristics and variations, and that, whereas they have only fitted one to the variations of the next, there is a third, a fourth, and fifth, each with its variations, which must all be fitted into the system. Thus, as far as our own note issue is concerned, an author succeeds in providing a scheme between issue and circulation, forgetting however that bullion, the rate of interest and reserve, are all in mutual relationship. He may even succeed in hinting at a combination between two factors and a third, but when the fourth and fifth are to be considered, the problem becomes confused. He concludes with some emphatic declaration, or quotes somebody else's opinion (dating from last century perhaps), and feels confident that his suggestions are valuable. So much for the short authoritative pamphlets, which, in the aggregate, make up a respectable library.

In writing this longer book, in which I, on my part, shall endeavour to lay before you certain facts in fair order, and point out the factors involved, I am fully aware that I am open to the charge of writing at too much length.

This charge will be increased when I mention to you that I have already written another book on the subject, to which allusion is made in this publication. I must bow to the reproach, but as my intention is that of instructing persons not thoroughly familiar with all the features of the case, I have not only written at greater length than would suit a practised economist, but I have purposely, when I thought proper, repeated matters for the sake of enabling the inexperienced reader to maintain the string of facts.

Ostensibly, this publication is addressed to the Stockholders of the Bank of England, and my respect for them and the Directors of the Bank induce me here to make the following declaration : In trying to point out the error in the present note issue system of the Bank, I am necessarily obliged to show certain matters in the criticism of which I attack the "admirers" of the present Act. It might, therefore, be imagined that I attack or speak disparagingly of the Directors. *Nothing is farther from my intention;* but the controversy requires that the critic should occupy an opposing point of view. Any man of candour, who professes fully to understand the nature of the issue, rather than blame the Directors, must, on the contrary, recognise that they have done well with the difficulty before them. The more he enters into the conception of the error, and its palpable serious consequences, the more he must admit that the nation should be grateful to the set of men who have thus far so well succeeded in counteracting a persistently ruinous system. Very few are able to understand this, for the confusion and helplessness into which the subject under discussion has fallen are so great, and the demoralisation of intelligence on this subject has gone so far, that there are actually persons who lay the whole blame on the shoulders of the Directors, and say, "the Bank is mismanaged." In a mercantile community like ours,—so rich and prosperous,— at the head of which stand the Directors of the Bank of England, chosen from the highest ranks of commerce, such a charge of personal failing in intelligence is an absurd one, and must be repudiated with indignation. The Directors of the Bank must guide the operations of the institution, in accordance with the Act of 1844, the law itself, and they have responded to its requirements as far as it was possible for them to do. For the error in this Act they are less responsible than the statesmen and the host of economists who framed and uphold it. They cannot undo the law, on the contrary, it is their province, not only from right, but from dictates of prudence, to be conservative—rather to maintain that to which they are accustomed and have shaped their practice, until they feel themselves on fairly safe ground—than listen to other schemes which may necessitate a total reversal of action in so precarious a problem as that here to be discussed. All the fearful sacrifices which are made on behalf of this just policy, as I shall demonstrate them to you, are, after all, to be preferred to any of the wild schemes started by amateurs. The question here is: What is the Act of 1844 itself; what is the experience made under it, has it worked with ease and satisfaction, or with difficulties and mischief—is it indeed so constructed that human intelligence can deal with it without gigantic efforts?

I hope to be able to show you that the Act of 1844 contains a practical error which baffles all efforts at proper management, and extends its disorganising influences far beyond the range of our own national interests. I may also succeed in showing you that the remedy is in the Act itself, and that a slight alteration in one of its minor clauses will set aside the error; leaving the Act in full force in other respects. It might be supposed that if the alteration is so slight, a few lines would suffice to explain it. But if you read through *Part I. of this book*, which deals with the anomalies caused by the error, you will find that its core could not be laid bare until the overlying masses of evil effects were removed first, when, in *Part II. of the Book* the remedy and a better system of adjustment can be laid before you for your consideration.

CONTENTS.

(N.B.—A perusal of this abstract of contents will enable the reader to obtain an idea of the plan and general tenor of this Book. The reader who is already acquainted with the controversy may pass over certain matters, and fix his attention on what may seem noteworthy to him.)

PART I.

The Want of Progress of the Bank of England.—Wealth must increase as if by a natural law —— The test of figures can be applied —— England's wealth, "local" and "international" —— England's decided supremacy in international wealth —— The manifest universal increase in all directions —— Import and export trade increased fourfold —— The only exception in this universal increase is the Bank of England —— The Bank of England must not be wantonly abused —— But there are facts bearing upon a long-standing controversy —— Concerning plain practical matters —— State of the controversy as regards the Bank —— Vain attempts at reform —— Natural conservative tendency of the Directors —— Baneful influence of dogmas of bygone times —— Dogmatic wisdom versus figures and facts —— The most fatal of the dogmas concerns "speculation" —— The Bank is unable to keep itself free from its effects —— That is plain proof of either its participation or its weakness —— A fault in the nucleus of a system repeats itself many thousandfold —— The mere appeal to strength of capital does not solve a problem —— Patriotic declamation cannot override figures —— These figures show that the Bank of England is not in accord with prosperity generally —— The interests of the stock-holders in this matter as regards dividends —— The author will suggest nothing wild and speculative, and reasonable suggestions ought to receive attention   ·   Pages 1 to 8

Comparative Figures.—*Table 1.—Note circulation—Deposits—Bankers' balances—Bills discounted, &c.—Exports and imports—Deposits of four joint stock banks—*Page 10 —— The whole increase not equal even to the single item of increase of population —— No increase from 1844 to 1866 —— Increase since 1866 owing to Bankers' balances —— Deposits actually declined —— False reasonings must be set aside first — - The allegation that commerce has increased at the expense of the Bank is quixotic —— The plea of conservatism cannot be stretched to the excess of which the figures given are evidence —— This kind of rough treatment of the question is not worthy of economical truths —— The rapid growth of other banks proves the very fact that the Bank has missed its opportunities —— The deposits at the Bank ought to have increased with general increase, independently of the question of allowing interest for them —— *Table 2.—Showing the increase, in the business of the Bank of France at the end of February each year—*Page 15 —— The "public" duties of the Bank are quite separate from its own rights as a Bank —— The progress of the clearing system has the tendency of increasing deposits —— Systems akin to clearing are in operation in France and Germany —— The insufficient increase of bullion as the real metallic Reserve —— Not in accord with our increased commerce; still less with the discovery of the Californian and Australian gold fields —— More gold ought to have accumulated at the Bank of England   ·   ·   ·   ·   ·   Pages 9 to 19

The Dividend of the Bank of England.—The dividend of the Bank of England cannot be called satisfactory —— The Bank's capital is very large, but the Bank has enormous privileges —— It holds its deposits free of interest —— It has the extra issue of fifteen millions of Notes —— Its investments exceed the deposits —— It keeps the State accounts, &c. —— *Showing the proportions here arising at the Bank ; and London and Westminster Bank* —— Another method of comparing results —— The London and Westminster Bank makes four times the profit —— Making due allowance for the difference of position between the Banks in question —— It is nevertheless not unreasonable to suggest that the Bank of England ought to have paid higher dividends —— If only by 2 or 3 per cent —— All the world has profited, excepting the holders of Bank Stock

Pages 19 to 23

The Discount Business of the Bank of England.—The great business of this country is conducted chiefly by bills of exchange —— These instruments of exchange are the staple of banking —— They amount to 1,200 millions sterling per annum —— Of which 300 to 350 millions are current at a time —— The Bank of England might be supposed to be the principal holder of such bills —— In some proportion at least to its resources —— But, in reality, the Bank holds but a comparatively insignificant amount of bills—Frequently below 3 millions —— *Table 3.—The Bills under discount at the Bank of England from 1845 to 1872*—Page 27 —— The temporary advances average 2 millions —— The total average of bills discounted is 6 millions only —— The general public and economists are not aware of this extraordinary matter —— The Bank appears to do a profitable discount business only when crises and panics set in —— Commerce has a higher right of enquiry into these facts —— The Bank of England is bound to invest in Government securities —— But not to the overwhelming disadvantage of bills —— Government securities require fresh contracts for their conversion —— Bills of exchange are the ultimate creators of currency —— Bills of exchange are continuous contracts already in existence —— Issues of Bank notes on credit are chiefly made for the support of active commerce —— Other central Banks have a much greater share in commerce —— *Footnote. —The account of the Bank of Prussia*—Page 32 —— The matter involves even the question of morality —— No dogmatic and pompous statement can go against the facts here shown —— The conflict requires the earnest consideration of all economists —— The undecided action of the Bank as regards advances to discount brokers —— The method in which brokers profit from advances of this kind —— In spite of the long practice, no definite policy has been established, such as our valuation requires —— The Bank stands between two sides, each of which has legitimate claims

Pages 23 to 37

Where is the Error ?—These remarkable accounts presuppose the existence of a subtle disturbing error of system in either the Issue or the Banking Department —— The error cannot be in the Banking Department —— although the operation of that Department may be seriously hampered by a subtle and hidden fault in a system with which it is connected —— The violent fluctuations of the Bank's Reserve and Bullion are not due to the Bank's investments —— The losses on investments are insignificant —— Nor the withdrawal of deposits, for these increase rather than diminish —— The question of fresh advances is independent of this matter —— The fault lies solely in the system of the Issue Department —— The enigma involved in the present seemingly so perfect arrangement —— Its evident conflict nevertheless with facts —— The remedy is possibly hidden by a misconception, engendered in the practice of the system

Pages 37 to 42

The Present State of the Controversy.—The absurd schemes being dismissed —— The party divisions on the Bank of England issue remain —— The only practical party is that which seeks reform *inside* the present system —— The subdivisions of this party —— There are five leading opinions in the controversy —— Class 1 is impracticable and impossible —— Class 2 admits of no reform —— Class 4 has an uncouth ground —— Class 3 now rules the situation —— The main characteristic of this proposal is "extension" only —— Whereas both contraction and extension are required —— The primary cause of the evil is the surplus created by the 15 millions —— The supposed strength of large note reserves is in reality the weakness of the system —— The idea of caution involved in the 15 millions fixed issue is fallacious —— Other causes are independent of this matter —— The plethora remains in force —— The excess drives bullion from us —— The scales must fall from the eyes of the authorities —— Mr. Fowler's proposals involves the immeasurable ruin of our valuation —— The compensating system alone will satisfactorily solve the problem —— The "concentrated" point of the controversy —— Increase of issue only —— *versus* —— Decrease and increase of issue —— The alteration of a clause of the Act is only required —— Clause 2 of the present Act already contains the spirit of the reform —— The succeeding portions of the pamphlet enter into closer detail.

Pages 42 to 50

The Origin and the Main Principle of the Act of 1844.

—The "mixed" basis of all good bank note issues —— The term "fiduciary" portion of a bank note issue —— The disastrous experiments with over issue of fiduciary bank notes —— The crude ideas prevailing even to this day —— The stockholders of the Bank of England are concerned only in the issue as practised by the Bank of England —— The old Bank of England Act. —— The Act of 1844 —— Its cardinal principle of limit —— The Government debt and securities for the fiduciary issue —— Separation into Issue and Banking Department —— All issue above 15 millions to be made against bullion —— The real and the deceptive merits of this method of issue —— The convertibility of the note —— Convertibility must be secured first of all —— The security of the State and "other" securities held against the 15 millions fiduciary issue —— The same security will be given in the scheme of the author —— The separation of the Issue from the Banking Department —— The same system of separation will be maintained by the author's scheme —— A discussion on the points enumerated is not necessary. The "real" point will appear all the more readily —— The main point to be considered, viz., the 15 millions fixed issue —— The supposed merit of the limit of 15 millions fixed issue —— The great charm involved in the limit —— Its apparent principle of caution and prudence —— The extent of its liberality —— Its want of pliability ·   ·   Pages 50 to 59

The Demerits of the Fixed Limit of 15 Millions.

—The origin of the amount of 15 millions —— The fallacy of the average in matters of this kind —— The variations have since been most excessive —— *Table 4.—Returns showing the amount of total circulation of Bank of England notes, with the amount of bullion held during the years 1834 to 1843, two in each year; and the years 1845 to 1871, four in each year; (at the respective periods mentioned before) and the consequent fiduciary circulation, and the Reserves of notes.—* Pages 62-3 —— The previous average relied upon has been totally destroyed —— A lamentable picture of confusion of results has followed —— The higher state of the bullion average is due to our enhanced trade —— The Bank itself has been unable to increase the stock of bullion proportionately —— But it has kept large idle Reserves of notes.

Pages 59 to 66

The Demerits of the Reserve arising from the Fixed Issue.

—The great misconception involved in the Reserve so arising —— A regular steady Reserve must be kept —— The question here concerns only the Reserve arising under the present system —— That Reserve drives away bullion —— Every million of more note issue keeps away a million of bullion —— The Reserve is useless for all practical purposes —— The manifold mysteries of the money market afford one or two simple main points —— To what are due the enormous divergencies in the rate of interest? —— They are not due to the numerical increase of circulation or actual use of more money —— The amount of money used remains the same, the rate of interest being in question only —— The only causes are the extreme variations in the stock of bullion which the Bank fails in preventing —— The task and the instrumental power to perform it —— The rate of interest is the automaton and unfailing power —— The Bank is absolutely free in exercising this power

—— As any regulating force can be exercised with due watchfulness —— The lamentable failure of the Bank in this respect —— The Bank is too late in raising the rate, and too quick in lowering it; and cannot even keep a margin for unknown contingencies —— The idle and useless reserve of notes are the sole cause of the impossibility to keep interest at proper levels —— Example showing how the present system works —— The Bank of England poises the rate in accordance with the amount of actual note Reserve —— The diminution or increase of fiduciary issue in lieu of the fixed amount —— Will regulate the rate of interest, and consequently regulate the stock of bullion —— The plainest intelligence can discern the rights of this matter —— The post facto action of the present system —— The voluntary of reduction the fiduciary issue would have the effect of retaining bullion in its stead —— This rule applies to all conditions and states of the market —— The almost ludicrous consequences of this Reserve of notes —— So long as this fallacy as to fixed fiduciary issue exists, a settlement is impossible, and all our policy is false —— The principle of reduction must have precedence over increase of issue —— *Memorial addressed to the Directors of the Bank of England* —— Substantial facts are given in the following portions of this Book .   .   .   .   **Pages 66 to 79**

The Effect of the 15 Millions of Fixed Issue on Bullion and the International Exchanges.—The laws of international exchange as connected with rates of interest must be appreciated —— False allegations as to the causes of withdrawals of bullion —— The world does not come to the Bank of England for gold —— Our bullion market is open to the Bank of England as well as other Banks —— Other nations are important traders and dealers in Bullion, as the foot note shows —— *Footnote.* —*Table 5.—Imports and exports of bullion and coin of England, from 1850 to 1872 inclusive.*—Page 81.—*Table 6.—Imports and exports of bullion and coin of France, from 1850 to 1872 inclusive.*—Page 83.—*Table 7.—Gold exports and imports between England and France.* —Page 84 —— The suggestion that foreigners prey upon our gold coinage is utterly false and contemptible —— The great international movements of bullion rest upon the purest basis of arithmetical truths —— The balance of trade determines the rates of exchange —— Arbitrations of exchanges precede shipments of bullion —— Their refinement and delicacy at the present day —— The action of the rate of interest in regard to exchanges —— The regular and legitimate action of true rates of interest —— The influence of undue rates of interest —— The absolute force of the established rate —— The insidious nature of an unduly low rate of interest —— The export of bullion in defiance of the balance of trade —— The consequent necessity for sudden and extreme rises in our rate —— The extreme efforts required for balancing fluctuations caused by extremes —— The moderate efforts required for the maintenance of a *status quo* —— The breaks in the chain of progress in bullion and note issue .   .   .   .   **Pages 79 to 91**

The International Rate of Interest, the Market Rate, and the Bank Rate.—Variations in the international value of money —— Instancing the supply of precious metals since 1848 —— The effect on increased production —— The counter effect of increased production —— The changes in the valuation —— The variations in the international rate of interest are gradual —— The want of accord between the international rates and the Bank of England rates —— The annexed table shows the result —— *Table 8.—Showing the variations in the Bank rates of interest in England, France, and Prussia, from September 1844 to December 1873 inclusive*—Page 94. —— The continental bank's protecting action is more efficient —— The key-note for the reform of our system indicated by this table —— *Table 9.—Showing the number of changes in the rates of interest, and the number of weeks during which the rates lasted, of the Banks of England, France, and Prussia, from 1st September 1844 to 31st December 1873*—Page 98 —— The Bank of England ought to be able to keep bullion with lesser efforts than foreign banks —— The reverse being the case, a false principle must be reversed —— The conflict here concerns bullion only as subject to international competition or guardianship by rates of interest —— The wretched result as far as England is concerned —— The consequences fall chiefly on our own industry and commerce —— The losses occurred on behalf of the recovery of bullion exceed the amount forced back —— The angry confusion and just complaints to which this gives rise —— The unhealthy and untrue expedients proposed —— The London exchange market has become powerless through its want of true rates of interest —— All reciprocity ceases in this case . . . . . . **Pages 91 to 106**

The General Circulation and that of the Bank of England Note.—

The question of the use of money by the home trade of the country —— The false impression that the demands of trade cause scarcity of money —— The comparative regularity of the home circulation —— The gross amount of money in the country —— Partly in circulation, partly in Reserve —— Characteristics of the constituents —— Firmness of the gold coin in circulation —— A sudden addition to the circulation cannot take place —— The subtraction of gold coin from circulation is resisted —— A general gradual increase has taken place —— Silver and copper coin —— Country bankers' issues —— The Bank of England note circulation; is the supernatant constituent of the general circulation —— The variations in the total circulation concentrate in the Issue Department of the Bank of England —— Table 10.—*Showing the extreme variations of the Bank of England Note Circulation in each Quarter (from 1st January) of the years 1845 to 1871 (in millions £ sterling)*—Page 113. —— The regularity of the circulation of Bank notes within three or four millions —— In spite of all movements, failures, crises, and panics, the public does not away with money, or uses too much of it —— On the contrary, it keeps what there is, and steadfastly resists all attempts at inflation —— Through the continual offer of the Bank's Reserve of idle notes —— The paramount importance of this fact —— The inexorable firmness of the circulation —— There is practically no scarcity of money, nor use for any surplus —— The lessons to be derived from this fact —— The misuse of the term "elasticity." It concerns gradual increase only —— The freedom of supply of gold and development of the demand —— In accordance with the principles of international valuation —— The absurdity of schemes for indefinite or definite supplies of Bank notes —— They would destroy the true elastic force of our currency —— The same spirit at work in all such schemes, ignorant of and incapable of citing facts —— A current fallacy as regards the distress for money —— Its untruth and the real truth —— The real cause of panic —— The true causes of the restoration from a panic . . . **Pages 106 to 120**

The Availability of the Reserve of the Bank of England.—

The difficulty of discussion as to Reserve —— The abolition of the present Reserve —— The substitution of a better system, explained in Part II —— The connection between circulation and Reserve —— The clear definition of the purposes of Reserve —— The reasonable considerations by which the use of the Reserve can be measured —— The requirements of the Bank of England —— The use of the Reserve for the accommodation of the public —— Is comprised in and identical with the circulation —— The importance of this fact and its confirmation by the most severe tests —— The public refuses altogether to make use of the surplus of fiduciary issue —— The Reserve of the Bank against withdrawals of deposits —— The right of inquiry into this matter by a reasonable method —— The capital and rest of the Bank offer overwhelming security —— Gradual withdrawals of deposits are met by realisation of securities —— Sudden withdrawals of deposits —— The capricious and unbusinesslike nature of the supposition —— What would be its effects? —— It would have no effect on the amount of money required —— The final suggestion of general bankruptcy —— Such an event would lead to a plethora in the already existing supply —— The remarkable fact of the increase of deposits in times of pressure —— Demonstrating the real strength of the depositors —— The extreme irregularity of the Reserve shows its failure —— The supposed purpose of the Reserve to replace withdrawals of bullion —— Its seemingly natural application —— Its real mischievous action is the cause of all the difficulties —— To demonstrate this is the object of this Book . . . . **Pages 120 to 129**

False Suggestions Founded on Reserve.—The remarks made before establish the reliability of the factor circulation —— False suggestions as regards Reserve —— False method of estimating Bankers' liabilities against cash Reserve —— Without reference to circulation —— The real state of the case of Bankers' Reserves —— Concerns the character of the investment made —— Failures and want of confidence result in matters of account only —— They do not destroy currency —— No legislation can stop errors of judgment in banking —— Reliance on express Reserves increases liability to commission of greater errors —— The supposed insecurity of contracts should be traced to its real original source —— The term "Banking Reserve" —— Attempts to connect Liability and Reserve —— The purposeless nature of these estimates —— The wide differences in the Bank's Reserve —— *Table 11.—Showing the highest and lowest per centage of Reserve (including Coin) to Liabilities (including 7 days' Bills) of the Bank of England for each rate of interest—Page 135.* —— The impossibility of finding a guiding principle in such proportions —— Example of the guess method, by Professor B. Price —— The vagueness of these guesses —— The attempt to lump all in one factorship —— The hotch-potch resulting therefrom —— The final refuge in mere assertion —— The ignoring of the first requirements as to bullion —— The clear result when this requirement is provided for . . . . **Pages 130 to 138**

The Destruction of Bankers' and Others' Solid Cash Reserves by the present Bank of England Reserve.—The real destroyer of all Reserve —— By using up her own and other people's Reserves —— The alleged insufficiency of Bankers' balances at the Bank of England —— Irrespective of the amounts prescribable —— The Bank's action in reference to these Reserves concerns us here —— *Example of ordinary good account* —— *Analysed account* —— Supposed safe position —— Departure of bullion and utter disappearance of Issue, Bankers' Reserve and deposits in the vortex —— The absolute Nothing and Minus —— *Example of crisis and no Reserve* —— *Bankers' Reserves 8½ millions, Bank's Reserve ½ million* —— The sudden increase in the Bank securities —— The erroneous current explanation of this fact —— The Bank of England loses Bullion and Reserves —— Replacing them by using up Deposits and Bankers' Reserves —— The danger to the Deposits —— The injustice of economical principles, explaining the Bank's nervousness and slow progress —— Imagine a per centage of the Deposits withdrawn —— The Bank of England is liable to the charge of over investment —— At other occasions than crises, the Bank encroaches upon the Bankers' Reserves —— *Table 12. Showing the Reserves of Notes at the Bank, selected from each half-year, with Bankers' balances as included therein, and consequent Bank Reserve without them —— Showing the frequent minus and variability of the Bank's Reserve—Page 146.* —— The heavy spasmodic profits made by the Bank —— The harvest of the Bank when it has caused crisis and panic —— Contrary to fair business ideas —— Denial that this is the unavoidable consequence of circumstances —— Examples of contrary action —— Why the Bank is able to do this will be shown in next chapter —— The inherent destructiveness of the present note Reserve illustrated by example —— The fixed issue would annul every attempt to secure a Bullion reserve or a level of Bullion —— The mathematical force of this acts with something like contempt for the sacrifice made · · **Pages 138 to 152**

The Money Market and its Special Phases apart from Bullion Withdrawals at the Bank.—Certain phases in the money market—which appear to be independent of the question of bullion —— What is their nature and influence? —International contracts separated from local contracts —— All international contracts concentrate their results on the stock of bullion in the Bank —— International contracts have no direct influence on the currency of the moment —— Local contracts not affecting the currency —— Loans and discounts —— The current source of supply —— The current demand —— The differences in daily supply and demand constitute the special phases —— The matter must be narrowed to the contracts in direct connection with actual money —— The presumably clear average amount of these movements per

day —— Their actual connection with cash —— Comparative regularity of production
and regular growth —— Degrees of regularity of demand and its gradual increase ——
The retention of currency in our industrial districts a source of satisfaction —— The
consequently longer contracts and smaller average of due dates —— The cause and the
amount of daily divergences —— The legitimate, moderate and beneficial office of
fiduciary issue here made apparent —— The present nervousness of the market —— This
should not be so —— The legitimacy of these phases in the money market —— Their
moderation, and the easy way with which they should be equalised —— The great contrast
of the effects of withdrawals of bullion —— The coincidence between requirements of
this kind and bullion withdrawals —— The misuse of the fiduciary issue for sudden
business at the Bank .   Pages 152 to 163

The Competition between the Bank of England's Note Reserves and the Daily Supply of the Market.

—The general competition
of natural supply with the note Reserve arising from the fixed issue —— Its continual
competition with the sufficient current supply —— The uselessness and unfairness of this
competition —— The submission of the market rate enforced —— The consequent rapid
and extreme decline in the rate of interest —— The market is obliged to be beforehand
with the Bank Reserve —— The "reverse" phase of the market —— The sharp competition in anticipation of practice —— Such practice being well known in the market,
and cannot be departed from —— The impossibility on the part of the Bank to hold a
rate higher than the practice of the present Reserve dictates —— The wantonly destructive
but useless conflict —— These matters cannot answer the purpose of Bankers —— Their
interests demand a reform —— Such reform will only enhance the convenience of the
mechanical arrangements   Pages 164 to 168

The Influence of the Idle Note Reserves on Speculation and Mercantile Morality.

—The dogma regarding speculation —— The tendency to
speculation admitted ; but the sweeping charge must meet with protests —— The morality
of the whole trading community in question —— with the immaculacy of one establishment —— Against this charge the British public can defend itself with sound reasoning
—— The Bank cannot hold its own assets, but uses up the Reserves belonging to others
—— The art of Banking consists of knowing how to guard assets —— The Bank of
England's supposed legitimate influence in controlling speculation —— By its power
to regulate the value of money —— Entirely nullified by practice of the present system
—— On the contrary the present system deliberately encourages speculation —— Until
in the desperate struggle of crises it beats down good and bad business —— The periodical
return of the same events —— Three-fourths of the effects of speculation due to the
system itself —— The show of reasons here apparent —— The unavoidable general effect
of a surplus of money upon commercial doings —— The disappearance by itself of the
surplus of idle note Reserve —— The law of valuation here acts in mercantile matters
by a similar process of arbitration as in exchange of money —— The price of money is
the true contract basis —— The contracts based on money unduly cheap —— The general
commerce based on abnormally cheap money —— The economical law involved in all this
is independent of morality —— The time allowed for the final break down of contracts
on money unduly cheap —— The enhancement of speculation by way of reaction ——
The clear causes and effects —— For the consideration of economists   Pages 168 to 178

The Direct Loss to the Bank on the Issue.

—The validity of the rule of
mutuality —— The supposed double profit on the issue —— No profit on bullion issue ——
The 15 millions of fixed issue are the supposed source of profit —— The expenses of the
issue —— Administrative and technical expenses —— Stamp dues and share of profits to
State —— Account furnished to Parliament —— The variations according to changes in the

fixed amount of issue —— The profit on bullion is apart from this —— *The net profit of the issue department* —— The supposed profit of the 15 millions in the banking department —— The heavy Reserves show that this profit cannot be made —— *Calculation of these profits* —— *Table 13—Total of interest earned by the Bank on the notes in circulation above the amounts of bullion held* —— The profit from both sources leaves a loss of £100,000 per annum —— The interest on securities on the issue is a separate matter —— The question lies between expenses and profits on the 15 millions —— *Table 14—Showing the annual charge on the issue, the annual interest, and consequent profit and loss per annum* —— The large profits only made in years of panic and crisis · · **Pages 179 to 186**

The Falsity of the Supposed Automaton Operation of the Issue and the Unnatural Accumulation of Reserve in the Banking Department.

—The principal allegations made —— The assertion as to the purely automaton character of the issue —— The invocation of the laws of supply and demand —— The formidable character of these pleas—— Apparently backed by the weekly Bank statement —— But nothing can be more false than this method of showing the case —— The lifeless character of the Issue Department —— The Banking Department is the moving force —— The impossibility of transferring the Issue Department to the State —— Without the State becoming also the Banker of the Nation —— Freed of the issue the Bank would require but a moderate regular Reserve —— The Issue Department is carried on at the charge of the Reserves in the Banking Department —— Supposed case of liquidation of deposits —— *Statement showing the effect on the Bank's capital* —— The asset of idle Reserve of notes left —— Showing the great loss to the Bank by the issue —— With any given amount of Reserve —— *The enforced incompetence of the Bank's Capital by the Reserve* —— The ludicrous aspect of this matter —— The reduction of Reserve brings the capital into use **Pages 187 to 194**

The Violation of the Rules of Supply and Demand, and Conclusion of Part I.

—The argument concerning supply and demand —— The undue accumulation of gold coin would be prevented by its international value —— Freedom of factors of supply and demand —— Arbitrary partial limits and characteristics depending on other factors interfere in their agreement —— The supply of notes mixed with the fixed limit of 15 millions —— Other factors require adjustment —— Before the system becomes truly self-acting —— The great error of this is suernust first be recognised —— Resumé of the evidence showing the error —— General reflection on the Bank's strength and splendid condition —— The small effort required for the recognition of the error and the remedy —— The subtlety, yet simplicity of the matter · · **Pages 194 to 200**

PART II.

The Principle of Timely Reduction of the Fiduciary Issue.—

The facts given might lead to the natural inference —— That the plethora rate of interest of some years is the direct cause of extreme scarcity and high rates in others —— The Bank is guided by the state of the Reserve —— It has the initiative —— Amounts of Reserve and corresponding rates of interest —— Result of tables showing the ranges of Reserve with the corresponding rates of interest —— Definite proportions of Reserve and interest by way of illustration —— Experience as to a fairly satisfactory state of Reserve, say of 10 millions and 4 per cent. —— The plain principle of reducing surplus of Reserve to some such level —— The whole secret of the difficulty, and the remedy involved in timely reduction —— Of the surplus of legal tender notes —— The maintenance of the *status quo* thereby made easy —— The law of compensation involved in the reduction or increase of issue —— The true fiduciary Reserve thus arising will be moderate, but ample at all times —— The conservative nature of the principle of timely reduction ——

Pages 201 to 207

The Principle of Decrease and Increase of Fiduciary Issue, and the late Proposals for Increase only in times of Crisis.—

The contrast between these proposals —— The nature and origin of the proposal for increase of issue —— The perversion of logic and *causes* here made manifest —— The perversion of actual facts —— Their accidental nature —— The restoration of confidence —— The real nature of this one-sided increase of issue —— The laxity in the valuation thereby established —— International exchanges would cease to respond to our demands for bullion —— The overwhelming withdrawals of bullion —— The greater nervousness of the money market; and reversal of present experience —— Effect on speculation and over-trading —— The common sense objection —— The proposal as to increase of issue only, is a sign of the demoralisation of enquiry into the question —— It would be better to prepare for a general scramble —— The proposal as to temporary increase have, however, broken the ground for enquiry —— The acknowledgment of the necessity of reform —— They admit the possibility of regulating the matter by clauses of the Act —— The subtle point of the whole controversy —— The slightest turn of economical thought will provide the remedy . . . . Pages 207 to 214

The Temporary Decrease and Increase of the Fiduciary Issue Provided for in the Present Act, and why it could not be put in practice.—

Clause 2 of the Act distinctly provides for a diminution of the issue —— Wording of the clause —— Distinct provision for a diminution of the issue —— Such diminution to be "from time to time," and "again to increase." —— Reasons why the sentence in question did not meet with sufficient consideration —— Sir Robert Peel would now acknowledge the importance of this matter ——The inability of the Bank to act in accordance with this part of the clause —— Clause 6 of the Act. Providing for a regular share of profit to the State —— Of £195,000 a year —— The actual loss made by the Bank —— The great variation in the actual use of the issue —— The unfairness of the regular charge —— The Bank has no inducement to reduce the issue —— It already bears the high technical charges —— The general statement of loss repeated —— The balance of accounts as regards the securities in the issue department *Table 15.—Showing the gross produce of the fixed issue, less technical expenses, and the supposed balance of profit for division between State and Bank, and Loss*—Page 221 —— The regular deduction of £195,000 per annum is irreconcilable with principle and practice —— The forces of bad arrangements here operate together against sound practice —— The State should take the share of actual profits —— Which with the reform might become fairly regular, if not larger than at present . . . . Pages 214 to 223

The Practical Solution of the Question contained in the Amendment of Clause 8 of the present Act.—The subject reduced to its simplest form —— The amendment of clause 8 gives the practical solution —— All other clauses on the Bank of England may remain absolutely intact —— The maintenance of the limit and Reserve satisfied —— The limit of 15 millions can remain as a nominal one —— The Reserve would be equally maintainable —— If the adjustment of the circulation and bullion stock took place without reference to it —— It would "float" over the substrata and continue to do so without harm —— The continual availability of this Reserve and the employment of the Bank's real resources —— Examples showing the difference to the Banking Department —— The larger profit made by the Bank —— Suggestion as to a rangement   .   Pages 223 to 229

The Control of Interest Regained by the Reduction of large Reserve to a temporary small Indicating Reserve.—The principal advantage given by reduction of the idle Reserve of Notes —— The Bank would regain its liberty of action —— And act in accordance with the market rate —— Undue withdrawals of bullion will be stopped thereby —— What shall gui lo the Bank in raising t's rate? —— The Bank had full liberty under the old Act —— But under the old, errors of omission were committed - —— The Banks of France and Prussia do better, but have no perfect system —— Sir Robert Peel's endeavour to create automaton action —— By increase and decrease of the issue —— To create a standard of Reserve —— In favour of anticipatory action —— The action was changed into post facto with both extremes —— The regular Reserve protects bullion and serves only as indicator for higher rates —— Clause 2 gives liberty of action together with indicator —— A true indicator cannot fail to guide discretion rightly —— Its clearness and certainty —— The problem solved by the amendment of Clause 8 of the present Act   Pages 229 to 234

The System of Compensating Interest and Increasing Reserve.—The search for adjustments and rules —— Its failure for want of reference to all factors —— The due appreciation and the reduction to the adjusting points —— The six factors of the system: Circulation, Commerce, Bank Notes, Bullion, Interest, Reserve —— The free scope given to the demands of circulation —— The encouragement of the circulation by continual offer for real equivalents —— The folly of demanding money without equivalents —— The independent concurrence between general circulation and commerce —— The Bank of England note issue not absolutely required for this purpose.—— We may dismiss these first two factors as concentrated in the Bank of England note circulation —— The factor reserve is also a separate one —— The guiding factor now becomes the amount of circulation of notes —— Bullion must be maintained in proportion thereto —— Proportion of circulation to bullion the true guide —— The simple office of the rate of interest to keep bullion at a level —— The finding of its level —— The test by practice —— Its proof by theory   .   .   .   .   .   Pages 234 to 242

The Principles of Compensating Interest in the combination between Bullion and Fiduciary Bank Notes.—Arbitrary assumption for standard rates are fallacious —— The true abstract ground for such rates lies in the valuation itself —— The point of agreement between amount of bullion and amount of circulation —— The truly normal character of the equality of bullion and circulation —— The abstract and neutral ground thereby established —— The frequent occurrence of this agreement at the Bank of England —— The deduction of the rate from this normal state of the valuation —— From the broad practice of the Bank —— By testing the excesses —— The practical test results in the rate of 2½ per cent. —— as that on which the excesses below are committed —— The deduction is abstract and not arbitrary —— The ratio of increase of interest to protect bullion —— Determinable by experience within the known ranges of interest —— Subject to the natural control of duration of time of each change —— The practice of the Bank affords a distinct available guide —— The theory of adjustment points to a distinct rule —— Viz., the doubled bid, to obtain the desired level —— Its applicability to the case of attracting bullion —— The true automaton action of the double bid —— Examples of its working —— The simple rule —— Construction of a table to show its working —— *Table 16.—Showing amount of circulation and bullion, with rates of interest to correspond*—Page 252 —— *Table 17.—Degrees of agreement and excesses between the practice of the Bank of England from 1845 to 1871, and the rule enunciated compared with basis of 2, 2½, and 3 per cent. as lowest rates on 198 instances of changes*—Page 254 —— The liberty of the Bank to keep interest at a suitable level to international rates —— The practically lowest rate for the maintenance of the issue —— Sufficient to cover the technical costs of the issue —— The fair rate resulting from the moderate issue —— Its accord with international rates —— Its fair level for the issue itself —— Its agreement with the market rate —— On the removal of idle Reserve —— Higher rates of interest —— Our average level may be slightly below others —— The legitimate advantage of our position —— The proper proportion of bullion to notes in circulation —— The plain principles here made evident as self-acting —— The starting point of lowest interest dissolves again in the system itself —— The order and certainty resulting therefrom and its corrective —— The corrective of time and reserve

Pages 342 to 261

The Reserve of the Compensating System of Bank Note Issue.

—The necessity of Reserve and its clear purpose —— If Bullion can be secured in due proportion to circulation, the same force can secure the addition of Reserve —— By proportionate increase in rates of interest —— Illustrating its operation —— *Table 18.—Showing the rates of interest required to secure Reserves from 0 to 15 millions upon a circulation of 25 millions, commencing with 25 millions down to 10 millions of Bullion. (Millions 00,000 omitted)*—Page 263 —— The proportionate increase or decrease —— Suitable to all amounts of circulation —— And desirable Reserve —— Illustration in another form —— *Table 19.—Showing the effect on rise in rate of interest by successive reserves of 2, 5, 7, 10 and 15 millions on circulation of 25 millions* —— Ranges of interest dependent on Reserve chosen —— The essential difference between the present Reserve and the proposed Reserve —— The true use of fiduciary issue —— The decline of present Reserve and enforced realisation of claims —— The continual hold by the proposed Reserve upon such claims —— Subject to instantaneous action —— The dis-union or union of the factors —— The simplicity of the matter —— The substitution of subtraction for addition —— The common sense and plain logic involved —— The reversal of present practice and the safety resulting therefrom —— The degree of safety —— Abolition of undue low rates —— Provision of proven pro rata action —— Its first corrective of time —— The supernatant corrective of Reserve —— Illustrating its absolute firmness —— The Reserve becomes the regulating force of all contingences —— The inviolability of this Reserve —— The strength of the defensive attitude —— The presumed amount of such Reserve —— Will be determined by natural indications —— In reality by rates of interest —— The balancing of this Reserve will give the legitimate scope for discretion by the Bank Directors by superior considerations —— Doing away with petty expedients —— Application of the system to great emergencies —— Orderly expansion and contraction of its factors

Pages 261 to 270

The Amendment of Clauses 2 and 8 of the present Act, in accordance with the proposed System.

—The desirability of prescribing orderly action —— The Bank might "practice" it without reform of the Act —— Impropriety of this suggestion —— The necessity for reform in Clause 8 —— The sense of order and refinement prevalent in England —— Incorporation of the system in Clause 2 —— Involving but removal of 5 words —— And substitution of a short sentence —— Leaving the discretion in Reserve —— The principle of rates of interest —— Admitted by Parliament —— Legitimacy of lowest rate —— Precautionary action better than *post facto* action —— No absolute necessity for abolition of the fixed limit —— No need for maintaining it · · · · · · · · Pages 271 to 274

The Advantages of this Reform to the Bank of England and the Public.—The freedom of its resources secured —— Disappearance of the idle Reserve —— Plainer statement of the accounts —— Example without specific Reserve —— Desirability of temporary moderate Reserve —— The issue department to state circulation and Reserve —— Example with five millions of "first" Reserve —— The balance over "first Reserve" still available —— The expenses covered by first Reserve —— The same liabilities and assets —— Example with less bullion —— Profit on more fiduciary circulation —— Consequent larger profit to the State —— Example with small stock of bullion —— The check on unduly large issues —— The compensating action of the whole system —— Advantages to the Bank —— Regularity of bullion —— Lesser range of interest —— Satisfaction to circulation —— Regularity of Reserve —— Greater scope of business —— Increase in deposits —— Larger dividends —— Advantages to bankers —— Less competition with Bank —— A better average of interest —— Advantage to discount brokers —— Advantages to general public —— Scepticism for want of contemporary comparision —— Realisation of the strong facts shown in this book —— Demonstrating the grave fault —— The history of this country teems with the surprisingly beneficial results of reform . . . . **Page 275 to 283**

The Country Bankers' Issues.—Reform of country issues not absolutely required —— Their anomaly —— The only plea in their favour —— Suggestion to satisfy this plea —— On issues on gold coin —— The true meaning of this improvement and the margin for expenses —— The Act of 1858 an insult to Peel —— Country bankers profit at expense of valuation —— The plea of vested right —— Is proof of the need of reform —— The damage to our valuation —— Enlightened men must deal with the whole subject **Page 283 to 295**

Conclusion.—The matter here elucidated a fair subject for inquiry —— Enquiry unfettered from dogmas —— The necessity for this exhaustive treatment —— The high position of the Bank Directors —— Their success with a proper system certain —— Other publications of the author —— Contain matters in support of this book —— The Author willing to correspond with competent parties . . . . . **Pages 295 to 298**

PART I.

THE WANT OF PROGRESS OF THE BANK OF ENGLAND.

A MONG the manifold duties incumbent upon wealth, that of maintaining and increasing itself is the foremost. The most refined intelligence, the highest economical principles, the utmost truthfulness, should be brought to bear upon the furtherance of individual as well as national wealth. In every community where equitable laws prevail, and free scope is given to production, the increase of wealth is a positive gain, of which all have the benefit. A certain set of transactions, although equitable apparently, gives, it is true, advantage to the one to the disadvantage of the other (among these latter the State Debts take their place), but the vast majority does not involve the vulgar notion that the wealth of the one means the poverty of the other—the positive and the negative. It may be said that all the factors and forces contributing to the accumulation of such positive wealth, advance together like an army, and in their respective ranks take the shares they are entitled to. These participations find expression in practical results, which can be measured by figures, and the agreement between such figures confirms the active and perfect co-operation of each factor. Indeed the "mutuality"

Wealth must increase as if by a natural law.

1

involved in this rests on a law of nature, which *must* manifest itself, unless one of the parties concerned is unable to keep pace with the rest. It follows that when the figures connected with one of these factors stand much below those of others, there is reason to suppose that it has lagged behind the general advance, and if that factor be an essential one, it is not unreasonable to inquire whether its tardiness does not hamper the general advance, and give occasion for disturbances and quarrels.

The test of figures can be applied.

England affords a striking example of the truth of these general reflections. The accumulation of its wealth has proceeded at a most rapid rate. The question whether the division of this great store of positive wealth is fairly conducted, whether the whole mass of the people is, on the average, more or less happy and comfortable than other nations, is entirely a local or domestic matter; but there can be no discussion as regards the supremacy of English " international" wealth. Apart from the accumulation of riches now bodily present in the country in all sorts of commodities and treasures, England has invested a considerable portion of her wealth in claims on other nations, from which a large income is derived. Her investments in foreign state debts, in foreign railways and other enterprises, in the current commerce with all parts abroad, according to the best estimates, exceed 1,000 millions sterling, and they are steadily increasing. This is what is meant by the expression " supremacy in international wealth," in contradistinction to " inferiority of international wealth," under which labour the nations who hold no such claims, or who, on the contrary, owe them. Among the nations possessing this international wealth may be counted, next to England, Germany, Holland, Belgium and France, the latter country still holding considerable claims

England's wealth, "local" and "international."

England's decided supremacy in international wealth.

against its own recently enlarged debt. Among those who are internationally poor and indebted to them, the United States, Russia, Austria, Italy, and other States, worse burdened, may be mentioned.

To every Englishman this decided supremacy of his own country must be most satisfactory and re-assuring. The figures are at hand to justify such feeling of satisfaction. Throughout the length and breadth of the land there has been almost universal progress. Not only has the population increased, but (in spite of higher prices) the production and the consumption of commodities of all kinds, from those required for food up to the highest efforts of art and intelligence, has doubled and trebled, especially within the last thirty years. One test is afforded by the exports and imports, which, amounting in 1844 to 130 millions, exceeded 600 millions in 1872. And whether the inquiry as to this universal increase be directed to all kinds of business where figures are available for comparison, such as that of insurance companies, joint stock banks, and other public companies, the advance is general, and in almost the same ratio as that exhibited by our trade returns; all have progressed together. *There is but one solitary exception to this rule,* concerning one of the most important factors—viz., *the Bank of England.* During the last thirty years the Bank of England accounts show but little variation, and the utmost extension of its business within the last few years is totally inadequate and out of proportion to the general increase of business and prosperity. And, as you are also aware, there are periods in our commercial history, notably at times of so-called crises, when disturbances take place so grievous to the steady prosperity of the country, and when quarrels and dissensions arise as to the Bank of England and the Act of 1844.

[Marginal notes:] The manifest universal increase in all directions.

Import and export trade increased fourfold.

The only exception in this universal increase is the Bank of England.

As holders of the Stock of the Bank of England

you feel conscious, no doubt, that you are not only in possession of a valuable security, but that your capital is instrumental also in assisting and promoting the commerce of the country through an institution managed by gentlemen of the highest standing; and the saying, "as safe as the Bank of England," you deem perfectly justified. I am far from being inclined to throw a shadow of doubt upon the security and solidity of the Bank of England, or to disparage the integrity and wisdom of its management under the Act of 1844. Any attempt to do this would meet with

instant and just rebuke. But there are certain striking facts to be brought before you upon which you may reflect; and these facts have an important bearing upon the controversy which, as you are aware, has been going on since the Act of 1844, under which the Bank is bound to perform certain duties. This controversy, in the first instance, concerns the Issue Department. Parliamentary inquiries, Royal Commissions have sat on the matter, books and pamphlets innumerable have been written, abortive attempts at reform have been made—all in vain. The problem is not yet solved, and the quarrel continues. I shall be able to show you that the range of this question is not confined to the Issue Department or Bank-note grievance itself, but that it has an influence extending far over the other operations of the Bank and the mercantile community.

You will find that what I have to say concerns plain practical matters, that the suggestions I have to make do not involve anything revolutionary or speculative.

But ere I enter upon this task, permit me to

call your attention to the fact that the controversy as regards the Bank of England is in a state which renders the task of obtaining a hearing extremely difficult. So much has been said and written, so many

wild and extraordinary schemes have been started, so
violent, on the other side, has been the dogmatic defence
of the present state of things, that the case seems
almost hopeless. If proof were wanted of the desperate state of confusion and demoralisation into which Vain
attempts at
reform.
the question has fallen, the lately proposed (but since
abandoned) amendment by the Chancellor of the
Exchequer may be quoted. People have become tired of
the whole thing, and among them your own Directors
are probably the most unwilling to listen to new reasons. Natural
conserva-
tive ten-
dency of the
Directors.
They may prefer the present state of things, under the
idea that the utmost conservatism is the only course
open to them, and have recourse to the dogmas to
which we are accustomed. I say so with all due
respect to the Directors of the Bank, conscious that
they have the power to come before you and condemn any suggestion by the mere force of their personal position. But with all due respect to the host Baneful
influence of
dogmas of
bygone
times.
of economists of the last generation, whose opinions
and assertions are so continually quoted by their
present pupils, for want of original thought, let me
remind you that these men lived at a time when the
aspect of things was different, when other matters,
such as the mere convertibility of the Bank Note, for
instance, were uppermost. If we are bound to follow
their opinions, most of which involve nothing more
than some crooked result, painfully eked out for want of
clear thought, but uttered in an authoritative manner,
there is an end to all progress and all reform. Many
of the controversialists of the present day, among
them several of the highest standing, frequently have
recourse to quotations, which modern economy is Dogmatic
wisdom
versus
figures and
facts.
able to condemn as unmitigated sophistry, as the result
of desperately false reasoning. Against all these
opinions and quotations, none of which are accompanied
by facts and figures, you can hold up the accounts as

they present themselves to you and ask, " What is the use of all that wisdom if better results cannot be shown?"

The most prevalent, deep-rooted, and fatal—but weakest—of these dogmas is that founded on the assertion—" all our difficulties and crises are owing to the speculative tendency of our merchants; that the Bank Act itself is perfection." It is but necessary that one of the authorities holding this view should say so in the usual style, supporting the Bank Act by the customary quotation of " sentences " pronounced years ago, and the majority of weak-minded people will assent. Nobody can deny that speculation is a serious evil. But there is one *primâ facie* reflection, which should raise doubts even in the minds of those who are thus easily overwhelmed. If speculation alone is the cause of the mischief, if the Bank of England is immaculate, why is the establishment either in jeopardy in times of panics and crises, or subject to the effects of speculation at all? If the system of the Bank is absolutely faultless, it must keep itself absolutely clear, not only of direct participation in speculative matters, but of all their indirect influences on its resources. To use a familiar example :—The pretending temperance man should remain serene and undisturbed however intemperate his associates may choose to be.

Thus, if the Bank Act were as immaculate as is alleged, speculation ought not to withdraw Bullion from its stores, or place the Reserve in danger. The evidence that the Bank is unable thus to guard itself shows either that its system, in spite of all virtuous protestations, is somehow productive of speculation, or, to say the most favourable thing, that it is too weak to defend itself against the effects of overtrading. As in everything else concerning the ramifications of commercial intercourse, the law of mutuality is opera-

The most fatal of the dogmas concerns "speculation."

The Bank is unable to keep itself free from its effects.

That is plain proof of either its participation or its weakness.

tive here, and the results loudly proclaim its truth. Give way only to the suspicion that it might be so—that the Bank Act is not perfect—and you will at once perceive that, inasmuch as the principle therein involved concerns the nucleus of *supply*, it follows that any fault, large or small, clearly perceived or difficult of discovery, multiplies its evil effects many thousand fold in the *demand*, as each unit serves in the thousands upon thousands of transactions. Unless you consent for once to abandon the assertion that speculation alone is to blame, the "old refuge for the intellectually destitute," you will never discover the error.

A fault in the nucleus of a system repeats itself many thousand-fold.

I venture, moreover, to request you not to admit as valid any boast or allusion to the strength and wealth generally of the Bank, based upon its capital and position, or upon results which are one sided, because no concurrent comparison can be made. Nothing is more fatal to the truth than the endeavours to swamp the search for great economical principles by a rough appeal to wealth and strength. When this method of defence assumes that well known quasi patriotic style, when the defender " points with pride," and, at the pitch of his enthusiasm enforces a cheer, sound reasoning is apt to be set aside. I allege that there is nothing to be very proud of in the accounts of the Bank of England, and that, on the contrary, its want of sufficient progress is evident. I hope that you, in this controversy, will not be influenced by the mere declamation that all is satisfactory, whilst in reality the figures show a comparatively regretable state of things.

The mere appeal to strength of capital does not solve a problem.

Patriotic declamation cannot override figures.

If you should appreciate the remark which I have ventured to make at the beginning of this chapter, respecting the duty of wealth in regard to its maintenance and increase by the application of refined intelligence, high economy and logical truth, you will

insist upon the reasonable consideration of indisputable facts or figures. These facts or figures, already
alluded to, I shall lay before you in a more definite
shape. They prove that the Bank of England has
scarcely made any advance, and is now far behind the
prosperity of the country, and its real, practical, dearest
interests. That alone should fix your attention, if it
were merely a problem of science to be solved. But
beyond this stands your own interest, as holders of
14 millions of Bank Stock. If it can be shown to you

that the Bank of England does not occupy the position
which it ought to hold, that its influence on the affairs
of commerce is not so complete and satifactory as it
ought to be, that with the advantages apparently
enjoyed by it it does not pay you dividends large
enough, you may probably be willing to listen to
suggestions which will point out the cause and its
effects, and which will indicate the remedy. If it can
be shown to you that by the removal of the cause of
mischief the Bank will be able to attain its legitimate
position, increase its business and dividends, you may
be able to confer great benefit upon your own income,
and that of thousands of families whose fortunes are

invested in the 14 millions, a capital of national
importance. And if an economist, who wants nothing
wild and speculative, can show you that by the proper
adjustment of your own Bank of England system the
disturbances and crises to which the commerce of the
country is now subjected, and which bring so much
misery to the mercantile and labouring classes, can be
dealt with in a better way; if he proposes to demonstrate that the quarrels and conflicts between the
public and the Bank, together with all the vain and
wretched attempts at legislation which have been made,
need not be renewed, you may at least deem it worth
while to listen to what he has to say.

COMPARATIVE FIGURES.

The table herewith submitted contains the items of the Bank of England accounts from 1845 to December 1872, which determine the extent of the active business. Table I.

First. The circulation of Notes. ⎫
Second. The amount of Bullion. ⎭ Note circulation.

For the sake of convenience, the average for each year has been given, as sufficiently indicative of the general advance.

Third. Total Deposits, viz. : — Public and Private Deposits (including Bankers' balances) and Bank Post Bills, as indicating the actual advance made by the Banking business. The variations in this business make it expedient that four items per annum should be given, taken from the returns. In selecting these, care has been taken to avoid the customary extremes at the periods of half-years, and the fairness of the selection is subject to control. Deposits.

Fourth. Bankers' balances, as included in the Total Deposits. Bankers' balances.

Fifth. Bills discounted and ⎫
Sixth. Temporary Advances, ⎭ Bills discounted, &c.

which indicate the amount of connection between the current commerce of the country and the Bank of England. It is understood, of course, that beyond these items the Bank invests in, and advances on Government Securities and "other Securities," such as railway obligations and kindred matters. The Bills Discounted and Temporary Advances are also given in four items per annum to fairly represent the case.

Seventh. Contains the annual total of our export and import trade, as indicative of the general increased prosperity of the country. The "exports" have been corrected in accordance with McCulloch's system. Exports and imports.

Eighth. Contains the total deposits of the four chief London joint stock banks, viz., the London and Westminster Bank, the London Joint Stock, the London and County, and the Union Bank. Deposits of four joint stock banks

TABLE I.

£ Sterling. Millions and Decimals (000,000) omitted.

| Years | From the Bank of England Returns. | | | | | | | Total of Exports and Imports. | Total Deposit of the Four Chief Banks. |
| | Averages of | | Four Periods each year of | | | | | | |
	Note Circulation	Bullion	Deposits	Bankers' Balances	Bills Discounted	Temp. Advances	Dividend		
1845	21·1	15·0	19·0	1·1	2.3	0·8	7	161·6	9·6
			14·2	1·0	3·1	4·1			
			17·8	1·0	5·3	1·9			
			18·7	1·6	9·4	1·1			
1846	20·3	14·2	25·5	2·0	13·1	4·1	7	149·8	9·3
			20·3	1·1	10·9	1·3			
			23·1	2·0	9·2	1·3			
			18·5	1·2	6·5	0·7			
1847	19·1	9·7	18·7	1·2	8·8	0·9	8	169·8	8·6
			13·6	1·8	9·9	0·9			
			15·3	1·2	8·5	3·6			
			14·7	2·0	12·3	1·6			
1848	18·6	13·6	16·2	2·4	5·7	1·6	9	164·6	9·3
			17·6	1·6	4·7	1·7			
			14·9	3·3	3·6	1·2			
			17·8	1·6	3·1	1·1			
1849	18·3	14·3	17·0	1·9	2·8	0·8	7½	194·8	10·7
			15·7	2·7	2·7	0·7			
			18·7	1·5	2·2	0·9			
			20·5	2·0	2·3	1·6			
1850	19·5	16·1	18·0	1·6	2·3	0·5	7½	193·7	11·9
			20·3	1·5	2·3	2·6			
			17·8	1·6	2·4	0·6			
			20·4	1·3	3·2	1·1			
1851	19·4	13·9	18·1	1·8	4·1	0·9	7½	208·7	14·7
			15·1	1·7	3·8	0·6			
			18·2	1·4	5·1	0·8			
			18·6	1·4	5·7	1·4			
1852	21·7	20·0	20·1	3·2	3·1	0·5	7½	210·6	17·4
			19·1	4·8	2·7	0·2			
			22·0	2·0	2·9	1·4			
			21·8	2·6	3·8	0·8			
1853	22·9	17·3	22·5	1·5	5·9	1·7	8	240·7	21·7
			18·4	2·5	4·5	0·2			
			20·0	2·5	6·7	2·1			
			22·1	2·1	7·6	1·1			
[1854	20·7	13·3	17·2	2·7	5·9	0·1	9	267·2	25·6
			13·8	2·2	7·2	0·3			
			18·1	2·3	5·8	0·3			
			15·8	2·7	5·3	0·2			
1855	19·8	13·5	15·4	2·3	6·1	0·2	8	260·0	28·3
			18·1	3·3	3·7	0·2			
			17·6	2·7	3·9	0·2			
			16·5	2·5	9·0	0·8			
1856	19·6	10·2	18·5	2·5	8·0	1·5	9½	311·7	33·0
			14·4	2·9	5·4	1·6			
			15·3	2·5	3·7	0·9			
			15·1	2·7	9·4	0·5			
1857	19·2	9·4	16·7	2·8	8·0	0·9	10	339·0	37·7
			18·1	2·7	8·1	2·4			
			14·7	3·3	6·8	1·0			
			21·8	5·1	17·1	3·2			
1858	20·0	17·0	22·2	8·8	9·8	0·9	10	304·3	35·3
			20·2	5·1	4·0	0·6			
			19·3	5·0	3·6	0·3			
			21·8	3·9	3·0	0·3			
1859	21·3	17·3	22·5	3·4	3·8	0·4	8½	334·8	35·0
			24·0	5·8	6·5	0·7			
			22·4	3·5	6·1	1·5			
			20·4	3·5	5·5	1·0			

TABLE I.—continued.

Millions and Decimals (000,000) omitted.

| Years | From the Bank of England Returns. | | | | | | | Total of Exports and Imports | Total Deposit of the Four Chief Banks |
| | Averages of | | Four Periods each year of | | | | | | |
	Note Circulation	Bullion	Deposits	Bankers' Balances	Bills Discounted	Temp. Advances	Dividend		
1860	21.3	14.5	23.0	3.1	8.4	2.5	9½	375.0	39.0
			20.5	3.6	8.4	0.8			
			19.5	5.2	8.1	0.8			
			18.9	4.7	7.5	1.4			
1861	20.9	12.2	16.7	3.2	8.1	1.1	10	377.1	45.0
			16.8	3.6	7.9	0.9			
			16.9	5.2	7.2	1.1			
			19.1	6.0	4.8	0.6			
1862	20.9	15.6	20.6	4.1	5.1	1.0	8½	391.8	45.5
			22.2	5.2	6.5	1.4			
			23.5	6.7	7.0	1.5			
			23.2	5.9	7.5	1.5			
1863	20.5	13.7	20.7	4.5	7.0	1.1	8½	445.8	54.4
			23.6	4.4	6.7	3.4			
			24.3	4.7	8.0	2.7			
			22.2	4.7	9.0	2.8			
1864	20.6	12.8	21.1	4.1	7.6	1.4	11	487.5	67.5
			22.7	4.8	8.2	2.6			
			19.5	5.5	9.4	1.3			
			18.1	5.9	9.1	1.5			
1865	21.1	13.7	23.7	4.7	7.5	3.6	10½	489.9	67.0
			22.1	4.6	7.8	2.4			
			20.9	4.5	9.8	2.2			
			17.6	4.4	9.4	1.7			
1866	23.1	14.0	17.5	4.3	7.8	1.4	11¾	534.1	69.0
			18.1	5.0	7.3	1.8			
			27.0	7.8	16.5	7.5			
			26.0	7.5	7.8	2.5			
1867	23.6	20.3	25.3	7.2	7.1	1.9	10	500.9	58.3*
			28.5	8.1	6.7	1.8			
			27.6	7.5	4.6	1.3			
			25.1	7.3	4.5	1.1			
1868	23.8	19.5	28.6	9.2	4.5	1.1	8	522.4	57.3
			27.5	7.3	6.6	1.5			
			23.3	6.2	4.3	1.2			
			24.7	7.1	4.1	1.1			
1869	23.4	17.7	23.4	6.2	7.1	2.2	8¼	532.4	57.1
			23.3	7.3	7.4	1.7			
			22.3	7.2	5.0	1.0			
			21.9	6.0	4.8	1.4			
1870	22.5	19.1	26.6	6.9	5.8	3.4	8½	547.3	63.9
			24.8	5.5	6.0	3.2			
			26.5	9.2	9.2	2.6			
			24.5	7.3	5.2	2.2			
1871	24.3	22.8	29.0	7.0	7.6	3.9	8½	614.4	73.9
			32.7	12.4	5.9	3.4			
			27.4	10.8	6.7	2.7			
			29.0	10.7	5.2	1.5			
1872	25.2	22.5	28.4	7.9	3.9	1.7	9½	669.2	79.4
			31.9	8.3	8.7	6.7			
			33.2	13.0	8.5	7.3			
			25.4	7.2	6.0	2.6			

* The apparent reduction from this year is owing chiefly to the separation in the accounts of the "acceptances" of the Union Bank, which are thence excluded. The London Joint Stock Bank does not separate the acceptances. The two other banks separated them before.

The full import of these statements will be more understood if it is borne in mind that the population of England and Wales increased from 16 millions in 1844 to 23 millions in 1872, and that the rise in the prices of commodities generally is probably not less than 35 per cent. Besides the four banks, whose deposits in 1844 were 9 millions, and in 1872 amounted to 79 millions, numerous other banks have been established, and the old bankers, as well as insurance and all other enterprises, private and public, have *trebled* and *four-folded their business.*

The whole increase not equal even to the single item of increase of population.

The table accordingly shows that, *whereas from* 1845 *to* 1872 *our trade has increased from* 160 *to* 669 *millions,* the *Bank of England has not only made scarcely any progress* in its accounts, *but that it has gone backwards.* In 1845 the circulation was 21 millions; it was the same in 1865; from 1866 to 1872 the increase is 3 millions. The deposits in 1846 were 25 millions; twenty years later they were 20 millions; in 1867 and 1868 they increased to 23 and 27 millions; in 1869 they declined to 22 millions; in 1871 and 1872 they increased to 30 and 33 millions, declining again to 25 millions; *but bear in mind this:*—As you see by the columns headed Bankers' Balances, these increases are owing only to such larger balances, which in 1846 were 1 to 2 millions, and rose in 1871 and 1872 to 12 and 13 millions. You may recollect that during the late controversy, the other banks were abused for keeping but small balances at the Bank of England. If these be deducted you will see that the deposits of the Bank during the last 28 years have *actually declined,* although the trade and prosperity of the nation has fourfolded.

No increase from 1844 to 1866.

Increase since 1866 owing to bankers' balances.

Deposits actually declined.

What is the cause of this manifest want of progress of the Bank of England? In any controversy where the real reasons for disorganisation lie deep, and are

False reasonings must be set aside first.

not discernible by the ordinary inquirer, other unreal but more convenient reasons are advanced. These must first be dismissed, so that they no longer obscure the view. It may be said—

First. That if the Bank of England has progressed slowly, and the wealth of the country rapidly, the Bank has made a sacrifice, on the principle that having gained less, the country has gained more. Apart from the quixotic nature of this suggestion, let it be distinctly understood that in all these matters reciprocity rules supreme—that, as I have stated at the beginning of this pamphlet, all the factors concerned in the accumulation of wealth *must* benefit therein—and if the Bank for its part has not done so, there is, on the contrary, *primâ facie* suspicion that it has not benefited the country as it ought to have done.

Second. It may be alleged that the Bank is too conservative, and has remained behind from prudential reasons. Granted, in general terms, that "the age is too fast," that people press too much in advance, and that it behoves an important institution like the Bank to be conservative against this tendency, how much conservatism would suffice? Between extremes lies the *right* course which, practically, is more than sufficient; and the conservative balance is fully secure, if, figuratively speaking, the Bank remained one or two per cent. more on this right or safe side; but when the actual results show that, comparatively, such conservatism is 100 or 200 per cent. in arrear, they prove an excess which cannot be brought into accord with natural truth. There are certain financiers who will tell you the Bank is quite right in keeping back, in acting as counterpoise, in discouraging business, &c. Men of that class are not economists; but their uncouth notions do infinite mischief to the whole question. Arguments of that kind, you must admit, have not done any good to the Bank of England itself. Considering that the whole aim of social and commercial intercourse is that of progress, and that such progress has had actual solid results in a fourfold measure, it might well be asked, what would be the aim and purpose of the Bank, or even the reason for its existence, if the idea of conservatism is to be forced to such a pitch of rough sophistry?

Third. It may be alleged that the rapid growth of other joint stock banks and banking generally, has absorbed business which would otherwise have come to the Bank. The practical acknowledgment that there was this large field conveys at the same time the reproach to the Bank that it has been unable to take advantage of the favourable contingencies themselves, the very cause of the progress, and this would seem to confirm the above suggestion as to ultra-conservatism! The Bank of France* has made enormous progress, in spite of the numerous large public banks started in competition with it during the last twenty years, and the much larger number of successful private bankers. Some of these French banking institutions do business as large as that done by our oldest and first-class joint stock banks.

The rapid growth of other banks proves the very fact that the Bank has missed its opportunities.

Fourth. It may be said that the other joint stock banks owe their success to the fact, firstly, that they actively solicit business; and secondly, that they pay interest on deposits, whereas the Bank of England pays no interest to its depositors. It is alleged, in that general manner so easily adopted, that the deposits of the Bank of England represent the " floating capital," the " balances for the moment

The deposits at the Bank ought to have increased with general increase, independently of the question of allowing interest for them.

---

* The following table shows the increase of the business of the Bank of France during the sme period. (The returns from the Bank of Prussia, and all other State Banks show similar results—

available only " of the commerce of the country.
Considering that these "floating balances" exhibit a
large continuous average, that the Banking Depart‑
ment is supposed to be as independent an institution
as other banks, this saying as to the dignity of the
Bank in waiting for business, and the non‑availability
of its deposits, is simply moonshine. The Banks of
France and Prussia hold a precisely similar position
in the commerce of their countries. The question as
to the Bank's inability to pay interest on deposits I
reserve for consideration, and I shall show that it is a
secondary matter; but granted that it be an original

viz., a more or less regular but decided increase of their affairs in
accordance with the progress of commerce.)

TABLE II.—*Showing the Increase in the Business of the Bank of France
at the end of February each Year.*

[In Millions and Decimals Sterling, 000,000 omitted.]

	Circulation	Bullion	Deposit	Bills Discounted	Dividend
1844	10·4	11·7	6·2	5·1	10·7
1845	11·0	12·2	7·5	6·7	13·3
1846	11·7	9·8	7·8	10·1	15·8
1847	11·0	4·2	3·8	11·1	17·7
1848	10·1	8·8	7·4	9·6	7·5*
1849	16·8	12·6	6·8	5·5	10·6
1850	18·2	18·9	8·0	4·5	10·1
1851	20·8	20·4	8·3	5·7	10·5
1852	22·6	23·4	10·0	4·6	11·8
1853	26·8	19·8	11·8	11·9	15·4
1854	24·5	11·2	9·2	17·9	19·4
1855	25·4	17·4	10·9	18·2	20·0
1856	25·4	8·5	7·5	17·4	27·2
1857	23·6	8·6	9·4	20·1	27·4
1858	22·9	12·3	9·8	18·3	11·4†
1859	28·4	21·8	14·5	18·6	11·5
1860	28·8	21·8	18·1	19·8	14·0
1861	30·4	17·2	10·7	19·4	14·7
1862	33·5	15·9	15·8	26·6	15·8
1863	31·5	12·8	9·4	21·6	16·5
1864	30·5	8·0	7·6	26·4	20·0
1865	30·9	12·6	10·2	22·8	15·4
1866	36·0	18·6	10·0	24·6	15·8
1867	42·5	30·8	16·8	24·8	10·7
1868	47·5	47·6	21·9	17·8	9·0
1869	53·5	46·2	19·7	21·5	10·7
1870	56·5	50·4	21·6	22·2	8·4‡

* The capital raised from £2.5 millions to £3.6 millions.
† The capital raised to £7.3 millions.
‡ The war began.

reason, and that the deposits at the Bank are such floating balances, they should, considering the enormous increase of wealth, have increased accordingly, without reference whatsoever to the question of interest.

Fifth. It may be alleged that the Bank has to perform public duties. It is difficult to perceive why these duties, which consist simply of the management of the National Debt and Government public accounts, for which the Bank receives adequate remuneration, and which are a source of profit, should interfere with other business, especially when the non-official character of the banking department is so strongly insisted upon. In other countries the central and quasi State Banks perform duties of that kind.

The "public" duties of the Bank are quite separate from its own rights as a Bank.

Sixth. It may be said that the progress of "Clearing systems" has reduced the deposits of the Bank of England. Nothing can be more false. The Clearing systems save *Currency* only, and they may contribute a reason why the active Note circulation has not shown so great an increase; but as to deposits, or capital so deposited, the Clearing system has the contrary effect, viz. it promotes the accumulation of such *free* deposits, and if these free balances have not come into the Bank in the measure which they ought to have done, it is simply owing to the fact that the institution was unable to do justice to them. But although the Clearing system does undoubtedly save currency, and although this serves as the current explanation why, whilst our trade has four-folded since 1844, the circulation of the Bank has only increased by a moderate per centage, we must not carry the idea as to the absolute force of the Clearing system too far. The rule of reciprocity is also valid here, and with the increase of Clearing a certain increase of circulation,*

The progress of the Clearing system has the tendency of increasing deposits.

---

* The increase of sovereigns in circulation since 1844 may be taken at 40 per cent., equal to increase of population. The

as satisfactory evidence of the greater prosperity and active life in special classes of trade should also have taken place. The Bank of France, and other banks abroad, show a decided increase of their Note circulation (and more decided in Bullion) simultaneously with the increase of banking institutions. The allegation, that neither in France nor Germany the principles of the Clearing system are applied, is utterly false, and shows ignorance of the real state of the case. In the Bank of France a special Clearing department, called the " Bureaux des Viréments," turns over from 3 to 4 millions sterling per diem, on pure " Clearing " principles, between bankers, and the systems of " Recouvrements," both in France and Germany, are in advance of our arrangements. I am quite ready to admit that our own London system of Clearing is best developed, and saves more currency, but I deny that it can absorb so much as not to leave to the Bank of England a fair margin for increase of circulation, especially as upon such increased circulation the proper amount of Bullion is really dependent.

Systems akin to Clearing are in operation in France and Germany.

The table on pages 10 and 11 shows that the *Bullion* at the Bank of England has not increased as it ought to have done. It is quite true that, since 1871, when the German indemnity question arose, the Bank has managed to hold 3 to 4 millions more of Bullion, but previous to this—from 1844 to 1870—the average was nearly equal. Considering that the stock of Bullion at the Bank of England is supposed to be the " Reserve " for international trade, is it not reasonable to expect that this Reserve should have been much higher in 1870, when the international trade of the country was 540 millions and Bullion 19 millions,

The insufficient increase of Bullion as the real metallic Reserve

---

sovereign circulation is independent of the Bank of England Note circulation.

than in, say 1852, when the trade was 210 millions
and Bullion 20 millions? Make whatever allowance
you like for the effects of the Banking and Clearing
system, and you will yet admit, especially when you
consider the necessity of holding a Bullion Reserve
for the sake of the solvency and solidity of our vast
commerce, that the want of increase of Bullion in the
Bank of England is a remarkable feature, and that "it
should be otherwise," at all events to the extent of
some fair proportion. In addition thereto, you must
bear in mind that, since 1848, there has been an
enormous increase in the production of Gold and
Silver, Gold alone having doubled in amount. Why
should the Bank of England not have secured a larger
share than it holds now? Add again the changes in
the valuation and rise in prices, and you further
increase the force of this reflection. In France,
from 1848 to 1869, a sum of no less than 250
millions sterling in Gold was coined, against 110
millions here, and the Bank of France in 1870 held 50
millions of Bullion against 19 millions of the Bank
of England. It will be said probably, the French
use so much more Gold than we do, because we use
more cheques. Granted this, and the above difference
in coining will account for it,—the question of the Note
issue, or rather its foundation, "Bullion," in the Bank,
is another matter. As such, it is essentially apart even
from the subject of "Balance of Trade," for it concerns the plain and simple rules of natural proportions,
and where these are not responded to, an error prevails.
Such larger stock of Bullion is the real foundation
for more issue ; and more of such solid issue, if the
country can absorb it, is indicative of greater strength
and prosperity. If a regularly increasing stock of
Bullion were thus maintained, the country would
absorb it ; but the present spasmodic movements and

enforced contractions too frequently break the chain of progress in this direction.

Other "grounds" might be quoted upon which the admirers of the Bank Act pretend to explain the anomalies here pointed out. None of them, it will be found, touches the core of the thing, or admits the possibility of a fault in the system itself as the cause of all the evil, as I shall point it out to you, after alluding to the Dividend and Discount business at the Bank.

THE DIVIDEND OF THE BANK OF ENGLAND.

The Bank of England pays dividends to its shareholders ranging, since 1844, at from 7 to 11 per cent. No doubt it has been pointed out to you that for so large an institution such a dividend should be considered satisfactory, that the stock stands at 250, and so forth. Against this "matter of pride," permit me to place before you the following considerations :— *The dividend of the Bank of England cannot be called satisfactory.*

Other banks, such as the London and Westminster Bank for instance, have paid from 20 to 30 per cent. (and more). Of course, so it will at once be said, the capital of the Bank of England is 14 millions, or seven times as large as that of the London and Westminster Bank, so that if both have 25 millions of deposits, the shareholders of the latter bank must receive larger dividends on the smaller capital. That is very true, but, on the other hand, the Bank of England enjoys enormous advantages, outweighing this consideration. *The Bank's capital is very large, but the Bank has enormous privileges.*

First. The Bank of England holds its 25 millions of deposits *free of interest*, the London and Westminster Bank pays, say on the average, 3 per cent. per annum for them, so that if the average rate of interest is taken at 4 per cent., each million of the Bank's deposits is equal in profitable value to 4 millions of the London and Westminster Bank. *It holds its deposits free of interest.*

Second. The Bank of England has the Note issue
It has the
extra-issue
of 15 mil-
lions of
Notes.
of 15 millions, clear above all deposits, *i.e.* it has
invested (above deposits) 15 millions in Government
debt and other securities, which, after deducting expenses of issue, and the share of profit taken by the
State, leave a profit of about £90,000 per annum,
and place 15 millions of money at its disposal.

Third. The London and Westminster Bank *must*
Its invest-
ments
exceed the
deposits.
keep a Reserve out of its deposits and capital, it cannot
invest the whole of them, whereas the Bank of England
does not only invest the whole of its capital and deposits, but over and above them, a considerable portion
of the 15 millions of Notes. (The question whether the
Bank Reserve is due to increase of Deposits, or to the
Note issue, is part of the controversy).

Fourth. The Bank keeps the National Debt and
It keeps the
State ac-
counts, &c.
Government Accounts for a remuneration, a source of
profit not enjoyed by the London and Westminster
Bank.

The dividend of the Bank of England may be
Showing
the propor-
tions here
arising at
the Bank.
taken at 9 per cent. (the average is a trifle less). The
sum of £90,000 gained clear on the issue, together
with, say, £50,000 made by the Bank as net profit on the
remuneration obtained for the National Debt management, make up say 1 per cent. of this dividend, leaving
8 per cent. This is earned on the use of—

Capital and rest . . . £18 millions.
Deposits, &c. . . . 25 ,,
——
43 ,,

The proportion of Capital, Funds, and Dividend
being . . $14\frac{1}{2}$—43; or,

1 —3=8 per cent. dividend.

The deposits of the London and Westminster Bank
And at the
London and
West-
minster
Bank.
are 25 millions. If interest be taken at the average
of 4 per cent., the London and Westminster paying

3 per cent. to depositors, the value of this 25 millions, as compared to the free deposits of the Bank of England, becomes reduced to $6\frac{1}{4}$ millions; but assuming that some portion of current balances are also held without interest—

Taking then the free value at	. 10 millions	
To which the capital	. 2	,,
And reserve fund	. 1	,,

Be added, making 13 millions free value, the proportion of capital, funds, and dividend of the London and Westminster Bank would be—

$$1-6\frac{1}{2}=20 \text{ per cent. dividend,}$$

besides accumulation of reserve fund.

Another method of showing the distinction to you is this:—The capital and rest of the Bank of England, if "free" in the market, would yield you, say, 4 per cent. per annum (in Consols it would yield $3\frac{1}{3}$ per cent.)

Another method of comparing results.

The dividend of the Bank at	
9 per cent. on the capital of $14\frac{1}{2}$ millions . .	£1,305,000
Deduct 4 per cent. on capital and rest of 18 millions	720,000
	£585,000
Extra profit on issue, £90,000	
Do. on National Debt management . 50,000	140,000
	£445,000$=1\frac{r}{10}$%

which the Bank earns on

25	millions of deposits and	
15	,,	of Bank Notes,

or 40 ,, which it holds for nothing, *i.e.* free of interest.

The London and Westminster Bank dividend of 20
per cent. yields . . £400,000
Deduct interest on the 2 million
capital and 1 million reserve
fund at 4 per cent. . . 120,000

$$£280,000 = 1\tfrac{1}{10}\%$$

earned on 25 million of deposits for which interest is
paid, *i.e.* say three-fourths of the total profit absorbed.
This would show that the London and Westminster
Bank makes a profit on its funds four times as large
as the Bank of England, after due allowance is made
for the larger capital of the latter.

In presenting this matter to you in this light I am
fully sensible that, under all the circumstances, the
Bank of England must follow a more conservative
course than the London and Westminster Bank.
Although the Securities dealt in by the latter stand
as high as any, and from their very nature are probably even more convertible than Government Securities—although the London and Westminster Bank
has 3 millions of Capital and Reserve, wealthy shareholders, and is as safe as any bank in the country—
yet I will allow that the Bank of England cannot
follow precisely the same course. (But I deny that this
involves the question of Reserve to be held by the Bank
of England for account of others, for the state of the
circulations flatly contradicts such an assumption).

Making full allowance, then, for the difference in
position between the two Banks ; disclaiming all intention to urge the Bank of England to earn 20 and 30
per cent. dividend as the London and Westminster has
done—what I want to bring before you is this: In all
directions there has been progress in profits and in
dividends—good, solid, visible profit, as manifested in
the last 30 years by the trade returns—facts which no

twaddle can upset. Why should the Bank of England's dividend alone show so little improvement? Is there anything unreasonable in the suggestion that the Bank of England, under all these favourable contingencies, should have paid an average dividend of say 12 per cent. instead of 9 per cent. This proportion of 3 over the present 9 to 10 would be equal to £400,000 per annum; and if the exports and imports of this country *If only by 2 or 3 per cent.* during the last 20 years have risen from 150 millions to nearly 700 millions, with the local business and wealth in like proportion, the inability of the Bank of England to eke out of all such stupendous increase this comparatively small profit for the benefit of its shareholders, is a matter for serious reflection and legitimate inquiry.

In claiming that the Bank should have paid to you this larger dividend, bear in mind that the history of *All the world has profited, excepting the holders of Bank Stock.* the commerce of the last 25 years is a most remarkable one. Of the four-fold increase of our own trade you are aware. Remember also that California and Australia, and the Silver-producing districts of the world, have increased the store of precious metals by nearly 1,000 millions sterling. All the world has had the benefit of this in direct material and manifestly large profits, and especially in this country. *You alone*, the stockholders of the Bank of England, have not profited a whit by it. From these points of view the subject appears to be one to which your attention may fairly be directed.

THE DISCOUNT BUSINESS OF THE BANK OF ENGLAND.

I now bring before you a fact which furnishes a most decisive proof in support of the statements so far made.

You are aware, no doubt, that the great commerce of this country, and that of the world, are carried on principally by " bills of exchange." I trust that in talking of such bills you will clearly understand what is meant by them. People unacquainted with commerce hear of " bill transactions," of " accommodation paper," &c., and are not aware that these have no connection with the great and gigantic system of credit, and the settlement of business in local and international commerce by the regular first-class bills of exchange. The " first-class " bills of exchange, those in which the London discount market and bankers all over the country and abroad deal, are drawn either against sales of goods made by one party to another in the country itself, or against securities deposited, or they arise in international trade, drawn against shipments of merchandize on the way, or against guarantees and deposits furnished from abroad. Thus the great Manchester trade, and that arising in all our industrial centres, is carried on chiefly by bills drawn against sales of manufactures, or bills accepted against purchases of raw material. This business, for English home account alone, is enormous; but England, as the first trading, shipping, and financial nation, also acts as banker for almost all other countries. Shipments of goods between India, America, Germany, Holland, and other parts of the world, are made " by bills upon London," the acceptors here receiving the documents and guarantees, and when the goods are due, the necessary remittances from abroad. A continuous large stream of these bills thus concentrates in, and flows from London; the vast majority of them does not even involve credit in the common meaning of the term, they are " instruments of exchange," in the " clearing " sense of the word, the very life-blood of commerce and of banking.

(marginal notes:) The great business of this country is conducted chiefly by bills of exchange.

These instruments of exchange are the staple of banking.

Mr. R. H. J. Palgrave* states, that for the year (1870—71) the circulation in England

Of Inland Bills amounted to	£667 millions.		
Of Foreign Bills (accepted in England)	. . .	507	,,
Of Foreign Bills (drawn and negotiated in England	.	104	,,
		£1,278	,,

They amount to 1,200 millions sterling per annum.

Mr. Palgrave further says, that the aggregate of bills in circulation at one time varies between 300 and 350 millions sterling.

Of which 300 to 350 millions are current at a time.

Bearing in mind these great facts and figures, and knowing, as no doubt you do, that the Bank of England is so powerful an institution, with so large a capital and deposits, the right of the note issue as extra resource, not enjoyed by other banks ; that it is the leader in the discount market, and that it determines the rate of discount, so anxiously watched by commerce, you may suppose that out of the 300 millions of bills of exchange current, the Bank of England not only holds the comparatively largest share, but that this share is more or less regular, so as to give a practical foundation to the leadership which the Bank exercises in the discount market. In order to afford you a guide of what the amount of bills held by the bank ought to be, I quote Mr. Palgrave's figures (p 5 of Notes on Banking) wherein he gives the

The Bank of England might be supposed to be the principal holder of such bills.

Bank of England total resources at	67 millions.		
London Private and Joint Stock Banks	. . . . .	174	,,
Provincial Banks†	. . .	210	,,
		451	,,

In some proportion at least to its resources.

---

* In his admirable paper, "Notes on Banking." J. Murray, London.

† Country bankers employ a great part of their resources in cash advances, and against securities without bills.

Assuming now that out of the 300 to 350 millions of bills current altogether, there are 175 millions of first class bills of exchange in London, you can form some idea as to what share *the Bank of England* might *fairly be expected* to have in the active commerce of the country. According to the above estimate of resources, the Bank of England, upon the assumption only that it should share alike with other Banks, and without holding a superior leading position, ought to discount say from 30 to 40 millions of bills. Make extra allowances for the conservative nature of the Bank, and reduce the expected amount to one-half, if you like,

and compare

it *with the facts* shown in table on pp 10 and 11.

You will there find that the " bills discounted " by the Bank of England range between 2, 3, 5, *and* 9 *millions only;* that in the years notably of 1849—50—51—52, they were mostly under 3 millions, that in 1857 only they rose for *one week* to 17 millions, and in 1866 for *one week* to 16 millions. In 1872 (last year) they were as low again as $3\frac{9}{10}$ millions.

But, in reality, the Bank holds but a comparatively insignificant amounts of bills—frequently below 3 millions.

The following table has been compiled from the returns* asked for by Parliament. In these the " Bills Discounted " and " Temporary Advances," which in the weekly returns are included in the " Other Securities " of the Banking Department, are given separately, week by week. The table shows the number of weeks from 1845 to 1872, with the bills under discount, from 2 millions upwards.

---

* These returns, from 1845 to 1857, are found in the Parliamentary Blue Books on the enquiries of 1857 and 1858. They are reprinted in " Reform of the Bank of England Note Issue," a publication of which the author speaks on a subsequent page. Since then, during the present year, Mr. J. B. Smith, M.P. for Stockport, at the request of the author, moved for returns from 1857 to 1872, published on the 26th May 1873, No. 229.

TABLE 3.

THE BILLS UNDER DISCOUNT AT THE BANK OF ENGLAND.

Millions of Bills so held (000,000 omitted).

Millions £ of Bills	2	3	4	5	6	7	8	9	10	11	12	13	14	15	16	17
Years				NUMBER	OF	WEEKS	IN	EACH	YEAR.							
1845	12	14	11	.2	5	1	2	5	...	...	...	...	...	...	...	...
1846	...	...	...	6	12	5	1	6	7	6	8	1	...	...	...	...
1847	...	...	...	...	...	6	8	23	8	4	3	...	...	...	...	...
1848	...	31	12	4	2	3	1	...	...	...	...	...	...	...	...	...
1849	46	6	...	...	...	...	...	...	...	...	...	...	...	...	...	...
1850	45	6	1	...	...	...	...	...	...	...	...	...	...	...	...	...
1851	...	10	30	12	...	...	...	...	...	...	...	...	...	...	...	...
1852	32	20	...	...	...	...	...	...	...	...	...	...	...	...	...	...
1853	...	...	9	25	2	9	6	1	...	...	...	...	...	...	...	...
1854	...	...	2	22	22	6	...	...	...	...	...	...	...	...	...	...
1855	...	11	6	12	8	1	13	1	...	...	...	...	...	...	...	...
1856	...	2	13	7	5	0	13	6	...	...	...	...	...	...	...	...
1857	...	...	...	2	5	7	25	4	...	2	...	1	...	2	2	3
1858	...	35	7	2	2	1	1	1	1	...	1	1	...	...	...	...
1859	...	4	14	11	21	2	...	...	...	...	...	...	...	...	...	...
1860	...	...	...	...	4	25	17	2	4	...	...	...	...	...	...	...
1861	...	...	13	7	7	18	7	...	...	...	...	...	...	...	...	...
1862	...	...	3	17	22	11	...	...	...	...	...	...	...	...	...	...
1863	...	...	...	3	17	18	12	2	...	...	...	...	...	...	...	...
1864	...	...	...	...	...	11	24	16	1	...	...	...	...	...	...	...
1865	...	...	...	...	...	19	14	14	5	...	...	...	...	...	...	...
1866	...	...	...	...	7	14	9	6	4	2	1	2	2	4	2	...
1867	...	...	21	3	21	5	2	...	...	...	...	...	...	...	...	...
1868	...	1	32	11	9	...	...	...	...	...	...	...	...	...	...	...
1869	...	...	13	13	20	6	...	...	...	...	...	...	...	...	...	...
1870	...	...	2	21	21	1	2	3	2	...	...	...	...	...	...	...
1871	...	1	8	20	11	3	1	2	6	...	...	...	...	...	...	...
1872	...	3	3	8	9	12	14	3	...	...	...	...	...	...	...	...

The temporary advances average 2 millions.

Besides these "bills discounted" the Bank of England makes "temporary advances" on bills and other securities. These vary from a quarter of a million to 4 millions, exceeding 5 millions in 46 instances, and reaching once 9 millions. The total average of these is under 2 millions. But the essential portion here under our notice are the "bills discounted," of which, according to the above table, embracing 28 years, or 1460 weeks—the Bank held

For 135 weeks,	between	2 and	3 millions		
144	,,	,,	3 and	4	,,
200	,,	,,	4 and	5	,,
208	,,	,,	5 and	6	,,
232	,,	,,	6 and	7	,,
190	,,	,,	7 and	8	,,
172	,,	,,	8 and	9	,,
95	,,	,,	9 and	10	,,
38	,,	,,	10 and	11	,,
14	,,	,,	11 and	12	,,
13	,,	,,	12 and	13	,,
5	,,	,,	13 and	14	,,
1	,,	,,	14 and	15	,,
6	,,	,,	15 and	16	,,
4	,,	,,	16 and	17	,,
3	,,	,,	17 and	18	,,

The total average of bills discounted is 6 millions only.

That is to say, for nearly 700 weeks, or 14 years—one-half of the existence of the Bank under the Act of 1844—the Bank held bills ranging between 2 and 6 millions, or an average of 4½ millions. For 26½ years the bills discounted were under 10 millions, the average being under 6 millions; for 84 weeks, or 1½ years, they exceeded 10 millions—average under 12 millions; the total average for the 28 years being *about* 6 *millions.* As before stated, the bills current amount to 300-350 *millions*; the first class bills in London are certainly *not less than* 175 *millions.*

The general public, under the impression that the Bank of England is the great discounter of our money

market, will probably be surprised at the facts here shown, for bankers, financiers and economists, who for many years had inquired into the Bank of England matters, and had written pamphlets about them, when these results were shown them by the author, were perfectly astounded at their "*novelty!*"

The general public, and economists are not aware of this extraordinary matter.

The table submitted speaks for itself. It will be noticed that the discounts exceed 10 millions only in the years of panic and crises—viz., 1847, 1857 and 1866; and that only for one or two weeks at a time. Some persons will say, " Oh, that is something, at all events; it shows that the Bank can come forward and assist the public in times of panic." And here " the availability" of the Reserve of the Bank is brought forward. If the office of the Bank be chiefly that of coming forward every 10 years with a few millions of money—and we know at what sacrifices to the safety of the institution itself this is done—there is but poor comfort in the existence of the establishment. These narrow-minded sayings must be dismissed ; they emanate from the same class of rough, would-be economists, who have no other resource left than praising the Bank of England system for everything done, however anomalous it may appear.

The Bank appears to do a profitable discount business only when crises and panics set in.

Commerce however has a higher right in this matter, and must demand enquiry into this very irregular and incompetent, though pretentious, action of the discounts of the Bank. What explanation can possibly be given by the admirers of the present Act of this extraordinary state of things ?

Commerce has a higher right of enquiry into these facts.

The investigation of the returns show that the Bank of England's Banking Department invests the greater part of its deposits in Government securities, and among the "other securities " in that department,*

---

* Beyond this, there are the 15 millions of Government debt, and other securities in the issue department.

which include the bills discounted, there are advances on railway securities and other matters. Nobody will object to any Bank making investments and advances on Government securities; indeed, where such great interests are at stake, a good proportion of a Bank's resources should always be invested in such undoubted guarantees. Further, the Bank of England is bound to encourage, by advances on railway and other bonds, all safe and quasi national public and agricultural undertakings, but when the total of these kinds of investments exceeds the discounts in so overwhelming a manner as here shown, there is reason to suppose that something is wrong. Government, railway and interest-bearing securities of that kind represent transactions already completed—for which currency has passed before—and investments in, and advances thereon, can be conducted by "financial companies" without any great organisation for banking. Upon this view the active produce of such securities is confined to the annual interest they bear, which re-enters commerce for the exchange of commodities without any direct connection with the wants of currency. When this want of currency arises, as it will in times of crises, the investment in Government securities, albeit considered the safest, cannot of itself produce what is wanted, for whether the sale or conversion be difficult or not, it involves only a transfer of account within narrow limits. There have been times when advances on such securities were absolutely impossible. Again, the sale of Government securities involves the question of price and possible loss, the realisation cannot take place without *a fresh contract being made*, a contract of "local" nature only.

Bills of exchange, however, as the great mass of active instruments, determining not only the exchange of commodities, the profits in national and international

The Bank of England is bound to invest in Government securities.

But not to the overwhelming disadvantage of bills.

Government securities require fresh contracts for their conversion.

Bills of exchange are the ultimate creators of currency.

trade, and the very foundation of all prosperity, are the ultimate creators of currency, absorbing and reproducing it, adding the balance to the circulation and the wealth of the country. And it is but reasonable to suppose that these active agents, which enter and re-enter commerce by hundreds of millions, should form the chief basis of active banking operations.

Bills of Exchange, be it understood, *represent contracts in existence*, backed by the solid guarantee of commodities. They require no fresh bargain and discrepancy of price, and their safety hangs on 'the millionfold threads of commerce. For whereas the Government security has nothing but itself to support, the bill of exchange is connected with assets of real and *international* value, subject to the reaction of the Bank's influence, be it for the purpose of producing currency or of modifying price or activity. It is evident then that when a Bank like that of England fails to obtain its proper share of influence in this respect, it fails lamentably in its office generally. Nothing that can be paraded before you in regard to the present action of the Bank with Government securities (for the attempt to demonstrate its infallibility will no no doubt be made) can upset the truth of the remarks here made, or explain away this gross symptom of disease under which the Bank of England labours.

Moreover, issues of bank notes on the credit of securities or fiduciary notes (the 15 millions of Bank of England notes issued above Bullion, are the "fiduciary" portion of the issue) are principally made for the purpose of assisting the active current commerce by supplying the circulation with means, the requirements for discount demand their issue, the realisation of the bill of exchange at due date repays the advance made by them. In all States where the Bank-note is not used for actual Government necessities, where there is parity between Coin and Paper, money and commerce sound, this is distinctly recognised. Accordingly, any bank intrusted with a note issue, has the special duty of bringing this issue in regular contact with bills of exchange.

The banks of France, Prussia,* and others, continually hold large amounts of bills of exchange, indeed they form their principal investment. Let it not be said that in these countries there are not comparatively as many other public or private discount establishments as in England—indeed the increase of joint stock banking in France and Germany has led to a large increase of the discounts held by the central banks, as properly it should do. The Bank of France

(margin note: Other central Banks have a much greater share in commerce.)*

---

* The following is the account of the Bank of Prussia of 15th August 1873 (in Sterling) :—

Active.

Coin and Bullion...	...	...	...	£36,880,000
Sundry Bank Notes	...	...	...	770,000
Bills discounted ...	...	...	...	25,360,000
Lombards (Advances on Securities)		...		3,790,000
State Bonds and Sundries		...	...	540,000

Passive.

Notes in Circulation	...	...	...	£39,940,000
Deposit ...	...	...	...	4,300,000
Balances of State, Companies, Private Acounts, &c. ...	...	...	...	16,850,000

This is exclusive of Capital, &c. The comparatively small amount of advances on Securities, as against Bills discounted, will be noticed. The Bank of Prussia charges more on such advances than on Bills. The National Bank of Belgium on the 20th August 1873, held under discount fs. 247½ millions, or nearly £10,000,000. Both in Prussia and Belgium there are other powerful joint stock Banks, and a considerable number of private banking firms. Neither of these States are "international Bankers," like we are in England, and the amount of bills during the year in proportion to population is probably but one-third or one-fourth of what is done in England. (See Bank of France, p 15).

(see table on p 15) discounts commercial paper in a far more effective and regular manner, and if that institution manages to hold such bills at a regular average of, say, £20 millions, why cannot the Bank of England do the same, or better? English bills of exchange should not be inferior to French bills—independently of the question of greater severity in the bankruptcy laws.

It can be alleged, with good reason, that the fairly regular action of so important a factor in national commerce as the leading bank of a country influences even the " moral" aspect of this matter. The letter printed at foot* (addressed by the author to the *Times*, of the 8th July 1872), referring to French bills, may assist the reader in his endeavour to appreciate the

The matter involves even the question of morality.

---

* " A year ago the Bank of France, after an interval of nine months of sieges, again issued its weekly statement of affairs. This statement, for the 29th of June 1871, among the assets, contained the following item :—Commercial bills prolonged by law, 371,385,060f. ; and among the liabilities, the item—reserve for eventual losses on prolonged bills, and on liquidation of the branches at Metz, Mulhouse and Strasburg, 26,000,000f.

" At that time a reserve of 26 millions on 371 millions of suspended bills, and for the liquidation of three branches, appeared ridiculously small. The bills so prolonged declined however in the following ratio :—27th July 1871, 309,834,000f. ; 21st August, 147,701,818f. ; 28th September, 88,750,045f. ; 26th October, 26,593,372f. ; 2nd November, 7,149,440f. ; 9th November, 3,070,530f. After which the item disappeared, the balance being included in the usual ' commercial bills overdue,' *i.e.* bills which lay over for next day or the following days of grace against protest.

" The ' Compte-rendu ' of the Bank for 1871 states, that from the 13th of August 1870, when the law of prolongation came into force, until the 12th of July 1871, when the faculty to prolong ceased, 416,000 bills, of a total of 630 millions francs, took advantage of the law at the head office (a very large proportion of the best bills were duly paid even during the siege). Of these bills, 105,000, amounting to 361,000,000f., were paid by anticipation. On the remainder, 269,000,000f., 255 millions were duly paid, leaving 14 millions unpaid at the end of 1871. The bills prolonged at the branches

3

hint here given, and thoughtful men may be willing to concede that there is a strong *primâ facie* connection between regular and orderly action, clear of all suspicion of error in system, and commercial morality.

And when it is borne in mind that we, here in England, do not only carry on our own business, but that we receive and pay bills for the world's trade at large, that the supply of these first-class securities is far more considerable than elsewhere, the small share which the Bank of England has therein must appear all the more striking.

What can the admirers of the present state of things bring forth in explanation? They cannot say "these bills are not good enough," that would be

---

amounted to 238,000,000f., of which 1,640,000f. remained unpaid. The total of unpaid bills six months ago therefore amounted to about 15½ millions of francs. I am informed, on the highest authority, that the greater part of this balance has since come in, and that the eventual loss is not likely to exceed 2½ millions of francs, or £100,000.

"Thus, on a grand total of 868,000,000f., or £34,700,000 of suspended or prolonged bills, there is a loss of £100,000, or scarcely one-third of 1 per cent. It is supposed that even this loss would not have happened if a certain number of parties to the bills had not been killed during the Commune. Bear in mind, with all this, that France has fought a most gigantic, disastrous war; that her trade and industry have been suspended for more than a year; that a bloody social struggle crowned her misfortunes; and that she has already paid 80 million pounds sterling to her conquerors.

"Englishmen are proud of their financial solidity, but if such disasters as happened to France were to fall upon this happy land, and if the 'bill-cases' of our banks and the Bank of England were suddenly turned into 'suspended paper,' I question whether one-third of 1 per cent. would cover the ultimate total loss. The astounding and wonderful result thus shown by the portfolio of the Bank of France furnishes striking evidence either of the excellent management of the Bank's system of discount, or of the thoroughly honest, conscientious and solid character of French commerce. In my opinion, both are combined."—*Times*, 8th July 1872.

belying our gigantic prosperity, and the Bank itself does not hesitate, when interest is high, to invest as much as it can in bills! Ask them for such explanation, and you are likely to be treated to a string of dogmatic statements and sophistical arguments, against which you must place the facts here laid before you, and decide which is the truth and which is the farce! Facts like these require more than mere talk of confidence and strength, and you may be willing, in your own interests, and those of the country at large, to repudiate for once these attempts at stifling an enquiry into "realities." You can do no harm by it. From the most general point of view, what does this want of progress of the Bank indicate? Is it, to use a familiar term, "worthy" of England, the foremost nation in progress? You cannot but admit that the figures placed before you indicate a state of "mediocrity," from which the conclusion may be drawn that the evident conflict between the Bank and the public has a most practical foundation. The Bank may say "there is no conflict, we are right, we have promoted the commerce of this country in the most perfect manner," and in the absence of a competitor of equal rank, all this might be said with impunity. But the financiers and economists, who ever since the passing of the Act of 1844 have disputed its propriety, deserve respect, and if, before this, they had taken the trouble of analyzing the Bank's accounts as has here been done, they might have been able to demonstrate to the common sense of the British public the necessity for a reform.

One of the most singular features belonging to this conflict, of which the general public is not, but of which discount houses are well aware, is the policy of the Bank as regards "advances to bill brokers." Ever since 1844 the Bank of England has wavered on

[marginal notes:]

No dogmatic and pompous statement can go against the facts here shown.

The conflict requires the earnest consideration of all economists.

The undecided action of the Bank as regards advances to discount brokers.

the question whether it should make such advances or not. Sometimes large transactions have been entered into, at other times the Bank has suddenly declared its intention not to make them. I am credibly informed that, during the present year, the question was again mooted—" shall such advances be made or not ?"—and that no definite decision has been given; and, let it be remarked, even if such definite decision was made, it could not be maintained. The facts of the case are these :—Certain discount brokers occasionally come to the Bank, and ask for advances on parcels of first-class bills at Bank rate. They do this at times when they expect a reduction of the rate of discount, so as to be able to gather as many bills together for future re-discount at a lower rate. Within a certain period before dividend times the Bank freely makes such advances, at other times it refuses them, although there may be an ample store of Reserve. On several occasions the Bank has endeavoured to establish rules to guide this business, but they have not been kept, and the Bank now pretends to act according to circumstances. The Bank's right thus to act according to circumstances is indisputable, but there is a degree of looseness about the whole matter which is not in accord with the firmness of valuation required in a money market like that of London. The changes of policy which have taken place indicate that the grounds upon which such business ought to be conducted, namely, the character of the securities presented, and the supply of money, are not adhered to. The class of discount brokers who thus make use of the Bank's reserve present the finest bills, and consider this method of profiting by advances thoroughly legitimate. On the other hand, the system leads to a kind of inflation which ought to be avoided, and the Bank is placed in a position in which the legitimate desire

The method in which brokers profit from advances of this kind.

In spite of the long practice, no definite policy has been established, such as our valuation requires.

to employ the idle reserve profitably on first class securities conflicts with ulterior considerations, both sides involving certain true principles. The subject becomes more complicated through the Revenue accounts and other matters which should be incidental only. It will be shown hereafter why the Bank is unable to maintain a more definite position in respect to advances of this kind.

The Bank stands between two sides, each of which has legitimate claims.

WHERE IS THE ERROR?

The accounts laid before you in the previous chapters, this want of progress in the establishment in face of the great prosperity of all other institutions, this "modest," or, to use a harsher term, "this comparatively trumpery" discount business of the Bank of England, must convince even the greatest admirer of the present state of things that "something is wrong." Others may go further, and say that these accounts indicate a serious disease, and if we bear in mind how long the controversy has lasted, that nothing has been done to improve matters, that the attempts made were futile, we may fairly assume that the original cause of the disease lies deeply hidden.

These remarkable accounts presuppose the existence of a subtle disturbing error of system

It is important then that we should discover its locality, for in a controversy of this kind the blame is often shifted to causes, and laid on the shoulders of those who are perfectly innocent of any charge, and cannot help themselves. The Bank being divided into the Issue and the Banking Department, we must decide whether the fault lies in the one or the other. Can the original fault lie in the Banking Department?*

In either the Issue or the Banking Department.

---

* In certain quarters the opinion prevails that the public have no right to inquire into the Banking Department of the Bank of

To this question a decided *negative must be given.* The Bank has an enormous capital and rest, and therein lies a force which, in high-toned competition even, would meet with its adequate share of deposits and banking business generally, and consequent good dividends. The Banking Department conducts the Government accounts, it receives millions of deposits, the solid wealth of the country, and these branches of business are absolutely free from any possible hitch or suspicion originating in their own nature. Above all, the Bank of England is managed by a set of gentlemen, chosen from the highest ranks of the mercantile community, gentlemen who have inherited all the experience of bygone days, cautious and ready to carry out the highest policy of business and caution combined. What, may you ask, can be more perfect? Convinced of this perfection, with the

The error cannot be in the Banking Department.

England, that being, so to speak, a private matter, the Issue alone concerning the public. Other banks, such as the Bank of France (which has less connection with the State than our Bank, and has "private" shareholders), and the Bank of Prussia, regularly publish their accounts in an elaborate manner, so as to lay open to all the world the legitimate business they do. The instruction in social commercial science which is thus distributed is beneficial to these Banks, and to the public at large, and a principle of the highest economic value is thereby vindicated. The Bank of England (beyond the weekly formal statement prescribed by the Act) does not furnish any details of its business, a proceeding which, in a country like this, where open and free investigation should be encouraged above all things, is a blot upon our civilisation. The Directors of the Bank and the nation should feel proud of showing what a Bank of England can do, and you, the stockholders of the institution, may feel assured that your property would thereby only improve in value. The returns from which the above accounts are taken were furnished to Parliament (see foot note to page 26). Being thus made public, I have the undoubted right to analyse them, whether the fiction as to the Banking Department being a private matter be maintained or not.

indefinite feeling that with such perfection the *Bank must* always be right, there may be among you many cynics, who require the strong argument contained in the figures and facts given before they will listen to criticism.

Whilst therefore it must be acknowledged that the Banking Department of the Bank of England by itself rests upon elements too solid and clear to admit of any doubt, it is equally clear, as I have shown by the accounts, that this magnificent strength and wealth is unable to assert itself, that it is under some influence, or has some connection which disorganises and lames its action. In any system of machinery, however expensively and magnificently proportioned it may be, however perfect it may appear in all its parts, there may yet be one fault or misconstruction attached to one of the components, which, in its connection with the others, demoralises the action of the whole. Where such a fault lies at the surface, it is easily seen and corrected, but when it is hidden or obscured, and yet has so overwhelming and powerful an effect in disorganising strength, and counteracting mercantile wisdom, there is reason to suppose that it is a very subtle and poisonous matter.

The conclusive proof that the elements of business in the Banking Department do not cause the trouble, will appear in the following: You are aware that violent fluctuations in the Reserve and the Bullion of the Bank of England take place, movements whose range comprises several millions. The withdrawal or diminution of the Reserve of any Bank, not connected with the Bank note issue, can only take place, because :—

Firstly. By losses which the Bank incurs on its investments. The Bank of England invests the greater part of its resources in Government securities, and among the " other " securities the bills discounted form a comparatively insignificant portion. The losses possible on such bills are small, they affect but profit and loss account, and cannot even remotely influence the Reserve.

Secondly. The second cause for a diminution of the Bank's Reserve might be the withdrawal of deposits. Now, here one of the most remarkable facts in the history of the Bank of England must, *throughout the controversy*, be *continually borne in mind*. During a crisis the deposits of the Bank of England, *instead* of *decreasing*, actually *increase;* still, even in spite of such increase, the drain on the Bank continues.

Nor the withdrawal of deposits, for these increase rather than diminish.

Beyond these two causes there are none other which can possibly affect the *status quo* of any Bank in a forcible manner; the question whether the Bank will part with its Reserve for additional advances, is one which it may decide at its own option. It will be shown hereafter that these fresh advances to commerce, by the Bank of England, are comprised in the circulation of the Bank of England note, which, within certain limits, is of a more or less regular character, its divergences having but little connection with the original effect of the disturbances.

The question of fresh advances is independent of this matter.

That original effect is : the fluctuations in the stock of Bullion in the Issue Department; and having shown, in the foregoing, that these cannot possibly be due to the losses made by the Bank on its own investments, nor to the withdrawals of deposits—in other words, the Banking business proper of the Bank—it will be my business now to point out to you *the special fault in the Issue system* which causes these quick and spasmodic withdrawals of Bullion ; the necessity for violent efforts to recover it, and how all this re-acts upon the Banking

The fault lies solely in the system of the Issue Department.

Department; destroying the benefits which both the country and the Bank might derive from the wealth, strength and wisdom there congregated, and leading to the confusion and partial ruin of our otherwise uninterrupted course of national prosperity.

At the first glance it would seem almost impossible that an issue of Bank notes could have so pernicious an effect as I assert it has. The elements upon which it is founded appear simple and profitable. A bank holds, or purchases, certain valuable securities, which *bear interest*, and thereupon issues bank notes, which cost but the paper, the printing, and the administration connected with them—and such notes can be employed as money, again yielding interest. And when, as is the case with the Bank of England, the amount of such bank notes is limited to a seemingly moderate amount, secured by Government stock, when all bank notes issued above them must be represented by bullion—it would appear that all the necessary precaution had been taken to secure profit and safety—that nothing more perfect could be suggested by human ingenuity.

The enigma involved in the present seemingly so perfect arrangement.

Yet if you set against this seemingly so proper an arrangement the fact that ever since it came into operation it has given rise to violent discussion—that crises and panics have been more severe than ever, that Royal Commissions have sat upon it, publishing thick Blue Books; that vain attempts at legislative improvement have been made, until the contending parties, in sheer despair at a solution, have formed into the extremes of warm admirers *versus* violent opponents, you cannot but come to the conclusion that, in spite of all that can be said in its favour, the fault remains undiscovered. The acknowledgment " that something is wrong " is frequently heard, but it is always

Its evident conflict nevertheless with facts.

The remedy is possibly hidden by a misconception, engendered in the practice of the system.

accompanied by the question, who can suggest " something better ?" The subtlety of the whole subject is thereby made manifest, and nothing is less surprising than that all sorts of wild revolutionary suggestions should be made in the hope to overwhelm, nolens volens, the anomaly. It is possible however, as in so many problems of a similar nature, that the error itself lies in a narrow compass, that the obscurity which surrounds it is due to some *misconception* arising in the practice of the system itself, and that some of the remedies suggested on the ground of this practice are fallacious, because they are dated from a *consequence*, instead of being led back to the *cause*.

THE PRESENT STATE OF THE CONTROVERSY.

The absurd schemes being dismissed.

An account of the present state of the controversy will contribute to the discovery of the error. Dismissing from consideration the outrageous scheme proposed by Mr. Anderson, M.P. for Glasgow—whose warm advocacy of the American system has received a wholesome rebuff by the American crises of September and October 1873—and other kindred more or less absurd suggestions, we confine our attention to the Bank of England issue and its reform.

The party divisions on the Bank of England issue remain.

In this field there are two great principal party divisions, the one may be designated as that which advocates the total abolition of the issue department, so as to merge the two departments into one, and recommending the repeal *in toto* of the Act of 1844, and certain other sweeping reforms. The other party division recognises the importance and usefulness of the separation between the issue and banking departments, and approves generally of other features in the Act. The latter division is the only one that stands in

sound practical relationship to the easy reform, and
a better understanding of the matter will be much
facilitated if all other considerations are dismissed
and attention be concentrated upon the point: "that
any reform in the Bank of England Note issue must
be sought *inside* the present system, the principle of
the arrangement as to the separation between issue
and banking department remaining in force." You
will perceive that I belong to this category, viz., that
I approve of the separation, as indeed I approve of the
whole Act, excepting the one point of error which
I shall endeavour to demonstrate to you.

The only practical party is that which seeks reform *inside* the present system.

Upon this more narrow, proper, and only practical
ground, five different sets of opinions or classes appear.

The sub-divisions of this party.

1st. The class of economists who, in despair at a
solution, pronounce in favour of an issue *on bullion only*.

2nd. The class of economists who still maintain
that the present *limit of 15 millions* is the precise and
right thing.

There are five leading opinions in the contro-versy.

3rd. The class who thinks the issue ought to be
increased temporarily or otherwise. Be it well understood that this class speaks only of an *increase* of
issue, not of a *decrease*.

4th. The class who would lay down a *sliding scale* of
issue, fixed amounts of bullion to guide the rates of
interest.

5th. The class which I represent, together with
those who have given adherence to my reasoning, which
proposes *a decrease or an increase of the fiduciary issue*,
not upon the system of a fixed sliding scale, but upon the
well defined *co-operation of the factors involved*, viz.
the amount of circulation, the proportion of bullion,
the rate of interest, and the necessities of reserve.

Of these, classes 1, 2 and 4 can at once be dismissed,
for the following reasons :—

Class 1.—In favour of pure issue on bullion (the

most careful of all) is impracticable. A bank note
issue made on bullion alone would continually subject
the circulation to forcible withdrawals, and, paradoxical
as it may seem, would place the country in an almost
continual state of panic. A fiduciary issue *must* be
made so as to exercise, in conjunction with the rate of
interest, a regulating influence. Besides this, the
fiduciary notes cover the expenses of the total issue.
This class may accordingly be dismissed first, as being
altogether impracticable.

Class 2, which maintains that the present system
is the right one, and will not admit of any alteration,
is still very powerful. (The money article of the *Times*
represents it most effectually). This class takes its
stand upon the desperate conclusion that "nothing
better can be suggested, and so matters are better left
as they are," under the, at all events, instinctively
"just objection" that any increase of issue is mischievous. Inasmuch as the whole subject involves the
question of reform or of no reform, the maintenance of
the present evil state, or its improvement, this class,
which will not consent even to its discussion, is
practically also out of the question. It is noteworthy
of remark however that a great many of the hitherto
principal supporters of this class have lately admitted
the necessity of reform, among them several of the
Directors of the Bank of England, who, during last
session of Parliament, spoke in favour of some sort of
extension of issue, tantamount to occasional legal
suspension of the Act.

Of the two classes remaining,

Class 4, which bases its conclusion upon suggestions made by the late Mr. Tooke, as to a fluctuating
fiduciary issue, for which however Mr. Tooke did not
submit a definite scheme, proposes a sliding scale

Class 1 is impracticable and impossible.

Class 2 admits of no reform.

Class 4 has an uncouth ground.

more stiff than the present system, and utterly devoid of life, being a mere rough guess work. This class must be dismissed, although the idea of a fluctuating issue touches a key note of the reform required.

Class 3 is that which the secessionists from class 2 have joined, and, represented by Mr. Wm. Fowler, Mr. Lowe and Sir John Lubbock, brought forward the measure proposed by Mr. Lowe in the Session of 1873, which, together with the amendments, was finally withdrawn by Mr. Gladstone.

This class, be it now distinctly understood, is that which practically has the matter in hand, and rules the situation. The principle which it has adopted is this:—"The limit of the Act of 15 millions of fixed issue is too rigid; whenever a crisis threatens we are obliged to suspend the Act, in order to allow more issue; in future we will legalise these suspensions." *[margin: Class 3 now rules the situation.]*

The chief characteristic of this proposal is accordingly this:—

The present system, with its limit of fixed credit issue is to be maintained, but it shall be suspended when requisite, by an extension of this limit. And therein the promoters of the proposal see the solution of the matter. *[margin: The main characteristic of this proposal is "extension" only.]*

Whereas

Class 5, which I represent, here says: *the present system shall remain, but the credit issue, hitherto fixed at 15 millions, must be subject to diminution as well as extension.* Mr. Fowler's* party *thinks that the present credit issue of 15 millions suits the case* in every way, excepting in the event of a crisis, when it *should be extended,* *[margin: Whereas both contraction and extension are required.]*

---

* Mr. Wm. Fowler, M.P., first started the proposal as to extension of issue in the event of crises. Mr. Lowe founded a bill upon it, which, with its manifest absurdities, proved too much for Sir John Lubbock, who proposed amendments. The main principle upon which both bill and amendments rest are those promulgated first by Mr. Fowler, who deserves to be called the originator of the party.

for it considers that crises and panics are due to causes which are independent of the system of issue; strange and inconsistent though it may appear that, under such an assumption, an alteration of the issue itself should be at all necessary.

I, on my part, distinctly assert—

That the *primary cause of all our difficulties* is the strict maintenance of the *fixed issue of* 15 *millions credit* notes in the times preceding a crisis, when bullion is in good supply, and sufficient to give a firm foundation to the *circulation* of the Bank of England notes, when a more moderate issue of credit notes would give a regular, but more moderate, *reserve.* Also I assert that any *surplus* of notes beyond the necessities of the regular circulation, and a certain amount of reserve, which, by the nature of reserve, should also be regular, is the *sole cause of the spasmodic and heavy withdrawals of bullion* from the stores of the Bank of England, and that the laws of exchange must operate against us when a heavy surplus of artificial money is brought into constant competition with the solid bullion basis.

The experience of our market proves that there are times when the Bank of England holds very heavy Reserves of notes, and when interest is abnormally low, and, according to the views maintained by Mr. Fowler, the Bank *is then strong!* Here lies the whole fatal misconception; for I maintain that these are the times of danger. Such heavy idle reserves not only have the effect of driving Bullion from our market, but the abnormal cheapness of interest then prevailing leads to the negotiation of seemingly legitimate but speculative contracts; until the low state of that commodity, even with the 15 millions of credit issue—which cannot afterwards be maintained, as they require a greater absorption

The primary cause of the evil is the surplus created by the 15 millions.

The supposed strength of large note reserves is in reality the weakness of the system.

of Bullion for their liquidation than we possess— furnishes an amount of total issue insufficient to maintain the circulation already engaged, *when panic sets in.*

The truth of the matter is accordingly this: in spite of the idea of caution involved in the limit of 15 millions of credit issue, it is nevertheless the fact that this issue produces an *almost continual plethora*—deceiving and disorganising our market for a length of time, and causing, by the rule of reaction, the *subsequent crisis.* So, if according to experience, we see that a crisis repeats itself every nine or ten years, we find that during the preceding years there are four or five in which heavy reserves are in hand, others when the ups and downs are vexatious, until the crisis happens.

The idea of caution involved in the 15 millions fixed issue is fallacious.

That there are other causes which contribute to speculation and to mercantile disturbances; that the Bank of England, in order to guard against special political and other contingencies (such as the German demand for gold), must have a degree of independence in ruling the rate of interest, I freely admit; but the principle here enunciated—that a fixed artificial issue must be productive of a plethora—will be admitted by all who can estimate the situation, and the sense of caution governing the action of the Directors of the Bank of England naturally inclines to the keeping of Reserve; therefore the plethora is almost constant. The fixed issue of 15 millions deprives the Bank of the more direct and legitimate influence on Bullion; it altogether deprives the Bank of its independence. And if the admirers of the system say, "a large Reserve of notes at the Bank is strength," they labour under that great misconception which obscures the "subtle" point of error lying at the bottom of the whole matter.

Other causes are independent of this matter.

The plethora remains in force.

The excessive note reserves are not wanted for the cir-

for the circulation is more or less regular, and in its
range the question of accommodation is comprised; for
the safety of the Bank against possible withdrawals of
deposits a more moderate but *regular* reserve is
required by the nature of Banking. The combination
of 15 millions of fixed issue with 10, 15, 20 or 30
millions of Bullion cannot give this regularity; it must
give plethora in most instances, and scarcity in others,
to the prejudice of Bullion on the whole. This plethora
of note Reserve is supposed to furnish a set-off against
possible withdrawals of Bullion; in reality it is itself
the *chief cause why Bullion is driven from the country*.

Let us hope that the scales will fall from the eyes
of our bankers and economists, and that there are
logicians in the country able to appreciate the mathematical law and the practical truth before us. Unless
that takes place, the proposal of the Reform party,
headed by Mr. Fowler, are likely to carry their measure
through Parliament, when, as I assert, " the evils from
which we are suffering will be immeasurably enhanced.
Not only will the permanent action of the 15 millions
of credit issue in competition with Bullion be thereby
confirmed; but, with the prospect of *extension* of issue,
the preceding caution enforced by the present limit
will be lessened, and a contract basis be established,
leading to crises and panics, during which Bullion will
leave us, not as by a running tap, as at present, but as
if the bottom of the reservoir was knocked out."

But if, on the other hand, it be conceded that the
fixed credit issue must be abolished; that such credit
issue must be supplementary, and vary according to
the actual necessities of Circulation and Reserve, and
in accordance with the rates of interest required to
restore the equilibrium : " the whole question will then
receive its satisfactory solution. A system can be

The excess drives bullion from us.

The scales must fall from the eyes of the authorities.

Mr. Fowler's proposals involves the immeasurable ruin of our valuation.

The compensating system alone will satisfactorily solve the problem.

established which will bring all its factors into concurrent action, and which will afford a regular steady
reserve, whose influence will remain neutral."

I have led you so far, and foreshadowed the
proposal which I have to make, in order to show
you more clearly that the controversy has come to a
narrow point. Abandoning all wild schemes, concen-
trating our attention on the Bank of England issue
only, you will now see that the practically contending
parties even agree as to the general principle of the
separation of Banking and Issue Department, and that
the point in dispute concerns only the 15 millions
of issue, determined by Clause II. of the Act of 1844;
the questions being :—

Firstly. Shall this be maintained ? In which case
no reform takes place, and the present evils will
continue.

Secondly. Shall this be reformed ? In which case
the sub-questions :—

> *a.* Shall we adopt Mr. Fowler's proposal,
> maintaining the present fixed issue, and *pro-*
> *viding* for *extension* only,—in which case, as I
> assert, more evils and greater ruin will follow ?

OR

> *b.* Shall the fixed issue be abolished ? shall
> the principle of *diminution* and *increase* of the
> issue be called into life ? in which case, as
> I assert, the matter will find its absolutely
> correct and satisfactory settlement.

You will perceive that there is nothing revolutionary
or violent in these proposals—for the reforms can be
carried out by the amendment merely of Clause II.—
the body of the Act might remain as it is. If this

4

Clause 2 of the present Act already contains the spirit of the reform.

Clause II., of the Act of 1844, be read by you, you will find that it actually provides " for the diminution of the issue," but this is incompletely worded, and Clause VIII., determining the State share of profit not being in accordance, the Bank has been unable to carry out what seems to have been the instinctive feeling of Sir Robert Peel as regards the true nature of a credit issue.

The succeeding portions of the pamphlet enter into closer detail.

In the succeeding portions of this pamphlet, for the benefit of those not familiar with the principles of Bank note issue, I propose to lay down references to this subject, showing also how the present system has been engendered, furnishing more decisive proofs of the error which it envelopes. I shall give also the outlines of the system of contraction and expansion of the issue, which should be adopted in its stead.

THE ORIGIN AND THE MAIN PRINCIPLE OF THE ACT OF 1844.

The " mixed " basis of all good bank note issues.

The issues of bank notes of all States which are not compelled by political necessities to make large over-issues, to the ruin of the basis of prices, and consequent damage to their commerce with other countries, consist of the " mixed " basis, *i.e.* bullion and securities. Issues of bank notes on bullion alone are not practicable; firstly, because they want that element of pliability which the admixture of credit gives; and, secondly, they do not pay the issuer. The expenses attending the issue can only be recouped from the profit made on the notes based on credit. The notes issued against this joint basis of bullion and credit are all alike, and " promise to pay;" and, as a matter of course, the public have full faith in the notes so issued by the Bank of England and other great State Banks so long as they are regularly paid and remain "convertible into gold."

The word "fiduciary" is the proper technical term applicable to designate that portion of the issue basis which *does not consist of bullion*, but of securities and instruments of credit *held in trust*,* or as guarantee for their value and ultimate payment.

The term "fiduciary" portion of a bank note issue.

Ever since bank notes were introduced the question of "how much fiduciary issue shall be combined with bullion" has been discussed and experimented upon. The creation of money by so easy and costless, and, therefore, so enticing a process, as the mere printing of pieces of paper, ruined French society before the great revolution, through John Law's schemes, and contributed to the terror of that bloody period. In Hayti, 500 dollars in paper money are now worth *one* dollar in silver, and there are numerous other examples in the history of nations showing the fearful results upon prosperity of such fiduciary over-issues. In other States more reasonable proportions are adhered to, the necessity for some cash basis is recognised, as in Austria and the United States, but the baneful effects of such issues are apparent. Nevertheless, at the present day, there are would-be financiers (even in the British Parliament) who would make people "happy" by the copious issue of fiduciary bank notes. It is unnecessary that I should here explain why these crude notions still show themselves —how they originate in the utter want of appreciation of all that concerns the equilibrium of production and prices—how they are founded, in all probability, upon that "indefinable luscious longing" as regards money matters, in which certain leaders of social democracy

The disastrous experiments with over issue of fiduciary bank notes.

The crude ideas prevailing even to this day.

* See Johnson's and other Dictionaries of the English Language.

find so much satisfaction for the exercise of their superior inventive faculties.

The English nation and others in the front rank of civilisation have recognised by experience, as well as by theory, that there is but *one* truth in this matter, and they have practically adhered to bullion, as the leading element in bank note issues. To this fact is due, in a great measure, the "international wealth," which England enjoys by the realisation of the profits of her industry and commerce on the cash basis. And you, the stockholders of the Bank of England, should not speculate in the widest field of wild ideas which this question of fiduciary bank note issue involves, but confine your attention to the limits and the practicable matter of the Bank of England note issue.

The stockholders of the Bank of England are concerned only in the issue as practised by the Bank of England.

Before the operation of the Act of 1844 the Bank of England issued bank notes against a certain amount of bullion, and against securities comprised in what were called the "means" at the disposal of the establishment. The amount of notes to be thus issued, in proportion to bullion or securities, was entirely at the option of the Bank; in other words, the power of issue was "unlimited." Now, although the Bank of England never did anything that could be called foolish or extravagant, yet it was found that grievous evils resulted from this method. Rapid withdrawals of bullion took place, crises ensued, interest jumped up high, and confusion and ruin followed.* The charge was made that the Bank was unable to keep a hold on bullion, that the rates of interest were not managed so as to become operative in time, &c.

The old Bank of England Act.

---

* Nevertheless, under the old Act the increase of the Bank of England's business stood in somewhat better proportion to that of the country, and the rates of interest were neither as extravagantly low or high as since then. In saying this, the author does not imply that he is in favour of the old Act.

These charges were true, and the evidence shows that the fiduciary issues were allowed to attain proportions altogether inconsistent with the rate of interest. It was felt that the "unlimited power of issue" was not the proper thing to allow.

The Bank Act of 1844 (generally designated as Sir Robert Peel's), under which the issue is now con- ducted, therefore adopted a diametrically opposite principle—that of *strictly limiting* the fiduciary issue. Upon the computation that for a number of years before, the Bank of England had been able to keep " afloat" an average of 11 millions of "fiduciary" notes (above those issued on bullion), it was resolved that this should be a guide for the limit of issue. Certain reservations as to the falling in of certain country bankers' issues were made, under which the amount has since risen to 15 millions, but the *one cardinal principle* that this amount of fixed issue should be made and never be exceeded, was established. At that time the Government owed a sum of money to the Bank of England, and £11,015,100 were thus made a book debt, as guarantee for the issue. For the remaining £2,984,900 to complete the 14 millions (now 1 million more for the 15 millions) the Bank received authority to hold " other securities " as it might deem fit. It is necessary to call attention to these " other securities," because the impression prevails that the whole of the issue is made against an express Government debt. It is true that the Bank makes it a practice to hold Government securities against the £3,984,900, but Clause 2 of the Act, which provides the arrangement, does not prescribe this.

At the same time, by Clause 1 of the Act, the Bank was ordered to form two departments, the one called the Issue Department, where the bullion and securities were to be held against the issue

The Act of 1844.

Its cardinal principle of limit.

The Government debt and securities for the fiduciary issue.

Separation into Issue and Banking Department.

of notes,* the action of this department being presumably entirely "automatic;" the other to be called the Banking Department, in which the Bank presumably has full liberty to act as any other banker. Forms of weekly accounts are prescribed by the Act, as we are now in the habit of seeing them. The *other great cardinal feature* of this arrangement is that all the issue of Bank of England notes above the 15 millions fixed fiduciary issue must be made against bullion. Thus, if the Bank has in its vaults 5 or 10 or 15 or 20 or 25 millions of bullion, the total issues would respectively be 20, 25, 30, 35 and 40 millions of Bank notes.

All issue above 15 millions to be made against bullion.

What are the real and uppermost merits of the case, *just* merits on the strength of which the Act has met with either unqualified admiration, or the *deceptive* merits, which have caused so much mischief and discussion? It is essential that a perfect understanding should be arrived at in regard to these merits, for whenever the Act is under discussion, such merits are brought to the front and are commented upon, without there being any necessity to introduce them, the question under consideration here lying within the narrower compass of the mere amount of fiduciary issue.

The real and the deceptive merits of this method of issue.

One of the most important objects in view was that of securing the convertibility of the notes into gold. The traditions of the war with France, the history of French and other bank notes, were uppermost at that time, and the word "convertibility" reigned paramount. Granted now that (if we ignore the crises, notably that of 1857 when the danger to convertibility was imminent) this object has been fairly secured, it is evident that

The convertibility of the note.

---

* Certain other duties as regards the purchase of bullion at a fixed rate, and the control of the gold and silver coinage, as by a *quasi* agency for the Mint, are undertaken in that department.

the precise sum of 14 or 15 millions of credit issue does not contain an absolute principle, it must be admitted that a fiduciary issue of but 5 or 10 millions would have enhanced, whilst 20 or 25 millions of it would have diminished, the chances of convertibility; absolutely convertible the notes would be if they were issued wholly against bullion. Nevertheless, whilst I recognise this securing of the convertibility of the note as a just merit of the Act, you must permit me to ask you not to lay too much stress upon this matter of convertibility. Many old economists, who live in the odour of traditions, claim this as the sole specific merit of the Act, whereas modern economists have long ago recognised the necessity of securing convertibility first of all, and this subject is so well understood, that (in England at least) no scheme would be listened to which does not provide for this before all other things. The question which must be considered here lies much beyond the convertibility, and in asking you to leave this matter as understood, I require you to free your minds from it for the moment, so that the real point will no longer be obscured by useless reference to it. Convertibility must be secured first of all.

The second supposed great merit of the Act is that the 15 millions of fiduciary issue are secured by Government debt and security, so that, even if all the bullion went away from the Bank, the Government would, by repaying the debt or by implication of its liability, provide cash for these notes. To every Englishman the security offered by his own Government gives a feeling of comfort and satisfaction, the legitimacy of which I do not deny. Nevertheless it is open to discussion whether Government securities,* which are subject to fluctuations in price, difficult of sale during a crisis, and requiring a fresh contract for The security of the State and "other" securities held against the 15 millions fiduciary issue.

---

* See page 30.

their conversion into money, might not be supplanted by bills of exchange of the first order, *i.e.*, by contracts already made and directly connected with the acquisition of bullion. The Act, it must be borne in mind, covers only 11 millions of the issue by the State debt, the balance consists of "other" securities, as the Bank may see fit to place in the issue; this, at all events, shows that the idea of Government securities is not absolutely leading. It is often said: let the State repay this debt to the Bank. That could easily be done by the State taking over the portion of notes and not issuing them again; but this would be tanta-

The same security will be given in the scheme of the author.

mount to a mere annulling of the fiduciary issue. If this issue is to continue it must have some security, whether this be in State debt, or in consols or bonds to bearer, or first-class bills and other convertible securities, is a question for the Bank. In the scheme which the author will propose, the fiduciary issue will also be covered by Government securities, so that this point, of which so much is made by those who do not go deeply into the matter, needs no further discussion.

The third merit or peculiarity claimed on behalf of

The separation of the issue from the Banking Department.

the Act is the separation of the issue from the Banking Department as provided by Clause 1. The admirers of the Act pretend that the issue is thereby rendered entirely automatic, as a thing with which the Banking Department has nothing to do. Much discussion has arisen in reference thereto, the opponents declaring that this is all moonshine, that it is merely a matter of account, that both departments are at the charge of the Bank and its stockholders, that it is absurd to pretend that the left hand of the Bank does not know what the right is doing. The admirers of the Act forget that Clause 2 provides expressly for the transfer of the notes to the Banking Department, and that the "Reserve" of notes so arising as *not* in circulation, might be as well held in the Issue Department, when the two accounts would be practically united. Nevertheless the separation of the two departments is of real value and practical importance, and the action of each can be more clearly defined, as will be done in the scheme to be proposed by me. Sir Robert Peel conceived the idea upon just grounds ; the reason why it has, to a great extent, missed its point, will appear hereafter to you. Again, then, as my plan will re-affirm and more clearly define the separation of issue and banking, there is no need in discussing this matter as a special merit of the present Act.

The same system of separation will be maintained by the author's scheme.

My object in strongly urging you to set aside, for a moment, these matters concerning convertibility, Government securities, and separation of issue and banking, with which, as you see, I fully agree (as, indeed, you will perceive that I agree with every other feature of the Act) is, I repeat, that of leaving a clear space for the real point. As I stated before, whenever the Bank Act is under discussion, these subjects are sure to be brought forward. They are crowded one upon the other ; hasty conclusions are made, so that it is difficult to wedge in a word concerning the true nucleus of the matter. It is, accordingly, unnecessary that you should have reference to subjects about which I agree with you. The point under discussion, that upon which all the good and evil turns, that which disorganises the operations of the Bank, is simply *the fixed limit of* 15 *millions of fiduciary issue, both the fixity and the amount so fixed,* and the whole controversy centres again on the simple points as to either the *maintenance* of this limit, its occasional *extension,* or its *diminution* and *expansion.* (See page 49.)

A discussion on the points enumerated is not necessary. The "real" point will appear all the more readily.

The main point to be considered, viz., the 15 millions fixed issue.

We can now concentrate all our attention upon the fixed limit of 15 millions of fiduciary issue. What are its merits ?

All those acquainted with the subject, and the previous history of our banking operations, will probably agree with me that the leading idea under which the legislators of 1844 established the system was to the following effect :—

" We have found that over-issues of paper money have taken place, that speculation was thereby encouraged, that disturbances and crises followed ; we will *avoid* this in future by limiting such issue to 15 millions ; for all issue above this, the commerce of the country must provide itself with bullion through the Issue Department of the Bank. The commerce of the country must operate within these bounds ! "

It can be admitted at once that this idea as to caution involved in the limit is the *great charm* of the thing, of which a great many financiers have approved, and to which others readily give their consent. Nor is this to be wondered at. The idea of preventing mischief by erecting a strict barrier is one that, in the absence of better suggestions, would rise uppermost and assert itself, for it has the great merit of caution and the *apparent merit* of moderation, and with these elements secured it is popularly supposed

that no error can arise on the side of extravagance and mischief. No wonder that there are persons going so far as to admire even the genius which invented the plan, and who enthusiastically defend it. No fault then should be found with the earnest men who, acting upon the principle of caution, really thought that they had established a perfect and almost sacred system.

Nevertheless, we may ask ourselves, did they act upon refined and really intelligent reasoning ? It is so easy to say, " Here, this we will give you; mind you remain within bounds ; you shall not have a farthing beyond it, if everything goes to wreck and ruin—so please understand that!" To many the thought of having made and upheld such a proposition is really comforting; they feel they have done their duty, have nothing to reproach themselves with; at any rate— the "there, we have put a stop to excess!"—concludes the matter with them. I call upon all those who have favourably estimated the present arrangement to say whether this feeling, as a kind of argument, is not that which induces them to approve of the principle of the fixed limit. Whatever honour and credit we may now feel disposed to award to the conscientious men, who, by adopting an apparently so straightforward and severe, yet not illiberal, a system, we may yet at the first glance ask the question, why did they fix upon 15 millions (originally 14)—what was the charm which made them adopt that sum in 1844, when the trade of the country was one-fifth of what it is now? Where is the economical principle which, either in the abstract or drawn from practice, induced them to choose this amount? This will lead us on to the consideration of the *demerits* involved in the fixed limit.

Its want of pliability.

THE DEMERITS OF THE FIXED LIMIT OF 15 MILLIONS.

The demerits of the limit consist, in the first place, of errors- of calculation and anticipation, which, although not of overwhelming importance in themselves, yet show distinctly their fallacious nature, and lead to the inference that they cause a grievous wrong somewhere. The origin of the fixed issue was as follows :—For a certain period before 1844 the circulation of the Bank of England, not founded on bullion, had given an average of slightly above 11 millions, varying, from 1826 to 1843, between 7, 9, 10, 13 and

The origin of the amount of 15 millions.

15 millions. Upon the ground therefore that the Bank had been able *to float*, and the public in the habit of *using*, so much fiduciary issue, it was resolved to take the average of 11 millions as a starting point. Certain country bankers having given up their issue, 3 millions more were added to it, making 14 millions, since increased to 15 millions.*

The system of taking an average of a series of items is applicable to many cases, and Sir Robert Peel's advisers no doubt imagined that they were doing the right and liberal, yet strict, thing; and although they did not make any provision for an extension of such issue in accordance with the increase of our trade (since fourfold), they certainly imagined that this system of average would be responded to in future. All the evidence given at that time expresses this anticipation. Now nothing is more contradictory of the true state of facts than the *average* taken from *variety*. If previous experience shows greater or lesser amounts, and if that experience is to guide the future, the average, instead of doing this, actually belies and directly contradicts it. Modern economy utterly condemns such computations, and the merest tyro in the science must admit that such condemnation is just.

If the experience since had borne out that the 11 or 15 millions of issue above bullion could have been kept in circulation, or even some proportion differing within as much as 50 per cent., the matter might have turned out as practicable, but the variations since then are of the wildest description, ranging from the *nothing* (or even an excess of bullion over circulation, 1852, 1871,) to 15, and even 17 millions (1857) of fiduciary

The fallacy of the average in matters of this kind.

The variations have since been most excessive.

---

* 1844, 14,000,000; 1856, 14,475,000; 1861, 14,650,000; 1866, 15,000,000.

circulation, and exceeding the ranges of 1 to 15 by two millions in either direction. A more flagrant contradiction of the validity of average could not well be shown.

The table on next page gives the returns furnished, in Parliamentary Blue Book, 1857, Bank Acts, Part II. No. 220, page 91, &c., &c. These comprise the returns from 1825 to 1843 of circulation and bullion on the 28th February and 31st August, each year.

From 1845 to 1871, these items have been extracted by the writer, and for the sake of greater accuracy, four periods of each year have been selected, viz.: the returns from the end of February and end of August each year, as given in the weekly Bank accounts (the second and third number for each year) and two items, the lowest and highest fiduciary circulation (the first and fourth number of each year). The reader may ignore the latter, and adhere to the two former, as corresponding with the previous years.

The portion of fiduciary circulation has been extracted. In the old returns this is given under the head of "circulation;" in the new Bank Returns, the term "Notes held by the public" is used. Both mean the same thing, and are here given under the head "consequent fiduciary circulation."

Under the old Act no special reserve was kept, whilst since the limit was established such Reserve appears. But it must be distinctly understood that under the old Act the Bank had full power of issue tantamount to a Reserve, although not expressed in figures.

This must be borne in mind, for the column headed "consequent fiduciary circulation" is that by which the case must be tested.

The first portion of the table comprises the period from 1824 to 1843, which served for the computation of the fiduciary average to be allowed. What that circulation was you will see under the columns of " consequent fiduciary circulation." It rarely fell below 10 millions, being above 11 millions in most instances.

TABLE 4

RETURNS *showing the amount of* TOTAL CIRCULATION *of Bank of England Notes, with the amount of* BULLION *held during the years 1824 to 1843—two in each year; and the years 1845 to 1871—four in each year; (at the respective periods mentioned before) and the* CONSEQUENT FIDUCIARY CIRCULATION, *and the* RESERVES *of Notes.*

(£ Sterling in millions and decimals. 00,000 omitted.)

From 1824 to 1843.

Year.	Circulation.	Bullion.	Consequent Fiduciary Circulation.	Reserve.	Year.	Circulation.	Bullion.	Consequent Fiduciary Circulation.	Reserve.
1824	19·7	13·8	5·9	Under the old Acts no specific Reserve was kept, the Bank being able, at any time, to make what issue it pleased. This furnished Reserve for all purposes.	1834	19·2	8·5	10·7	Under the old Acts no specific Reserve was kept, the Bank being able, at any time, to make what issue it pleased. This furnished Reserve for all purposes.
	20·1	11·7	8·4			18·8	6·5	12·3	
1825	20·7	8·7	12·0		1835	18·3	6·2	12·1	
	19·3	3·6	15·7			17·8	6·2	11·6	
1826	25·4	2·4	23·0		1836	18·1	7·8	10·3	
	21·5	6·7	14·8			18·1	5·2	12·6	
1827	21·8	10·1	11·7		1837	18·2	4·0	16·2	
	22·7	10·4	12·3			18·7	6·6	12·1	
1828	21·9	10·3	11·6		1838	18·7	10·5	8·2	
	21·3	10·4	10·9			19·7	9·5	10·2	
1829	19·8	6·8	13·0		1839	18·0	6·8	11·2	
	19·5	6·7	12·8			17·8	2·4	15·4	
1830	20·0	9·1	10·9		1840	16·5	4·3	12·2	
	21·4	1·1	10·3			16·9	4·2	12·7	
1831	19·6	8·2	11·2		1841	16·4	4·4	14·0	
	18·5	6·4	12·1			17·5	4·8	12·7	
1832	18·0	5·2	12·8		1842	17·0	6·3	10·7	
	17·9	7·5	10·4			20·0	9·3	10·7	
1833	19·3	9·5	9·8		1843	20·2	11·1	9·1	
	19·6	9·8	9·8			19·3	12·2	7·2	

The second portion of the table now following comprises the period from 1845 to 1871; and you will observe that, whereas upon the assumption that the fiduciary issue would continue in the same measure, there ought to be some similarity, so as to show the correctness of the basis adopted; a glance down the column " consequent fiduciary issue " will show you the greatest divergences instead.

TABLE 4—*continued.* *From 1845 to 1871.*

Year.	Circulation.	Bullion.	Consequent Fiduciary Circulation.	Reserve.	Year.	Circulation.	Bullion.	Consequent Fiduciary Circulation.	Reserve.
1845	20·2	16·0	4·2	9·8	1858	20·3	16·9	3·4	11·0
	19·7	14·6	5·1	8·8		19·7	18·4	1·2	13·2
	21·0	15·0	6·0	7·9	1859	20·3	19·2	1·1	13·3
	22·0	13·4	8·6	5·6		20·2	19·0	1·2	13·2
1846	21·1	12·5	8·5	5·4		21·5	15·9	5·6	8·8
	20·0	13·0	7·0	6·9		22·4	16·3	6·1	8·3
	20·4	15·8	4·5	9·4	1860	23·4	13·9	9·5	4·9
	20·0	15·8	4·1	9·8		20·6	14·4	6·1	8·3
1847	20·6	13.2	7·4	6·5		21·1	15·1	5·9	8·5
	19·3	11·3	7·9	6·0		20·8	15·6	5·2	9·2
	18·2	8·5	9·6	4·3	1861	20·4	10·7	9·7	4·9
	20·3	7·5	12·8	1·1		19·5	11·3	8·1	6·3
1848	18·5	11·8	6·6	7·3		19·7	12·2	7·5	7·1
	18·1	14·1	4·0	9·9		19·4	14·7	4·7	9·9
	18·1	12·8	5·2	8·7	1862	19·8	15·6	4·1	10·4
	16·7	13·9	2·7	11·2		20·0	14·8	5·1	9·4
1849	19·2	13·4	5·7	8·2		21·2	16·8	4·3	10·2
	18·1	14·4	3·7	10·2		21·0	14·5	6·7	8·1
	18·4	13·7	4·8	9·3	1863	19·5	14·1	5·4	9·1
	17·8	16·2	1·6	12·4		19·1	13·7	5·3	9·2
1850	19·0	16·4	2·5	11·4		20·9	14·4	6·5	8·1
	18·8	16·3	2·5	11·4		22·0	13·1	8·8	5·8
	19·6	16·1	3·5	10·4	1864	20·4	11·7	9·7	4·9
	19·4	15·7	4·6	9·3		19·6	13·0	6·6	8·0
1851	19·8	12·6	7·2	6·7		20·7	12·2	8·5	6·1
	18·7	13·7	4·9	9·0		19·2	13·5	5·6	8·9
	19·7	13·7	5·9	8·0	1865	19·5	14·4	5·1	9·5
	18·6	16·8	1·8	12·1		19·6	13·7	5·8	8·7
1852	20·2	17·0	3·2	10·7		21·5	13·5	8·0	6·6
	20·5	18·7	1·7	12·2		22·3	12·0	10·3	4·3
	22·6	21·1	1.1	12·8	1866	26·0	11·4	14·5	0·4
	21·3	21·5	Nil*	14·2		20·8	13·3	7·6	7·3
1853	21·4	18·5	2·8	11·2		23·8	14·7	9·1	5·8
	21·9	17·6	4·3	9·6		22·1	17·7	4·4	10·6
	22·7	16·5	6·2	7·7	1867	23·1	17·9	5·1	9·8
	23·6	14·6	8·9	5·0		22·3	18·4	4·9	10·0
1854	21·9	11·8	10·1	3·9		23·6	22·3	1·3	13·6
	21·6	15·5	6·1	7·8		23·3	23·2	0·1	14·9
	20·0	12·9	7·1	6·8	1868	23·6	21·6	2·0	13·0
	19·0	13·4	5·6	8·3		23·1	20·1	2·9	12·0
1855	19·5	17·4	2·1	11·8		23·9	19·6	4·3	10·6
	19·0	12·3	6·7	7·8		23·5	17·0	6·5	8·5
	20·0	14·9	5·1	8·8	1869	24·0	15·5	8·4	6·5
	24·0	10·8	9·7	4·2		22·7	17·1	5·6	8·3
1856	19·5	12·4	7·0	7·3		23·2	20·0	3·2	11·7
	18·5	9·9	8·6	5·8		23·5	19·9	3·6	11·3
	20·1	11·7	8·4	6·0	1870	21·4	17·9	6·4	8·5
	19·9	9·0	11·3	3·6		22·2	18·9	3·3	11·6
1857	19·9	10·9	9·0	5·4		23·3	19·7	6·4	8·5
	18·5	0·6	8·9	5·5		22·8	22·0	0·8	14·1
	19·3	10·8	8·4	6·0	1871	23·5	25·6	Nil‡	17·1
	21·4	6·0	15·3†	Nil†		23·0	21·1	1	13·0
1858	19·6	12·7	6·9	7·5		24·8	24·3	0·4	14·5
	19·4	16·8	2·6	11·8		26·1	18·9	7·7	7·2

* Excess of £200,000.

† Extra issue of £2,000,000

‡ Excess of £2,196,000.

The table for 1824-43 shows then that from 1826 (after the crisis of 1825) to 1842, with fiduciary issue varied (with the exception of the crisis of 1837) between 10 to 12 millions—the average being slightly over 11 millions.

Since then (under the new Act) the variations differ by the whole 15 millions—and the total average (computed from the full returns week by week) is £5,800,000—or little more than one-third of what was contemplated. That the other 9 millions have gone into Reserve has nothing to do with this matter; the old Act had its own reserve power, as already stated. The question here touches only the actual circulation at both periods. Not only then has the average previously assumed at 14 and 15 millions not increased, as it was thought capable of with our increased trade, but it has actually declined to nearly one-third. If the matter were to be constructed for a new Act, upon the same plan as before adopted, the fixed limit would be only 6 millions. It is evident then that if the public formerly had the benefit of fiduciary issue, whatever such benefit might amount to, it has since had much less of it.

It might here be said, "if the public has used less of these notes than was anticipated, more Bullion has been used, and this is a favourable sign!" So it

would be, provided that the average of 6 millions had been maintained, or varied 1 or 2 millions either way only. But when, as you see, the variations, at their extremes in 1857 with 17 millions of fiduciary circula-ion—and in 1871 with no fiduciary circulation—but 2 millions in excess of Bullion—assume a total range of 19 millions—you will admit that all bounds appear to be lost, most certainly the bounds of 15 millions—independently of the question of Reserve. And so if you glance down the columns of fiduciary issue, since

1845, you will find irregularities of so extreme and irreconcilable a nature that you must altogether conceive that the method adopted for fixing the limit of 15 millions was an economical failure of the most flagrant kind—leading to a state of confusion, at the results of which Sir Robert Peel himself would probably stare with astonishment. The arithmetician who, from dates carefully laid down, anticipates a certain, or at all events a fair result, will here admit that there is a fearful mistake somewhere; the *serious* economist must review such results with terror. Yet there are persons who, to this day, defend that fixed amount as something almost supernaturally clever and wise. Will sensible Englishmen endorse such a " hocus pocus?"

It would here appear that, at all events, the average of Bullion held is higher than before 1844. This is true, but at what cost has it been maintained? How extravagantly has it varied! The higher average is due principally to times when Bullion was attracted with too much force, and a state of surplus created, during which the public did not have the advantage in circulation of the benefit of even a moderate, perfectly safe share of the issue. During 700 weeks, or one-half of the whole period, from 1845 to 1872, the fiduciary circulation did not exceed one-fourth of the amount allowed. The credit of practically using more Bullion basis is due to the public, which procured the gold, and enabled the Bank to issue notes against it.

The higher state of the bullion average is due to our enhanced trade.

As far as the Bank is concerned it has itself been unable to increase this Bullion in accordance with increased commerce, as mentioned on pages 17 and 18. The Bank has, indeed, been unable fairly to maintain the Stock which the public furnished, although it commands the rate of Interest for the maintenance of that Stock. Instead of Bullion, it has held an average of nearly 9 millions of idle notes. The Stock of

The Bank itself has been unable to increase the stock of bullion portionately.

But it has kept large idle Reserves of Notes.

idle notes has frequently increased to 12, 13, or 15 millions, absolutely useless for the purposes of the circulation, though most efficient in reducing the rate of interest below its natural level.

THE DEMERITS OF THE RESERVE ARISING FROM THE FIXED ISSUE.

The great misconception involved in the Reserve so arising.

It may now be said, " If the fixed issue has not answered the purposes of circulation as originally designed, it has been all the more useful in enlarging the Reserve of money." Of all the errors under which economists labour, the popular delusions by which a mercantile community is misled, this is probably the most flagrant. The error is so deeply rooted that on all sides the cries are heard—" We do not keep sufficient Reserve; more is required." One authority says, " The Bank of England ought always to keep 15 or 16 millions of Reserve, and not allow this to decline." In the face of all this wisdom— for in the idea of such Reserve abstinence, moderation, and prudence seem implied—bold indeed must be the man who tells you that all this cry for more Reserve is fallacious; that the present heavy Reserves are the chief causes which keep bullion out of the market, and bring about the whole mischief. Such a man will at once be accused of "not being a banker, for what is more natural than that every banker, especially the Bank of England, should keep a large Reserve, and without such Reserve where would our trade be?" In order to allay such an accusation, permit me here

A regular steady Reserve must be kept.

to tell you that I am not only aware of the necessity, and of all the claims for Reserve, but that I go farther, and say that such Reserve must be regular, and in the scheme to be submitted to you later on, such a

Reserve, *continually* available, of whatever amount it may be deemed advisable, will be provided for, yet in such a way that if not absolutely required, it will not unnecessarily influence the rate of interest. Having said this, you must discharge me of the above suspicion as to not knowing and appreciating the paramount importance of Banking Reserve, and you must wait until you see this appear.

The question here *only concerns the Reserve as arising from the present system,* under which we have formed conclusions and habits that are entirely wrong and contradictory, obscuring the real point; and there lies the difficulty of the whole problem. Bearing in mind then I emphatically repeat, that *this is not a question of whether Reserve* should be kept; admitting that Reserve *must* be kept, I want to impress you with the idea that the *Reserve arising or remaining under the fixed issue system (the present method)* is that which involves the error. You must pardon me for insisting so explicitly on this point, the fallacy under which we seem to labour in regard to this matter cannot be dispelled unless you clearly appreciate what is here indicated.

The question here concerns only the Reserve arising under the present system.

I open this matter then by telling you: firstly *the present fixed limit of 15 millions has the effect of keeping away from this country, or of causing the continual and spasmodic withdrawal of, several millions of bullion which would otherwise remain, if, instead of a fixed limit of fiduciary issue, we adopted the system of varying that issue in accordance with the demands of circulation and regular reserve.*

That Reserve drives away bullion.

Further

That every million of fiduciary issue, added to the present fixed issue, either temporarily or otherwise, is tantamount to a million of bullion kept off or withdrawn from the country.

Every million of more note issue keeps away a million of bullion.

And within the above sentences you may find the solution of the present enigma.

For nine years out of ten (or thereabouts) the 15 millions notes of fixed issue, when added to the Bullion in the Bank, are too much for our requirements;

The circulation cannot absorb them;

The Bank cannot use the Reserve of notes for the accommodation of the public, just because the circulation cannot take it;

As a Reserve to protect the Bank against withdrawals of deposits, it is either too low or too high, independently of the fact that the deposits increase in times of danger instead of diminishing;

Withdrawals of deposits would involve but changes in account, without increasing the currency.

As Reserve, it is supposed to be useful to the Bank, for the purpose of covering withdrawals of Bullion; whilst—and this indicates the fallacy—it is the maintenance of the Note Reserve itself which encourages this withdrawal of Bullion, driving it away with ease, and requiring redoubled efforts and sacrifices to recover it!

I am well aware that the assertions made above may appear startling to many, and that, sunk as we are in the mire of misconceptions engendered by the present system, it will take some time before the truth makes its way.

To the ordinary reader, who hears of the Money Market, of capital, supply or scarcity of money, bullion, the stock markets, the clearing-house, and all the numerous matters daily taking place, all this seems a maze; and when the Bank of England either raises the rate of interest to a high pitch, or lowers it to as extreme an extent, he is apt to suppose that all this is due to natural causes, however grievous may be the effects, however loud and continuous the complaints made as regards the very excessive movements in the value of money. Yet there are one or two simple considerations which will open the way into the understanding of these matters. Beginning with the extreme movements in the Bank rates of interest, by what are they caused?

Are they caused by scarcity of current money, *i.e.* a diminution in the circulation of coin and Bank notes arising from losses, or a sudden demand for more money? Popular delusion often ascribes the mischief to these, though it is a fatal mistake—for the causes do not even exist. The mass of coin and Bank notes in circulation is firmly held; the Bank is as unable to withdraw several millions from the circulation as it is unable to cram several millions into it. And in this matter of circulation all is comprised that concerns what is termed "accommodation" to commerce, for the sums current show what that accommodation amounts to practically. Thus the Bank of England note circulation, which overlies the gold coin, and corrects its movements, is more or less regular, and although capable of gradual extension or contraction, does not vary spasmodically within 3 and 4 millions. Those familiar with the circulation returns will confirm this. In a later chapter I shall submit to you the proof of figures. All other considerations as to events in our own special market and their consequences can be dismissed, for the Bank of England stands aloof from these. Lastly, it must be clearly understood that, as all the world knows, we are never short of money, the amount is always there, the question merely concerns the rate of interest that is asked for it. *The chief,* if not the *sole cause,* of the great divergences in the rate of interest is owing to *the inability of the Bank to maintain* a due proportion of bullion against the note issue, and

The only
causes are
the extreme
variations
in the stock
of bullion
which the
Bank
fails in
preventing.

the extent of this matter will at once be made clear if you bear in mind that bullion has been as low as 6, and as high as 27 millions, within a range of from 22 to 25 millions of circulation. This chief cause is now well recognised as such, so much even that financiers arise who, now and then, not understanding the question, propose that we should do away with bullion altogether. The reader and the writer are probably agreed upon the point that bullion cannot be set aside, and that the Bank of England must maintain the supply of this material.

The task
and the
instru-
mental
power to
perform it.

The question of ability or inability to perform a certain task naturally involves the use of instrumental power and its proper application. The task here set to the Bank is that of maintaining a stock of bullion proportionate to a certain amount of bank notes, the instrumental power by which this is to be done is *the rate of interest*. If the Bank of England *raises* the rate of interest, bullion is *attracted;* if the rate is *lowered*,

The rate of
interest
is the
automaton
and
unfailing
power.

bullion is *repelled* from this country. It must now be distinctly understood that the efficiency of this power is beyond question. Not only does the Bank practise it, not only has it never failed in its effects, not only is it provable by all that concerns international exchange matters, but it is regarded as that valuable automaton factor, which moderately or ruthlessly used, regulates the supposed automaton action of the issue department of the Bank of England in a manner superior to all consideration, as the corrective of all real or imaginable faults committed. Thus, when the rate of interest is raised from $3\frac{1}{2}$ or $4\frac{1}{2}$ per cent. to 7, 8, or 10 per cent., bullion always responds to the call.

The Bank is
absolutely
free in
exercising
this power.

Further, it must be distinctly understood that this power of raising and lowering the rate is absolutely and solely at the discretion of the Bank of England, that no outside influence can act directly upon it, the

public being absolutely powerless in determining the
rate. No objection on the part of the market can deprive
the Bank of its right to discount bills, or to state at
what rate it is prepared to furnish money against
securities. That being so, the Bank holds the position of the steersman, who need but direct the rate
of interest, so that bullion will be attracted or, at all
events, maintained, and the simple mechanical law
here involved might, for argument's sake, be compared
to Mr. Bessemer's plan of counteracting the effect of
the movements of sea-waves by the hydraulic appa-
ratus manipulated at the will of the man in charge of
it. All and every other consideration can be fully
dismissed, for here is a plain natural problem with
which common sense can deal. The lamentable
failure of the Bank, in respect to fixing the rate of
interest for this purpose, need scarcely be pointed out.
In the midst of seeming quiet, there suddenly arises
an export of bullion: up goes the Bank-rate to 8, 9,
and 10 per cent. Hardly has this been done, when
bullion comes pouring in, not only sufficient, but in
excess. Down then goes the rate again, often more
rapidly than it had gone up; excessively cheap interest
prevails, until, at a certain stage, the game commences
over again. Few people can deny that the movements in bullion at the bank make this impression upon
the beholder; as a matter of fact, the violent ups and
downs in the rate are evidence that it cannot be
otherwise. It is undeniable, then, that the Bank of
England is *always* too late in raising the rate, and too
quick in lowering it. To what must be attributed this
want of adjustment? If it be said that the Bank
cannot foresee these things, that this is not in the
nature of business, you must admit that between
extreme ups and downs a *margin*, on the principle of
insurance would fully suffice to absorb differences,

and every prudent business man would provide such a margin if he felt himself in the dark;—he would secure such margin before going too low, as a set-off for the future. Nor can the blame be laid on the wisdom of the Directors of the Bank, as is so often done by certain writers.

The *whole and sole cause* why the Directors of the Bank are unable to poise the rate properly, lies in the system *of Reserve of Bank notes*, which accumulate from time to time, and which are *absolutely* useless, for any purpose whatsoever, *save for* that of *lowering the rate of interest so much below its natural level*, that the contracts for, and the actual *export of bullion itself*, are continually going on. And when bullion has thus been contracted for, and reaches a certain delicate level, the effort to *recover it* must be made with more than *double force*. With the exception of a moderate portion of it, this Reserve is—

The idle and useless reserve of notes are the sole cause of the impossibility to keep interest at proper levels.

1st. Useless for the purpose of circulation.

2nd. Useless for advances to the public, for they are comprised in the circulation.

3rdly. Useless as Reserve for the safety of the Bank, for *withdrawals* of deposits from the Bank mean nothing *but changes of account* from one banking establishment to another, and do not increase the currency. It follows that any sum of note Reserve beyond actual need can perform no other office than that of uselessly and unduly lowering the rate.

It has frequently happened that the Bank held an idle note reserve of 14 to 15 millions. At such times the amount of bullion is equal to notes in circulation, amounting, say, to 25 millions, giving, with the 15 millions credit notes, a total issue of 40 millions. The rate of discount then stands, say, at 2 per cent. Now, when by exports of bullion, the stock is reduced from 25 millions to 20 millions, the total issue is also reduced

Example showing how the present system works.

to 35, and the reserve of notes to 9 or 10 millions. The bank then raises the rate of discount to, say, 4 per cent., and when bullion falls to 15 or 10 millions, giving but 30 and 25 millions of money respectively, the Bank raises interest very high, in order not only to stop further export of bullion, but also to recover it, for only through bullion can it regain the note Reserve; the whole action turning so far upon the amount of available issue. That is to say, we find that when the total amount of money in the Issue Department is at 40 millions, money stands, say, at 2 per cent., when at 35 millions it is, say, 4 per cent., at 30 millions 8 or 9 per cent. Now, inasmuch as the circulation of, say, 25 millions deducted therefrom, leaves 15 or 10 or 5 millions of Reserve, the Bank arranges the rate of interest in accordance with such Reserve.

That such is the case you need not be told. The sayings, the Bank is strong, because it has a large Reserve, or the Bank is getting weaker, because the Reserve is diminishing, are familiar to you. It is called the "barometer" of the money market, and when the barometer is high, at 15 millions, interest is at 2; when low, at 5 or 6 millions, interest goes to 9 or 10 per cent. The high, medium, or low state of the barometer, being solely due to either an over supply, or a satisfactory *status quo*, or an abnormally low and diminishing stock of bullion.

It may now strike you as singular that when there is say a stock of 23 or 25 millions of bullion, when the Reserve stands at 13 or 15 millions, we should be so little able to keep that amount of gold; but you will see that when we lower interest to 2 per cent., we actually invite and encourage its export. You will then say, "why don't we hold interest at 4 or 5 per cent., if these rates will protect it against exportation!" Now this we cannot do, because the Reserve is at 13 or 15 millions, and it consists of full valued legal tender money, created by the Act of 1844, by the mixture of 15 millions of fiduciary Bank notes and accidental amounts of bullion. This legal tender money has the same right and might in all that concerns supply and demand; it is not a mere matter of account, but an absolutely independent money element; you may even go so far as to say that you do not know whether the large surplus is owing to too much bullion, or to too much fiduciary issue. If the authorities at the Bank were to tell you that it is too much bullion, you might hang your head, and acknowledge that you regretted your imprudence in making any suggestion; but should you be a clear-headed man, you might say, " Nonsense, let us keep the bullion, and rather diminish the fiduciary issue for the time being." So that if, with a Reserve of 15 millions of notes, interest is at 2 per cent., if, with a reserve of 10 millions, interest would be at 4 per cent., and we think it right, for the protection of bullion, that such a rate should be maintained, let us abolish, or set aside for a time, 5 millions of the notes created by the Act. The Reserve *will* then be at 10 millions, and interest at 4 per cent. You will be ready to admit that certain arrangements with the Government debt can easily be made, in order to suit the cases of such diminution or increase.

Will regulate the rate of interest, and consequently regulate the stock of bullion.

In putting the matter to you in this light, I have not treated it theoretically or scientifically, nor is the plain common sense which you would show in endorsing such a suggestion anything extraordinarily meritorious. Many occasions in daily life compel us to seek for original sources of confusion, and to connect them, and this method of search, from effect to cause, guides the schoolboy in his arithmetical problem, and the cook in the concoction of her pudding.

The plainest intelligence can discern the rights of this matter.

The insufficient action of the Bank of England in

regard to poising the rate of interest will now be patent to you. It is almost entirely *post facto*—the actual forcible absorption by exports of bullion must precede a rise in the rate before, under the present system, the remedy is used.

But if instead of waiting for this forcible reduction by exports of bullion, the Bank reduced the total issue *voluntarily*, by setting aside 5 millions of the note reserve, thus creating beforehand (as far as the money market is dependent on the notes available is concerned) precisely the same effect as if 5 millions of bullion had been withdrawn, and making the same moderate rise in the rate of interest at once, would they not retain the 5 millions of bullion? No one can deny that this is correct, and that under the operation of the effective laws here at work, 5 millions of bullion would be retained in place of the 5 millions of idle note reserve *voluntarily* withdrawn.

I have chosen 15 millions of reserve, 25 millions of bullion, and 5 millions of reduction, for the sake of convenient illustration; the same principle applies to whatever other figures or situations that may occur. You will now understand the fatal policy involved in the present system, and you may admit that the economical error involved in the seemingly " prudent " (?) notion of the fixed limit leads to an almost hopeless demoralisation of the groundwork necessary to arrive at true practice.

You will then begin to appreciate the difficulty under which almost all the writers on the Bank of England are labouring. They cannot get rid of the idea that when the Government (which is but the nation itself) has created 15 millions of note issue on Government securities, it has done a wonderful thing both as regards the circulation *and the Reserve*. Mr. Micawber's I O U's, at all events, have the advantage

of being harmless instruments ; but the fixed issue of
the 15 millions of Bank of England notes remains not
only intentionally unpayable and practically unpaid,
is not only almost useless, but drives away bullion
from us, and finally destroys *itself*.

So long as
this fallacy
as to
fixed fiduci-
ary issue
exists, a
settlement
is impos-
sible, and
all our
policy is
false.

No wonder that with this fallacy, in which
the majority of our Economists appear to be hopelessly entangled, it seems impossible almost to come
to an understanding and to an intelligible solution
of the difficulty. It is this point, then, of the
controversy to which I call your attention, as the
hidden fault in the whole magnificent machinery of the
Bank of England, and there is no hope whatever of
any reform until it is recognised that *this kind of
Reserve* is false, and that all *the policy founded* upon, and
all the false craving for more of it, are but the consequence of the deep error involved in the fixed limit of
15 millions. The reduction of the fixed issue must
have precedence in this question ; without it a solution
is impossible. In saying this I again remind you that
I am no Bullionist, repudiating all fiduciary issue,
advocating, in despair, a mere issue on Bullion alone.

The
principle of
reduction
must have
precedence
over
increase
of issue.

On the contrary, I shall show that a fiduciary issue *must*
be made, but I maintain that it must be subservient to
Bullion, that it must vary, and on the proper system,
fiduciary issue of a few millions may at other times
reach fifteen or twenty millions with absolute safety
—so long as it is accompanied by the compensating
action of all the factors concerned.

On the 2nd July 1873 I ventured to address to the
Directors of the Bank the following memorial (published in the *Daily News*, 7th July 1873) :—

To the Honourable Court of Directors of the Bank of England.

The undersigned begs most respectfully to submit to the
Honourable Court of Directors of the Bank of England the following remarks on the question of the amendment of the Act of 1844.

The Chancellor of the Exchequer's proposal, and Sir John Lubbock's amendment thereto, contemplate an alteration of the limit of 15 millions in the one-sided direction of extension only. Almost all parties agree as to the extreme danger involved in this measure. They see in it a disturbance of the principles of prudence which, rightly or wrongly, are involved in the strict limitation established by Sir Robert Peel! and altogether a violation of the whole Act under which the Bank has hitherto been managed with such consideration and conservatism. Permit me, therefore, to point out to you that this violation of the Act, so repugnant to the sense of caution, can be entirely avoided, for the Act itself contains the provisions necessary for a better adjustment of the issue. In clause 2 of the Act, the one on which the system principally rests, there is the following sentence:—"But it shall be lawful for the said Governor and Company *to diminish the amount* of such securities, and *again to increase the same* to any sum not exceeding in the whole the sum of £14,000,000 ; and so from time to time as they shall see occasion." This sentence shows that Sir Robert Peel, whilst absolutely debarring increase, left a door open for decrease of the issue. In all probability he contemplated such reduction as applicable to the three millions (now four millions) of "other securities," these being subject to the direct action of the Bank ; whereas the State debt of eleven millions could not be so raised without other preceding arrangements. The 8th clause of the Act provides for the annual payment, or credit, to the State of £180,000 (now £195,000), in lieu of profit on the issue of fourteen millions, without making any reference to the "decrease" of such issue as contemplated in clause 2. Here is the conflict between the two clauses ; and if clause 8 had been amended in conformity with clause 2, you might deem it expedient occasionally to reduce the issue by four millions, for you would thereby effect an annual proportionate saving on the total sum now paid to the State. If consequently, you could now induce the Chancellor of the Exchequer to amend clause 8, and to forego that portion of the annual profit for the State, you might be inclined, from time to time, to lower the issue of 15 millions to 11 millions (notably when your reserve has accumulated to 14 or 15 millions), retaining the right of reissuing the four millions. The point here to be decided is this :—If at any time there are say 20 millions of bullion on hand (or more or less as the case may be), and if it is desirable that such status quo of bullion should be maintained, you will be better able to do so with only 11 millions than 15 millions of note reserve. A denial of this proposition cannot be made, unless it be said that the reserve is of no value at all, and unless it be declared that 15 millions of reserve have no more influence than eleven or five, or less. It is but necessary that you should continue the measures and policy requisite to uphold the supposed status quo of 20 millions of bullion and eleven millions of reserve, in order to retain four millions of bullion in place of the four millions of notes temporarily withdrawn, when the latter would become a free and available reserve within the range of the Act. I claim that this proposition as to the upholding of any desirable status quo (*i.e.*, as to the maintenance of a due proportion of bullion) can be submitted to the test of logic and practice. You may be disposed to perceive that if the evident intentions of the Act were thus carried out, you would forestal the necessity of the proposals of the Chancellor of the Exchequer and Sir John Lubbock. These proposals, based upon the experience of 1857 and 1866, may contemplate the temporary extra allowance of a couple of millions beyond the 15 millions; but if you had previously reduced the issue by the four millions, and then defended the status quo based upon the reduced issue of 11 millions (*i.e.*, protected bullion as effectually as you have done hitherto), you would still retain four millions of free reserve standing against crisis—a sum more than sufficient to meet the contingencies hitherto known. No violation of the Act need thus take place. The key of the whole mystery is contained in the simple amendment of clause 8 in conformity with clause 2. I venture to call your attention to this point, because it involves a plain practical matter which is easily appreciated, and can be quickly amended. If so amended, our money market would be relieved from occasional " plethora " in favour of future free reserve, and although the range as thus provided by the Act is but four millions, yet it will have the effect of modifying extremes to that proportionate extent. At some future time, when we have made more advance in the appreciation of the real value and use of fiduciary note issues, you might be disposed to take into consideration the system of issue which I have explained at length in recent publications on the subject, the recommendation herein contained being the first step towards the final adoption of such complete system.—I remain, your obedient servant,

1A Princes Street, 2nd July 1873.　　　　ERNEST SEYD.

To most economists of real freedom of thought, the hints here conveyed would be sufficient not only for the purpose of explaining all the unaccountable anomalies under which the Bank and the public have been labouring, but for the suggestion of a remedy. Substantial facts are given in the following portions of this book. But, inasmuch as this publication is written also for others, and inasmuch as I can bring forward a series of substantial facts confirming the evil effects of the present system. I propose to lay before you in succession—

The effect of the 15 millions of fixed issue on the stock of bullion at the Bank of England.

The evil of the variations in the Bank rate of interest, the international and market rate.

The circulation of the country, and of Bank of England notes : their connection with requirements of Reserve.

The influence of the 15 millions of fixed issue on our money market and bankers' Reserves.

The influence of the 15 millions of fixed issue on speculation and overtrading.

The *direct* loss suffered by the Bank of England itself by the issue.

And these matters will give me groundwork for the consideration of an amended system of issue in Part II. of this book.

THE EFFECT OF THE 15 MILLIONS OF FIXED ISSUE ON BULLION AND THE INTERNATIONAL EXCHANGES.

In the previous chapter we have ascertained that the inability of the Bank of England to maintain a fair The laws of international exchange as connected with rates of interest must be appreciated. *status quo* of bullion is due to the low rate of interest induced by the heavy reserve of idle notes, and I have stated that the undue export of bullion is the natural consequence. Few people unacquainted with the laws of international exchanges can understand " why that should be so." An explanation of the operation of these laws will, therefore, be useful, and will reveal the cause why the rebounds from extremely low to extremely high rates of interest must take place.

But before I enter upon this matter, it is expedient *False allegations as to the causes of with-drawals of Bullion.* that certain other allegations should be disposed of which are falsely put forward in order to account for these extraordinary movements.

It is frequently said—"We are the principal holders of Gold, through the Stock at the Bank of England. All other nations come to the Bank of *The world does not come to the Bank of England for gold.* England for gold, and this establishment must defend itself by rates of interest." This is a great error. It is quite true that our market has the greatest transit of gold, but that is quite another matter; for the Bank of England is one of the factors which can supply itself from the stream of gold in our market just like everybody else can do who bids for it, its stock being *Our bullion market is open to the Bank of England as well as other banks.* but a moderate one comparatively. In the foot note which I have herewith annexed, the exports and imports of gold of England and France are given, and you can form some opinion as to the relative importance of the markets. In this same foot note I also make allusion to the demand for gold in Germany and America, and show the real extent of the dangers to which we are open. The British public is so often and so willingly deceived by extravagant estimates of its own great *Other nations are important traders and dealers in Bullion, as the foot note shows.* overwhelming force, or alarmed by statements as to its danger, that these figures will be useful in order to show the real and practical limits here involved, and I give these in the foot note below, so that they may be referred to separately without breaking the chain of this chapter.*

---

* The following is a table of the Exports of Gold and Silver Bullion and Coin, from 1850 to 1872, and of the Imports into the United Kingdom from 1858 to 1872 (the registration of the Imports of bullion at the Custom House commenced only in 1858.)

It is also frequently said, " Foreigners prey upon us, export sovereigns, and do other dishonest things to cheat us; Bismarck among the rest." This sugges- tion as to our wealth and ability to patronise the foreigner may be flattering to the ignorant, but it is the most vulgar prejudice imaginable. In the first place, we are far too prudent to part with gold unless we obtain a proper equivalent for it; secondly, foreigners are not such rogues as we are too often inclined to

The suggestion that foreigners prey upon our gold coinage is utterly false and contemptible.

TABLE 5.

IMPORTS and EXPORTS of BULLION and COIN of ENGLAND, from 1850 to 1872 inclusive.

	IMPORTS.			EXPORTS.	
Year.	Gold.	Silver.	Year.	Gold.	Silver.
1850			1850	2,574,568	4,365,778
1851			1851	3,975,364	5,084,187
1852	The Imports of Bullion		1852	4,325,824	5,969,640
1853	into England were not		1853	12,751,778	6,154,975
1854	registered before 1858.		1854	16,552,845	6,033,723
1855			1855	11,847,213	6,980,965
1856			1856	12,038,299	12,813,498
1857			1857	15,061,500	18,505,468
1858	22,793,126	6,700,064	1858	12,467,040	7,061,836
1859	22,297,698	14,772,458	1859	18,081,139	17,607,664
1860	12,584,684	10,393,512	1860	15,641,578	9,893,190
1861	12,163,937	6,583,108	1861	11,238,372	9,573,276
1862	19,903,704	11,752,772	1862	16,011,963	13,314,228
1863	19,142,665	10,888,129	1863	15,303,279	11,240,671
1864	16,900,951	10,827,325	1864	13,279,739	9,852,561
1865	14,485,570	6,976,641	1865	8,493,332	6,599,192
1866	23,509,641	10,777,498	1866	12,742,059	8,896,552
1867	15,800,159	8,020,888	1867	7,889,030	6,435,487
1868	17,136,177	7,716,418	1868	12,708,308	7,511,706
1869	13,770,812	6,730,179	1869	8,473,699	7,903,829
1870	18,806,728	10,648,940	1870	10,013,521	8,906,169
1871	21,618,924	16,521,903	1871	20,698,275	13,062,396
1872	18,469,442	11,138,570	1872	19,748,916	10,586,945
	£269,384,218	£150,448,405		£202,950,250	£148,455,702

(According to this Table, 67 millions of Gold and 2 millions of Silver were retained in this country. But it is known that at least 5 millions of Silver must have remained, and the difference of 3 millions is accounted for by the fact that a great deal of *Gold* shipped from here is declared as *Silver*, in order to save freight. Accordingly we must deduct at least 30 millions from the balance of Gold, leaving 37 millions since 1858, which corresponds with the increase in Sovereigns, and the greater use of Gold in Arts and Industry.)

The table then shows that from 1858 to 1872 no less than 270

6

assert. And as to the export of sovereigns, supposed to be coined free of charge, this involves a fallacy which has long since been disposed of. Not only are sovereigns dearer than bar gold, and are exported only by a few foolish people who do not know better, but, as far as the melting down by foreigners is considered a charge against them, it is rather the other way. Of the masses of foreign coin melted down here in England, American eagles alone amounted to 70

---

millions of gold passed by the Bank of England, besides 150 millions in silver, which served us in lieu of gold for payment to foreign nations. In 1852 the Bank held a stock of bullion of 21 millions, in 1857 it fell to 6 millions, in 1871 it reached the highest point of 26 millions, in 1872-3 it fell to 18 millions. Considering now that between 1852 to 1872 there lies the period when the great historical discoveries of gold in California and Australia were developed, doubling the stock of gold in the world, does it not seem strange that the Bank of England should not only have been unable to obtain more bullion, but that out of the hundreds of millions passing, it should not have been able to retain at all events the few millions required to keep its stock, once obtained, at a more regular average?

But it will be said: "*All the world comes to the Bank of England for gold. We are so rich!*" &c., &c. Without wishing to disparage our wealth, permit me here to observe that the dry figures and facts are preferable to the bombastic declaration by which the British public is so frequently and willingly misled. The Bank of England stock of bullion has never exceeded 26 millions (this amount was reached in 1871 for three weeks), the stock of bullion in the Bank of France in 1870 stood at 52 millions, so that as far as amount is concerned, the latter institution is in advance, and even at this moment, in spite of the great indemnity paid by France, the bullion exceeds 30 millions. The stock at Berlin of bullion is £36 millions, and all these accumulations and stocks are quite as much subject to the operations of the demand by arbitrations of exchanges as the Bank of England stock. Although steamships carry more bullion to us *in transitu*, and ours is the larger market, yet the foreigners have their fair share, as you will see from the following table on the exports and imports of bullion of France. (This table is of value, having been obtained by the writer through

millions sterling from 1850 to 1872—far in excess of the export of our sovereigns to all other countries ever since sovereigns were coined.

The great movements in bullion which affect our market seriously are conducted by bankers connected with international trade, and the operations so carried on are in strict accordance with the laws of exchange, which, like a great clearing system, are inexorable and automaton in their action. Any sug-

The great international movements of bullion rest upon the purest basis of arithmetical truths.

the courtesy of the Bank of France, and having never before been published.)

TABLE 6.

IMPORTS and EXPORTS of BULLION and COIN of FRANCE, from 1850 to 1872 inclusive.

	IMPORTS.			EXPORTS.	
Year.	Gold.	Silver.	Year.	Gold.	Silver.
1850	2,511,429	6,231,382	1850	1,848,339	3,300,913
1851	4,660,108	7,155,453	1851	1,284,067	4,117,869
1852	2,407,049	7,207,830	1852	1,710,093	7,341,190
1853	13,485,976	4,528,317	1853	1,195,183	9,248,646
1854	20,250,529	4,002,402	1854	2,585,474	10,723,179
1855	15,920,920	4,957,282	1855	6,449,778	12,898,447
1856	19,314,930	4,397,912	1856	3,555,937	16,134,537
1857	23,478,808	3,964,089	1857	4,876,607	18,742,424
1858	22,759,471	6,422,664	1858	3,636,288	7,338,897
1859	30,063,372	8,385,505	1859	7,440,954	15,884,088
1860	19,451,436	5,219,580	1860	6,391,413	11,976,138
1861	9,720,937	6,889,441	1861	10,794,520	9,582,607
1862	12,571,922	5,293,935	1862	9,513,646	9,077,153
1863	14,916,225	6,484,767	1863	14,451,327	9,581,349
1864	18,737,513	10,853,336	1864	13,526,854	12,814,405
1865	16,925,842	9,721,780	1865	10,828,112	6,845,414
1866	32,206,817	9,902,050	1866	12,476,099	8,120,442
1867	23,507,819	10,077,056	1867	6,663,112	2,563,403
1868	19,540,436	7,645,057	1868	11,110,862	3,317,777
1869	18,002,024	7,635,464	1869	7,138,387	3,223,087
1870	12,259,507	4,199,177	1870	7,546,786	2,794,704
1871	5,357,168	5,971,620	1871	13,601,406	7,340,088
1872	5,181,372	9,903,878	1872	7,234,730	5,260,987
	£363,330,610	157,044,977		£165,859,984	£198,227,041

Accordingly France retained 200 millions in Gold, but exported 40 millions in Silver (to India). This fully agrees with the anticipations formed.

You will perceive that the amounts here represented as passing in and out of France render that country quite as important a market for bullion as England. The following table gives the imports and exports between England and France of *Gold*, showing

gestion that speculation in gold can be conducted in countries where it is the legal tender money is perfectly absurd, for speculation requires *advances* of money, and you cannot advance money on money with profit. The value of gold can be ascertained exactly to half a farthing in a lump of £1000; no hocus pocus is possible in this respect, and persons only thoroughly ignorant of the unfailing laws of arithmetic, or the pure, logical, and refined operation of interna-

---

that out of the 363 millions of Gold imported by France, 143 millions came from England.

TABLE 7.

GOLD EXPORTS and IMPORTS between ENGLAND and FRANCE.

Year	Imported from France.	Year	Imported from France.	Year	Exported to France.	Year	Exported to France.
			B.fd. £4,436,217				B.fd. £89,198,877
1850		1862	91,980	1850	1,367,864	1862	6,356,200
1851		1863	187,546	1851	1,211,194	1863	3,502,829
1852	Imports were not registered in England before 1858.	1864	573,913	1852	685,639	1864	7,775,111
1853		1865	307,765	1853	5,327,993	1865	4,263,286
1854		1866	2,843,356	1854	13,388,293	1866	8,465,243
1855		1867	387,319	1855	9,865,459	1867	6,034,340
1856		1868	280,170	1856	9,657,145	1868	7,189,646
1857		1869	695,851	1857	10,863,818	1869	4,194,430
1858	654,001	1870	315,767	1858	10,530,095	1870	3,505,448
1859	936,546	1871	3,708,203	1859	14,902,467	1871	1,569,171
1860	341,177	1872	2,116,557	1860	10,400,604	1872	1,040,448
1861	2,504,493			1861	998,304		
C.fd.	£4,436,217		£15,944,644	C.fd.	£89,198,877		£143,095,029

This Table is useful also in order to show the effects of the late war indemnity paid to Germany on the Bullion question in England. For whereas the French from 1850 to 1870 took Gold from us at the rate of 7 millions per annum, they re-imported to us in 1871 and 1872 (deducting export) 3½ millions, and from 1870 to the present time the stream was directed to Germany, as appears from the following :—

The export of England to the Hanse Towns from

1858 to 1870, was only - - - - - -	£3,700,000
Or per annum - - - - -	300,000
During the war 1870 - - - - - -	180,000
1871 - - - - - -	8,480,000
1872 - - - - - -	8,050,000
And during 1873 it may amount to about - -	10,000,000

A few extra sums may have gone by way of " other countries," but the substance of the statement is this—that whereas we used to

tional exchange matters can have the impudence to make assertions as to the possibility of unfair dealings in bullion. The transfer of bullion from this country to another takes place in accordance with the balances of trade indicated by the rates of exchange in our favour or against us. From certain countries they are permanently in our favour, notably those which are international debtors to us and other nations, and who, by additional state loans, only now and then, for

The balance of trade determines the rates of exchange.

---

send Gold to France, we now send it to Germany; our own position, as far as this settlement is concerned, is not much altered. It is worth while to bear this in mind, in view of the extreme alarm raised that the Bank of England must furnish the Germans with Gold exclusively from its own store.

It is further said that when France resumes specie payments, she will drain gold from the Bank of England. In the first place France can well afford to maintain a larger fiduciary issue, and if the present 90 millions of such notes are reduced by 50 millions of bullion, within 8 or 10 years, she will do well. In the second place, the Germans do not take the 200 millions in gold, a large portion will be invested in securities and transferred in commodities. The world's supply of 16 millions of gold per annum will be sufficient to enable France to resume specie payments (for there are yet 120 millions of gold in France), and to square Germany also, and if we continue to supply 7 or 8 millions of gold per annum, for our part, not from the Bank, but from the usual arrivals in our market, we do nothing more than what we have done from 1850 to 1870.

It is again said that America will resume gold payments, and that much gold will be required from the Bank of England for this purpose. Here the question of balance of trade arises, for unless the United States turn the balance of trade *in their* favour, they cannot obtain an ounce of gold from us. In order to afford you some points for judging of the probability of this event, you will find that the United States, from 1850 to 1870, imported £11 millions of gold from us, and exported £89 millions; further, that they exported to Europe about 800 million dollars, or £180 millions of their debt, receiving besides, say £40 millions capital for railways. Further that emigration to them is valued at £6 millions per annum in *cash* imported, or about £184 millions for the 23 years, besides which their mines of gold produced £7 millions per

a short term, turn the Exchange the other way. Austria, Italy, Turkey, and South American Republics belong to this category. Australia is not internationally indebted, but its gold production *must* be exported. The United States of America are large exporters of gold to us; but now and then, by a short spasm, they turn the Exchange in their favour. France, Germany, Belgium, and Holland, hold almost equal rank with us in international financial independence, and up to 1870 our exports of gold to France

---

annum, and from the silver mines no less than £24 millions were sent here since 1850. Bear now in mind that the United States have immense riches in produce, cotton, corn, &c., which *by themselves* ought to be sufficient to *balance trade*, and then reckon up the above sums *exported to* us as extra settlement of the balance of trade against them, viz. :—

From 1850 to 1872 balance of gold exports	·	·	£78 millions.
„ „ Exports of U. S. Loan to Europe	·	·	180 „
„ „ Capital for Railways, &c.	·		40 „
„ „ Imports of Cash by emigration			84 „
Gold produce of California ores, is included in the above Exports			
„ „ Silver produce	·	·	24 „
			£406 „

Or nearly £20 millions per annum used up, by an equivalent of imports of commodities and luxuries, by the people of the United States; squandered in wild, reckless social extravagance. If now you bear in mind that the debt thus incurred to Europe adds its annual weight of dividends in *our* favour, without calculating on the contingencies that the capital of the debt held in Europe must be repaid, you *can estimate* what social changes, what reforms in political and personal economy must take place before the United States people can recover their balance of trade, and so as to become a permanent claimant for gold bullion. The present and the rising generations must die before such a change in the morality and economy of a nation can be expected, or dire misfortune and bankruptcy must crumble the whole edifice to pieces. The French

were very large (see foot note p 84) ; they have since changed their course to Germany.

The mere turning of the Exchange in favour of one country does not immediately bring about actual bullion shipments. These take place only when the so-called arbitrations of Exchange have exhausted their effect. In order to explain this, you must imagine, say, England indebted to France, France indebted to Holland, and Holland indebted to England. Instead of making three shipments of bullion, the account is settled by England remitting her Dutch bills to France, the margins in the prices of exchange at each Bourse making this profitable, and the principle here brought into operation is that the *status quo* of bullion in each country remains undisturbed, kept free even from the demands of discount. This magnificent clearing system, when finally it resolves itself into bullion shipments for unsettled balances, is often misunderstood by ignorant local financiers, who fancy that the bullion merchant "is a mischievous man." In reality this business is conducted on the most refined and infinitesimal differences ; it involves profits of from $\frac{1}{10}$th to $\frac{1}{50}$th per cent., or £100 to £20

Arbitrations of exchanges precede shipments of bullion.

---

are a people of a much higher sense of national as well as personal economy, and will recover the balance of trade in a much shorter time, gradually increasing their metallic means out of what becomes naturally available.

I make the above remarks so as to enable you to estimate the alarm sounded by many of our economists in reference to these matters at its proper value. We have nothing to fear from these probabilities, but what we can guard against easily. I admit however, that the question of demonetisation of silver throughout Europe, will tend to make money dear, and that the Bank of England has done well in holding interest higher generally. It will do well in continuing to uphold an average rate sufficiently high, the best remedy for which would be the reduction (temporary) of the fixed fiduciary issue of 15 millions, which now competes with bullion.

on transactions of £100,000; whereas, the shipments of bullion would cost, in charges alone, ten times as much. And now-a-days, with telegraphic communications, with the number of competitors, this business has become so delicate and instantaneous, that ordinary contingencies in the European balances of trade are thus frequently cleared by telegraphic orders in the forenoon of a day.

I show the extreme delicacy of this arbitration of exchange, in order now to make you perceive the importance of the rate of interest in regard to infinitesimal differences, for next to the balances of trade, the value of money or interest guides the business of transmission of bullion. The rate of interest in one country may be lower than in another, for the real solid reason that the industry and commerce of the one has accumulated more money than it can use. In that case, the surplus goes away in return for claims on the other country and for valuable equivalents. That is frequently our case, and we accordingly invest the surplus of our wealth in foreign securities. But, and this must now be clearly borne in mind, when these investments are completed (and their completion by arbitration of exchanges and the stock markets, is often the question of a day), the *balance of trade is again restored*, so that for the time being, as far as the supply of solid money itself is concerned, we stand again on a level with others. This thoroughly legitimate operation of the rate of interest concerns the questions of valuation, prices, and general international financial relationship, as a matter totally distinct in principle and practice from the violent spasmodic movements in our Bank rates.

These spasmodic rates of interest are created by over supplies of money through artificial means, such as arise in our case with the fixed issue of 15 millions.

It is immaterial whether the surplus is due to too much Bullion (as the admirers of the system allege), or to too much credit issue, so long as the surplus *does* exist, relieved only by excessive scarcity as the best proof of its frequent existence. Such artificial surplus, entirely useless for foreign, if not for all kinds of business, must necessarily bring about very low rates of interest, such as we experience in England.

The influence of undue rates of interest.

The absolute force of the rate of interest enables us to attract bullion whenever we require it; its action is just as absolute when France, Germany, and other states raise the rate, and we, on our part, lose bullion when we lower the rate below others in just as an automaton and certain a manner, independently of the balance of trade. Imagine that the rate of exchange for the time being, between England and France, is at par, indicating that neither country owes money to the other, interest in both countries being at, say, 4 per cent. Now, if we in England lower the rate to 2 per cent., the 2 per cent. difference on the three months' bill on us will give a profit of $\frac{1}{4}$ per cent.; the Frenchman then offers the bill in his market, and the short par of exchange settles with a clear difference of $\frac{1}{4}$ per cent. against us. The more immediate effect of the change then concerns our discount market. The Frenchman, able to discount home bills or foreign bills, except ours, at 4 per cent., sends the English bill to London, obtaining money for it at 2 per cent.; the English holder of French bills also takes up money here in order to hold French and foreign bills at 4 per cent.; thus our discount market suddenly has a double demand upon it. All this can take place, as you see, whilst the balance of trade remains at par—to the disturbance of our money market—until, at a certain stage of balance of trade, the $\frac{1}{4}$ per cent. profit is amply sufficient to lead to the

The absolute force of the established rate.

The insidious nature of an unduly low rate of interest.

The export
of bullion
in defiance
of the
balance of
trade.
exportation of many millions of bullion. And, inasmuch as bills of three or six months can be renewed, a series of engagements can thus be kept hanging over our market which may burst upon us at any time. Accordingly it happens frequently that for many months our market remains with low interest, lulling us into false security, until the cloud breaks and bullion suddenly flows away.

The
consequent
necessity
for sudden
and
extreme
rises in our
rate.
Up then goes our rate to an alarming extent, stage by stage, until a maximum is reached, sufficient to turn the exchanges not only back to par, but much over the par, in order to bring bullion back to us—efforts, which foreign Banks partly counteract by corresponding temporary heightening of their own rates. That these movements in our rates of interest are so spasmodic, and altogether distinct from any effects which our gradually accumulating wealth can possibly have, is proven by their great frequency and their excessive ranges, and also by the fact that during certain months we allow bullion to leave our market, until within a few weeks afterwards we are compelled

The
extreme
efforts
required for
balancing
fluctuations
caused by
extremes.
to make efforts to get it back again. That this driving away and drawing back bullion increases the great divergences immeasurably, beyond the efforts required merely to maintain a reasonable *status quo*, you will see at once. It pits one extreme against another. First, bullion is sent away by the low rate of interest, but before it can leave, the exchanges must be forced down, so that freight and charges are covered. When, having settled to that stage, we require it back, the exchanges must not only be restored, but the charges for reshipment must be overcome as well. This can only be done by correspondingly extravagant rates of interest which are rendered higher still by the resisting continental rates. And so, in the endeavour to regulate its stock of

bullion, the Bank of England rates of interest range from 2 to 10 per cent. *without such regulation being properly effected*, whereas, for the purpose of maintaining merely a *status quo* (once reached and satisfactory) a moderate range of from $3\frac{1}{2}$ to $6\frac{1}{2}$ per cent., or from 4 to 6 per cent., or probably less, would suffice. What I have explained to you so far concerns only the international and bullion aspect of the matter, apart from any other effect on our own local interests. As regards bullion, the 15 millions of fixed credit issue do not only cause the violent fluctuations in interest, but they exercise a permanent prejudice against bullion. It is a one-sided thing—a positive without a negative, and logicians will understand what this means. Hence we have been unable in this country to maintain an amount of bullion at the Bank adequate to our larger trade, and the benefit of the Bank of England note itself has been restricted, because, besides the permanent pressure against it, the chain of progress (as regards bullion) has been so frequently and ruthlessly broken.

(margin: The moderate efforts required for the maintenance of a status quo.)

(margin: The breaks in the chain of progress in bullion and note issue.)

THE INTERNATIONAL RATE OF INTEREST, THE MARKET RATE, AND THE BANK RATE.

Variations in the rates of interest are not only unavoidable, but they are positively necessary for the adjustment of the proportions arising between supply and value of money, and supply and prices of commodities. The supply of the precious metals—which, when all considerations as to paper money, cheques, and clearing systems are duly appreciated, constitute the real basis of value—is a matter of universal or international importance. It is immaterial whether this supply arises, in the first instance, in California, Australia, or elsewhere; or whether it subsequently

(margin: Variations in the international value of money.)

(margin: Instancing the supply of precious metals since 1848.)

finds its way to specific channels or is generally distributed, the first effect of the supply is a lowering of the rate of interest all over the world. This was the case manifestly when, as in 1850 to 1853, consequent upon the Californian and Australian gold discoveries, interest ruled low almost in all countries.

The effect on increased production.

The stimulus given by prices to production—if Custom House statistics are a guide—has three-folded the latter ; and this is all the more remarkable, because the total addition to the stock of current metallic money in the world—estimated at 900 millions sterling (viz., 550 millions of silver and 350 millions of gold) in 1848—has been increased by 400 millions of gold only, to the present total of 1,300 millions : an increase of only 45 per cent. being accompanied by an

The counter effect of increased production.

increase of trade of 300 per cent. Now, when the level of production has thus risen or distanced the supply of money, a disproportion of numbers arises in the other direction, and money must become dearer, as it has done since. There is yet another distinct cause influencing the international rate—that of the change in the systems of valuation. The demonetisation of silver, which England commenced in 1816, which Germany is about to introduce, so that all European nations must follow their example, threatens an

The changes in the valuation.

enforced decline in the value of that metal, under which its use as money cannot be continued, even on the token system ; and if some international agreement as to the maintenance of silver as money is not arrived at, the stock of metallic money in the world may be reduced by 400 to 500 millions.* Prices

---

* The gravity of this matter cannot be overrated. It forms the substance of the controversy between "the single gold" and the "double," or "gold and silver" valuation, in which we in England appear to have less interest than other nations, and have not much considered the point. Our interests, however, are so

and production must therefore decline, to suit the numerical stock of gold remaining, and interest rule high until the adjustment is completed.

It will readily be admitted that these variations in the international value of money, as dependent on a certain per centage of fresh supply to the world, or on the corresponding slower increase of production, are not of a violent spasmodic character. They may at times, as they did in the period of 1850 to 1865, produce strongly visible effects; but these involve months and years. It is not in their nature that they should, like the rates of the Bank of England, vary from day to day, or week by week, or jump within a period of a few weeks between three and ten per cent. It would accordingly seem reasonable that any country having a share in international commerce should be able to maintain its share of gold by following the international rate of interest, as it can be ascertained from time to time by practice of business, or protected by certain conservative margins, and for the latter purpose that country which has the greatest wealth and investments, is placed in the most favourable position.

The variations in the international rate of interest are gradual.

England is that country; yet nowhere do the rates of interest differ so widely, so spasmodically, and so frequently from the international rate than the Bank of England rates! Our market rate, which is determined in the first place by the amount of money falling due from expiring contracts, and the amount of fresh contracts offering every day, has to compete

The want of accord between the international rates and the Bank of England rates.

much bound up with the world at large that any detriment caused in universal trade would strike us indirectly, but possibly with greater effect than we now perceive. Mr. Disraeli, in his speech at Glasgow University, in November 1873, alluded to this matter—a hopeful sign that English statesmen are beginning to understand this gigantic question.

with the large idle reserves at the Bank; you may further infer why the market rate of interest is thus placed between two combatant elements, in which it is perfectly powerless to follow the true guide (the international rate), and must bow and succumb to what the Bank of England, proud of its accumulated reserve, may choose to dictate.

The annexed table shows the result.

In order to enable you to appreciate this best, I herewith give a table, placing in juxtaposition the rates of interest from 1844 to 1873 of the Bank of England, the Bank of France, the Bank of Prussia. These three States are "internationally" wealthy, and efficient competitors with us in commerce. Belgium and Holland might also be included, but their influence is not sufficiently paramount, France and Germany holding the overwhelming competitive power. States like Russia, Italy, Spain, Turkey, the United States, and others, are internationally poor, and continually indebted to us and these four States. They are in a chronic state of dear money, and any bid of higher interest on their part does not only affect us, but also by way of arbitration, the four States placed alongside of England.

TABLE 8.—*Showing the Variations in the Bank Rates of Interest in England, France, and Prussia, from September 1844 to December 1873, inclusive.*

Bank of England.		Bank of France.		Bank of Prussia.		Bank of England.		Bank of France.		Bank of Prussia.	
1844.	%		%		%	**1857.**	%		%		%
7 Sept.	2½	1 Sept.	4	1 Sept.	4	16 Jan.	3½	14 Jan.	6	1 Sept.	4½
				16 Oct.	4½	23 ,,	4	,,		,,	
						10 April	5	,,		,,	
1845.						7 Aug.	5½	,,		,,	
15 Oct.	3	,,		19 March	4	11 Sept.	5	,,		,,	
8 Nov.	3½	,,		9 Oct.	5	16 Oct.	5½	,,		,,	
						30 ,,	8	,,		,,	
1846.						27 Nov.	7	,,		,,	
29 Aug.	3	,,		2 March	4	4 Dec.	6	,,		,,	
		,,		1 July	5	24 ,,	5	28 Dec.	4	,,	

TABLE 8.—continued.

Bank of England.	%.	Bank of France.	%.	Bank of Prussia.	%.
1848.					
29 Jan.	4	28 Dec.	4	27 March	5
17 June	3½	,,		15 July	4½
4 Nov.	3	,,		,,	
1849.					
1 Dec.	2½	,,		20 Feb.	4
1850.					
28 Dec.	3	,,		,,	
1851.					
1 Jan.	3	,,		,,	
1852.					
1 Jan.	2½	5 March	3	,,	
24 April	2			,,	
1853.					
8 Jan.	2½	,,		,,	
22 ,,	3	,,		,,	
4 June	3½	,,		,,	
3 Sept.	4	,,		,,	
17 ,,	4½	,,		,,	
1 October	5	7 October	4	30 Sept.	5
1854.					
13 May	5½	20 Jan.	5		
5 August	5	12 May	4	11 May	4
1855.					
7 April	4½	,,		,,	
6 May	4	,,		,,	
16 June	3½	,,		,,	
8 Sept.	4	,,		,,	
15 ,,	4½	,,		,,	
29 ,,	5	4 October	5	,,	
6 October	5½	11 ,,	6	6 Nov.	4½
1856.					
24 May	6	1 April	5	7 Jan.	5
31 ,,	5			6 May	4
26 June	4½			,,	
4 October	5	26 Sept.	6	3 Sept.	5
11 ,,	6½			22 ,,	6
15 Nov.	7			,,	
6 Dec.	6½			,,	
20 ,,	6			,,	
1857.					
2 April	6½			9 March	5
18 June	6	26 June	5½		
16 July	5½	13 October	6½	18 August	5½
8 October	6	20 ,,	7½	10 Sept.	6
12 ,,	7	10 Nov.	9	3 October	6½
19 ,,	8	26 ,,	8		
5 Nov.	9	3 Dec.	7	7 Nov.	7½
9 ,,	10	17 ,,	6		
21 Dec.	8	29 ,,	5	26 Dec.	6½
1858.					
7 Jan.	6			5 Jan.	5½
14 ,,	5			16 ,,	5
28 ,,	4	6 Feb.	4½	2 Feb.	4

Bank of England.	%.	Bank of France.	%.	Bank of Prussia.	%.
1858.					
4 Feb.	3½	18 Feb.	4	6 Feb.	4½
11 ,,	3	10 June	3½	11 Oct.	5
9 Dec.	2½	23 Sept.	3	13 ,,	4
1859.					
28 April	3½	3 May	4	5 May	5
4 May	4½				
2 June	3½			,,	
9 ,,	3			,,	
14 July	2½	4 August	3½	18 July	4
1860.					
19 Jan.	3			,,	
31 ,,	4			,,	
29 March	4½			,,	
12 April	5			,,	
10 May	4½			,,	
24 ,,	4			,,	
8 Nov.	4½	12 Nov.	4½	,,	
13 ,,	5			,,	
15 ,,	6			,,	
29 ,,	5			,,	
31 Dec.	6			,,	
1861.					
7 Jan.	7	2 Jan.	5½	,,	
14 Feb.	8	8 ,,	7	,,	
21 March	7	14 March	6	,,	
4 April	6	21 ,,	5	,,	
11 ,,	5			,,	
16 May	6			,,	
1 August	5			,,	
15 ,,	4½			,,	
29 ,,	4	26 Sept.	5½	,,	
19 Sept.	3½	1 October	6	,,	
7 Nov.	3	21 Nov.	5	,,	
1862.					
9 Jan.	2½	21 Jan.	4½	,,	
22 May	3	6 Feb.	4	,,	
10 July	2½	27 March	3½	,,	
24 ,,	2			,,	
30 October	3	6 Nov.	4	,,	
1863.					
15 Jan.	4	15 Jan.	5	,,	
29 ,,	5			,,	
19 Feb.	4	12 March	4½	,,	
20 April	3½	26 ,,	4	,,	
6 May	3	7 May	3½	,,	
16 ,,	3½	11 June	4	,,	
21 May	4			,,	
2 Nov.	5	8 Oct.	5	3 Nov.	4½
5 ,,	6	6 Nov.	6	,,	
2 Dec.	7	12 ,,	7	,,	
3 ,,	8			,,	
21 ,,	7			,,	
1864.					
20 Jan.	8			,,	
11 Feb.	7			,,	
25 ,,	6			,,	
16 April	7	24 March	6	,,	

TABLE 8.—*continued.*

Bank of England.	%	Bank of France.	%	Bank of Prussia.	%
2 May	8	6 May	7	3 May	5
5 "	9	9 "	8		"
19 "	8	20 "	7		"
20 "	7	26 "	6		"
16 June	6		"		"
26 July	7	9 Sept.	7		"
4 August	8	13 October	8		"
8 Sept.	9	3 Nov.	7	6 Sept.	6
10 Nov.	8	24 "	6	6 October	7
24 "	7	3 Dec.	5		"
15 Dec.	6	22 "	4½	5 Dec.	6
1865.					
12 Jan.	5½		"	14 Jan.	5
26 "	5	9 Feb.	4	18 Feb.	4
2 March	4½	9 March	3½		"
30 "	4		"		"
4 May	4½		"		"
25 "	4		"		"
1 June	3½	1 June	3		"
15 "	3		"		"
27 July	3½		"		"
3 August	4		"		"
28 Sept.	4½		"	4 Sept.	5
2 October	5	5 October	4	3 October	6
5 "	6	9 "	5	10 "	7
7 "	7	23 "	4		"
23 Nov.	6		"		"
28 Dec.	7		"		"
1866.					
4 Jan.	8	4 Jan.	5		"
22 Feb.	7	15 Feb.	4½	22 Feb.	6
15 March	6	22 "	4		"
3 May	7	23 March	3½	4 May	7
8 "	8		"		"
11 "	9	11 May	4	11 "	9
12 "	10	28 July	3½	13 July	8
18 August	8		"	18 "	7
23 "	7		"	26 "	6
30 "	6	30 August	3	3 August	5
6 Sept.	5		"		"
27 "	4½		"	29 October	4½
6 Nov.	4		"		"
20 Dec.	3½		"	13 Dec.	4
1867.					
7 Feb.	3		"		"
30 May	2½	31 May	2½		"
2 July	2		"		"
1868.					
10 Nov.	2½		"		"
3 Dec.	3		"		"
1869.					
1 April	4		"		"
6 May	4½		"		"
10 June	4		"		"
24 "	3½		"		"
15 July	3		"		"
19 August	2½		"		"
4 Nov.	3		"	29 October	4½

Bank of England.	%	Bank of France.	%	Bank of Prussia.	%
1870.					
21 July	3½	18 July	3½	15 Feb.	4
23 "	4	21 "	4	15 July	6
28 "	5	30 "	5	18 "	8
4 August	6	9 August	6		"
11 "	5½		"		"
18 "	4½		"	19 August	6
25 "	4		"		"
1 Sept.	3½		"	5 Sept	5
15 "	3		"		
29 "	2½		"		
1871.					
2 March	3		"	20 Feb.	4½
13 April	2½		"	6 March	4
15 June	2¼		"		"
13 July	2	20 July	5		"
21 Sept.	3		"		"
27 "	4		"		"
7 Oct.	5		"		"
16 Nov.	4		"		"
30 "	3½	3 Nov.	6		"
14 Dec.	3		"		"
1872.					
4 April	3½	27 Feb.	5		"
11 "	4		"		"
9 May	5		"		"
30 "	4		"		"
13 June	3½		"		"
20 "	3		"		"
18 July	3½		"		"
18 Sept.	4		"	18 Sept.	5
26 "	4½		"		"
3 Oct.	5		"		"
10 "	6		"		"
9 Nov.	7		"		"
21 "	6		"		"
12 Dec.	5		"		"
1873.					
9 Jan.	4½		"		
23 "	4		"		
30 "	3½		"	20 Jan.	4½
26 March	4		"	7 Feb.	4
7 May	4½		"	1 April	5
10 "	5		"	3 May	6
17 "	6		"		"
4 June	7		"		"
12 "	6		"		"
10 July	5		"		"
17 "	4½		"		"
24 "	4		"	28 July	5
31 "	3½		"	8 August	4½
30 August	3		"		"
25 Sept.	4		"		"
29 "	5		"		"
14 October	6	14 October	6	27 October	5
18 "	7		"		"
1 Nov.	8	8 Nov.	7	28 Nov.	7
7 "	9	20 "	6		"
20 "	8	27 "	5		"
27 "	6		"		"
4 Dec.	5		"	10 Dec.	6
11 "	4½		"	20 "	5

A noticeable feature in this table is the fact that many of the movements in the rates of the banks of the continent are *consequent* upon the movements in England, these banks finding it necessary to protect themselves against any sudden demands of bullion the Bank of England may make. In 1866 only, when the balance of trade in favour of France was so strong, gold went there in spite of our high rate. But in none of the cases were continental rates obliged to be raised to our pitch, nor on the other hand did they fall so low. I do not mean to say that the system followed by the great continental banks is a most perfect one; on the contrary, they all suffer more or less from defects in their practices of issue; nevertheless, it will be evident to you that they do not only succeed in holding their own bullion in better control, but that they are able to do so with more equable rates of interest. Some of the disturbances in continental rates are due to revolutions and wars, but by far the greater divergences are consequent upon *our own* temporarily extreme variations, which are the chief contributors of confusion.

The continental bank's protecting action is more efficient.

The original cause for these frequent and extreme changes in England are the unduly low rates of interest; and the keynote of the reform is struck when you reflect on the following:—" The Bank holds rates low when the Reserve of notes is 13 or 15 millions, the rate then falling to 2 per cent. Now, if with a Reserve of 8 or 10 millions, interest rules at, say 4 per cent., it follows that if we *voluntarily* reduced the Reserve of 13 or 15 millions to 8 or 10 millions, we should be able to maintain the rate of 4 per cent."

The keynote for the reform of our system indicated by this table.

The following tables show the variations and the number of weeks for each change, under each rate of interest, from 2 to 10 per cent., of the three Banks, from September 1844 to December 1873 inclusive :—

TABLE 9.—*Showing the number of Changes in the Rates of Interest, and the number of Weeks during which the Rates lasted, of the Banks of England, France and Prussia, from 1st September 1844 to 31st December 1873.*

BANK OF ENGLAND.

RATES OF INTEREST AND WEEKS OF DURATION.

2	2¼	3	3¼	4	4¼	5	5¼	6	6¼	7	7¼	8	8¼	9	9¼	10%
87	57	3	1	11	2	17	5	3	31	1	—	4	—	2	—	7
14	20	42	20	20	4	5	2	1	5	3		3		9		14
69	57	55	13	2	2	5	12	15	2	1		2		2		
14	16	53	12	6	12	31	2	4	11	6		5				
	2	19	1	1	4	36	12	1		2		3				
	20	43	1	1	2	1	2	1		1		4				
	27	5	1	9	2	4	1	2		3		1				
	19	1	7	24	4	2		1		2		1				
	2	9	1	3	3	2		1		2		5				
	8	7	1	1	1	4		11		3		2				
	1	11	2	9	5	1		3		2		7				
	11	2	1	23	4	4		7		3		1				
	22	6	7	5	1	5		5		6		1				
	9	16	3	1	1	2		4		1		1				
		18	2	8	2	4		1		3		1				
		5	2	6	1	1		5		1						
		37	1	5	1	5		7		3						
		2	1	2	3	3		1		2						
		6	8	2		5		2		1						
		1	8	1		3		4								
		16	3	2		1		2								
		4		2		2		2								
		3		4		4		4								
				2		1		1								
				2		1		1								
				1		2										
				6		2										
				1												
				1												
				1												
134	271	364	96	162	54	153	36	89	49	46	—	41	—	13	—	21

Number of Weeks 1,529
Number of Changes 212
Range of Interest from 2 to 10 per cent.

(The Bank has actually done business as low as 1¾ per cent., and as high as 12½ per cent.)

BANK OF FRANCE.

RATES OF INTEREST AND WEEKS OF DURATION.

2½	3	3½	4	4½	5	5½	6	6½	7	7½	8	8½	9 %
163	83	15	124	2	50	16	25	1	2	3	1	—	2
	32	66	217	7	16	1	39		9		1		
	18	32	15	2	1	1	2		19		3		
	39	5	72	2	25		1		1				
		12	16	7	6		7		1				
		7	13	1	28		1		5				
		5	7		9		6		3				
		1	10		8		15		2				
			6		4		1						
			18		3		49						
			4		2		17						
			1		6		3						
			10		1		1						
			4		15								
			10		85								
			1		3								
			2										
163	172	143	530	21	262	18	167	1	42	3	5	—	2

Number of Weeks 1,529
Number of Changes 83
Range of Interest 2½ to 9 per cent.

BANK OF PRUSSIA.

RATES OF INTEREST AND WEEKS OF DURATION.

4	4½	5	5½	6	6½	7	7½	8	8½	9 %
7	22	21	5	24	5	8	6	1	—	9
29	81	9	2	2	2	19		4		
17	32	15		4		1				
240	22	19		6		1				
78	26	17		1		1				
18	6	3		10						
36	2	23		6						
20	8	2		1						
224	11	9		3						
28		11		12						
142		18								
21		5								
80		4								
7		12								
		19								
		24								
		18								
		5								
		2								
		4								
		4								
947	205	244	7	69	7	30	6	5	—	9

Number of Weeks 1,529
Number of Changes 68
Range of Interest 4 to 9 per cent.

The number of changes in the rate of interest since 1st September 1844, were accordingly

At the Bank of England . . . 212
,, Bank of France 83
,, Bank of Prussia 68

But a reference to the preceding statement in the years when our rates varied most, shows that the two foreign Banks were obliged to follow ours to some extent so as to protect their exchanges. This, after making due allowance for counter effects, is clearly traceable in 28 instances as regards the Bank of France, and in 19 instances for that of Prussia, so that their actual changes may be reduced to the number of 55 and 49 respectively.

The following exhibits the rates and numbers of weeks for each of the three banks enumerated :—

%/₀	2	2¼	3	3½	4	4½	5	5½	6	6½	7	7½	8	8½	9	9½	10
England	134	271	364	96	162	54	153	36	89	49	46	—	41	—	13	—	21
France	—	163	172	143	530	21	262	18	167	1	42	3	5	—	2	—	—
Prussia	—	—	—	—	947	205	244	7	69	7	30	6	5	—	9	—	—

Taking the range of from 3½ inclusive to 6 inclusive as already a pretty wide one for variations, it would appear that out of the total of 1,529 weeks there were comprised within this range—

For England	...	590 weeks	{	769 being below 3½ per cent.
				170 ,, above 6 ,, ,,
For France	...	1141 ,,	{	335 ,, below 3½ ,, ,,
				53 ,, above 6 ,, ,,
For Prussia	...	1472 ,,	{	none ,, below 3½ ,, ,,
				57 ,, above 6 ,, ,,

Or if 4, 4½ and 5 per cent. are taken as fair mercantile rates, it would appear that this range prevailed—

In England	...	369 weeks	{	865 being below 4 per cent.
				295 ,, above 5 ,, ,,
In France	...	813 ,,	{	478 ,, below 4 ,, ,,
				238 ,, above 5 ,, ,,
In Prussia	...	1396 ,,	{	none ,, below 4 ,, ,,
				133 ,, above 5 ,, ,,

In looking at these figures, and speculating on the probable causes of this restlessness of our rates, the old argument may again be used, "Everybody comes to England for gold, hence the Bank of England *must* make greater movements in the rate." *The exact contrary should be the case.* The bullion which comes to England, and is offered in the market, is not only just as available to the Bank of England as to other foreign banks, but more so, for the Bank of England has the *first* offer of the copious arrivals, of which it need but retain a small per centage, so as to keep the stock in the Issue Department at a fair level. A reference to table 5, on page 81, will show you that the annual passage of gold through this country is like a continual stream, from which the Bank can help itself before anybody else. And whereas the Bank of England need but poise the rate of interest so as to obtain its share of the current flowing by, or of maintaining, at the least, its own stock already in hand, the foreign exchanges must overcome the charges for transmission before they can take away from that which is on our market, and which our Bank would not require. The foreign banks are bound, accordingly, to make greater efforts by greater bids, or they must wait until the Bank of England has served itself. I appeal to your common sense for the justice of this view, and if you agree with me in this, the extraordinary divergences in our rates will come into stronger relief. The claptrap argument as to the *undue* drafts of bullion on the Bank of England must give way to the thought that there is an error somewhere in the Bank's system which totally reverses sound reasoning, and that the correction of this error necessarily involves the reversal of the present practice. In this conflict between the international and Bank rate (to which latter the market rate must submit),

The Bank of England ought to be able to keep bullion with lesser efforts than foreign banks.

The reverse being the case, a false principle must be reversed.

bullion alone is in question, *i.e.* the due proportion of Bullion to be maintained by the Bank on the note circulation. With the latter, our home trade deals without having any immediate concern in the precise amount of bullion which the Bank of England should keep. The *Bullion question itself is entirely an international* one. In the competition for bullion among nations of equal, or nearly equal, rank of prosperity, that which bids the highest rates obtains the most, even to surplus; that which maintains the most regular rates keeps the most regular stock; whilst that which loses most, and is obliged to recoup its losses, *suffers from the greatest divergences in its rates of interest.* That is our case; and if you want to discover where the error lies, you must decide between cause and effect, the cart and the horse. Should bullion guide the rate of interest, or should the rate of interest guide bullion? It is hardly requisite to tell you that interest must be the active factor, and the avowed intention of the Bank in using its force for the very purpose needs no comment. It follows that the bad practice which the Bank makes with the rate of interest—causes this utter failure of its guardianship; and if you bear in mind the Bank's exceptionally favourable position in regard to the facility of obtaining bullion at its own doors, and then refer to the facts, as they present themselves before you, both by the extreme fluctuations in the Bank of England stock and the rates of interest, you must come to the conclusion that the error which leads to this must be a very wretched and economically contemptible one indeed.

If these struggles for bullion on the part of the Bank of England affected but the establishment itself, or foreigners, we might leave the Bank to do as it liked. But, unfortunately, the brunt of the mischief falls upon the legitimate trade and industry of the country. For the sake of a few millions of bullion —which the Bank is incapable of maintaining—thousands of millions of transactions current, and contracts incurred, must suffer by the spasmodic changes in the value of money. Hence, Manchester, Yorkshire, and all our manufacturing centres, whose business is that of a purely mechanical nature, which, with our advantages in resources and industrial ingenuity, is bound to be profitable, are subjected to the changes of prices in raw and ready goods brought about by these abnormal jumps in interest. In the world's great market, and our own, the ordinary conditions between supply and demand do not warrant these movements in the value of money, nor give them a natural character, free of suspicion of error. And where such error exists, manifesting itself by such abnormal results, most of the evil, including the suffering of the industrial classes, falls to its charge, notwithstanding the dogma which taunts commerce with speculation. If the variations in supply and demand, as far as the world's trade is concerned, give a field for speculation, how much more extensive must that ground become under the spasmodic changes in the rate of interest, and lay our otherwise regularly constituted industry open to an unjust charge ?

The consequences fall chiefly on our own industry and commerce.

The effect of these variations in the rate of interest in reference to one branch of business alone, exceeds in seriousness the original cause. Of the 300 millions of bills current (see Mr. Palgrave's book alluded to on page 25), about 160 are local bills; so that any change in discount chiefly affects local interests. About 140 millions are foreign drawn bills, of which a change of interest may fall back on foreigners for a small

The losses occurred on behalf of the recovery of bullion exceed the amount forced back.

portion, say 50 millions ; the rest concern contracts completed, or running, for which we have accepted definite terms. A change of interest from 4 to 8 per cent., on 250 millions of bills, involves 2½ millions clear loss to the discount market, and the loss in other branches of trade may be still larger. All the bullion *lost* by the Bank may not be more than 3 or 4 millions, and to get this back again the above losses must be incurred by other parties. The angry confusion to which this gives rise, the extraordinary and inexplicable dealings in our discount markets, the singular policy of the Bank, and the trumpery yet variable discount business of that institution, find their explanation in this miserable and unjust conflict, and loudly call for a reform which will separate the interests here concerned.

The angry confusion and just complaints to which this gives rise.

Indeed, among the hundreds of remedies proposed, it has even been suggested that the Bankers should emancipate themselves from the Bank of England, and form a new institution to take charge of their Reserves. Independently of the waste of force and economy implied in this suggestion, the Bank of England, would be able to override any such scheme of opposition, by means of the fixed issue of 15 millions, itself." It has also been suggested that the Bank of England should not publish its rates, or make *no* rate, that it should make advances or discounts at whatever rate it pleased. Independently of the impossibility of keeping rates secret, of the immorality involved in charging different rates at the same time on securities of equal rank, the principles of the valuation require, at all events, some *prevalent* rate, for otherwise our dealings in exchange and the settlement of international accounts would be impossible. The Bank of England cannot hold itself aloof from this rate ; as the issuer of notes, by a contract with

The unhealthy and untrue expedients proposed.

the State, it is bound to bring *this issue* in connection with current business, and must state the terms upon which it is prepared to do so. The life of our commerce depends upon the firmness of the factors for the calculation of profits and insurances, and the principles of our valuation require the Bank of England to contribute to its firmness by declaring its rates of interest.

Of the advantages which the foreigner derives from the undue and frequent variations of our rates of interest, I have already spoken. Our special disadvantage is our loss of influence on rates of exchange. As the wealthiest nation, with perhaps more than 1,000 millions invested abroad, with the command almost of the bullion market, it is *we* who ought to guide exchanges so that they benefit us first; but the London exchange market has ceased to be a guiding one, it is made utterly subservient to the exchanges as they are quoted abroad. Every exchange broker will confirm this fact, but we cannot blame the foreign banker who follows up the profit offered to him by the thoroughly legitimate arbitrations of exchanges, the buying in the cheapest, and selling in the dearest, market, which the variations of interest with us afford him. The foreigner thus takes money from us at one time, and returns it to us at another, appearing as if he came to our relief. Although in the course of international business, we may occasionally become temporary debtors, we need no such assistance from foreign countries. Persons who pride themselves upon the fact that foreigners do lend us money as a sign of confidence in us, are just as ready to blow the other way if the argument suits; they forget that we should not allow the foreigner who thus favours us, to do so at heavy cost to

The London exchange market has become powerless through its want of true rates of interest.

ourselves, for this must be firmly borne in mind, the greater intensity of the movements in our rates of interest, the greater are the chances of profit made abroad. Not only will the banker abroad take a profit on the transaction, by which he *receives* Bullion, but he will take a second profit on what he *sends back*.

All reciprocity ceases in this case.

The wide mouthed argument, that in trade nothing is done that does not suit either party, that we in England obtain set-offs of equal value, entirely fails in a one-sided case like this. The whole comfortable thought of equivalents, all the pretty arguments about reciprocity, break down when under crises and panics and the terror of the moment, we must, *nolens volens*, take every accumulated evil into the bargain, and thank our stars it was not worse.

THE GENERAL CIRCULATION AND THAT OF THE BANK OF ENGLAND NOTE.

The question of the use of money by the home trade of the country.

The foregoing chapter will have shown that this matter of due proportion of bullion is one standing by itself, dependent only on the proper rates of interest, turning simply on the Bank's ability or inability to manage such rates for the efficient protection of its *status quo*. To what extent now is the commerce of the country guilty of the movements in the money market and the distresses caused to the Bank of England? During the confused controversies in times of crisis, you hear of failures, loss of confidence and credit, scarcity of money, of high rates of interest, and of ruin and panic.

Your first impression will probably be that the commerce of the country, or the speculators in it, or somebody else, has wrongfully and wilfully made

away with, say, several millions of good money—that
these have disappeared, and that the high interest
"serves us right." You may hear that we have
something like 170 millions of money in circulation in the country, and imagine the scarcity is due to
the fact that, say, 10 millions have been made away
with. You may think that the great variations
in interest from 2 to 10 per cent. are hardly
justified with a change of per centage of about 6 per
cent. in the total amount of money on hand, nor
can you probably account for the rapidity with
which 10 millions of money are thus destroyed and
brought back again. Still, looking at what takes
place, you may think that no other explanation of
the enigma of the extreme dearness of money can
be given than that our commerce is most extravagant
and irregular in its use and demands for money.
Accordingly, as the money is employed for the purposes of circulation, *the state of the circulation* is that
by which the matter must be tested.

On investigating the returns of the total circulation, you will then find that you are *completely in the
wrong in thinking that money had been made away
with* in the manner suggested, or that too much
has been used. You will find not only that the
divergences in the circulation, within the periods
comprising the enormous changes in interest, do not
vary by anything like 10 millions, but that in the
times of the most severe crisis the variations in
total circulation are comparatively insignificant, showing that commerce is not guilty of the charges
alluded to. The circulation maintains this regularity
even in spite of mercantile failures; for the very
natural reason that such failures do not involve
destruction of currency, but are mere matters of
account.

The false impression that the demands of trade cause scarcity of money.

The comparative regularity of the home circulation.

In order to make you understand this clearly, the
The gross amount of money in the country. following analysis of the elements of our circulation is worthy of your attention :—

At the present time we have in England—

£105 millions in coined gold, <small>(according to the best estimates.)</small>

 18 ,, of silver and copper coin,

 37 ,, of Bank of England <small>(on 22 millions of bullion.)</small> notes.

 16 ,, of country notes, <small>(authorised issue.)</small>

say £176 ,, in money.

Of the 37 millions of Bank of England notes, there are at present, say, 22 millions issued against bullion, so that our total stock of gold, coined and uncoined, amounts to 127 millions. I take these figures, together with the 22 millions of bullion at the Bank, as occasional facts—their state, when this is read, may not agree—my purpose being to show that, out of the total of 176 millions of money, after deducting these Reserves, there are, say, 161 *firmly engaged in circu-* Partly in circulation partly in Reserve. *lation*, whilst, say, 10 millions of Bank of England notes and 5 millions of country notes, together 15 millions are *held in Reserve, i.e.* not in circulation.

Accordingly we have :—

Money in circulation . . 161 millions ;
do. in Reserve . . 15 millions.

The characteristics of each of these constituents of
Characteristics of the constituents. the *circulation* will show their mutual relationship to each other and to the whole :

1st. *Coined gold.* The greater part of the gold
Firmness of the gold coin in circulation. coin is in the pockets of individuals (a limited proportion hoarded), in tradesmen's and bankers' tills. Portions of it are held by country bankers against increased issue of notes. Parcels of sovereigns go in and out of the Issue Department of the Bank of England, notes and gold substituting each other in

circulation. The sovereigns in the tills of London bankers are not required as Reserve against investments, such Reserve being kept at the Bank of England, but they serve principally as stock for the daily wants of customers. The whole of this stock of gold coin is accordingly firmly engaged in the circulation, and any *sudden* fresh addition to it, or any *sudden* subtraction is impossible. If five millions of sovereigns were imported fresh to-day and spent in the purchase of goods, the whole amount would, in the evening or the next day, find its way to the Bank of England. A considerable time would elapse before the country could absorb one or more millions of gold coin, a corresponding change in prices and production, or some other contingency, must manifest itself before the circulation would *engage* such an addition. A few hundred thousands of pounds are periodically required for harvesting time in exchange for notes; they *return* in due course.

A sudden addition to the circulation cannot take place.

Equally impossible is any sudden forcible subtraction from the gold currency. In times of crisis, when the Bank of England bids high for money, certain limited amounts held by bankers may come in, but the overwhelming portion held by the public remains firm in service. In times of panic, the disposition to hold gold coin instead of notes, and a tendency to increased circulation show themselves, and make subtraction quite impossible. Nothing but a governmental Act, by way of forced taxation, could wrench the gold coin so engaged from circulation. This fact must be clearly borne in mind, any ordinary exchange of gold against notes, or *vice versa*, does not affect the existing basis of gold coin as a whole.

The subtraction of gold coin from circulation is resisted.

But whilst sudden additions and subtractions are thus impossible, the *gradual* increase of the gold coin circulation nevertheless takes place. In 1850 there

A general gradual increase has taken place.

were but between 60 to 70 millions of sovereigns current in Great Britain; in 1872 there were between 100 to 110 millions.* What I want to impress upon you here is, the difference between the *gradual increase* concurrent with production, prices, population, and other compensating effects, *as against* any *sudden expansion* or contraction, as the spasmodic movements of the Bank rate would presuppose. In twenty years time another 40 millions may have come into use, but for the time being, the 105 millions stated may be considered as being thus *firmly engaged*.

Silver and copper coin.

2. The amount *of silver and copper coins*, of a comparatively small per centage to gold, is even less liable to sudden movements. These coins are not legal tender money (beyond £2 for silver and 1s for copper), and although a portion now and then is held by bankers, above what they may want, they can neither give it to the Bank, nor when silver is in request, when even a demand arises, can they obtain a sudden supply. A general increase in these coins in circulation has nevertheless taken place, especially during recent years, and at this time an amount of 18 millions (according to the best estimates) is *firmly engaged* in circulation.

---

* This satisfactory evidence of the greater life in our interior intercourse is noteworthy, if only for this reason: many people think that the banking and clearing house systems in this country save currency, and that in time they may diminish it. That these systems save currency, is no doubt true, but however large this saving may be, and become, it will never actually diminish the metallic currency. The progress in clearing is immense, and it is *one of the rules of progress*, that all the useful factors of an organisation should share in it. Hence, to the astonishment of many people, our gold circulation has also increased. The law of mutuality is again in operation here, like in so many political and social matters of progress, in which this country has made similar experiences.

3. *Country Bankers'* notes, of which the authorised issue amounts to 15¾ millions sterling. When Scotch bankers issue more than this aggregate, they must hold gold coin against them. Such gold coin, exchanged for notes, is practically part of that in circulation out of the Bank of England, re-exchangeable into coin on notes being drawn on it. The absorption of coin by these banks does not alter the amount of circulation; the gold is merely temporarily replaced by notes, and the note holders have the first claim on it. It is necessary to say this, for such gold coin in issuing country banks, is often miscalled " cash reserve." The consistent general element to be considered in country issue is the 15¾ millions authorised issue clear above the gold coinage. Country notes are not legal tender money, their influence is confined to the immediate neighbourhoods of the issuing Banks, and although they "replace" a certain amount of sovereigns, they do not directly affect the London market. Their effect on the valuation is not beneficial to the country as a whole, however useful £1 notes may be. Country bankers keep a certain proportion of reserve, the circulation, above sovereigns, exhibiting this singular characteristic, that in times of crisis it diminishes (in 1866 by 1¾ millions). The Bank of England is then called upon to supply notes instead. For the practical purposes of this enquiry the 5 millions of country notes, which on page 108 I have assumed as being in Reserve, can be set aside.

4. The *Bank of England* note circulation is the superior or *supernatant constituent* of our circulation. By it are absorbed all the possible vagaries to which gold, silver, and to a certain extent country notes, may be subject. Thus gold coin may be in request for Ireland, or other districts, at harvest time; notes in circulation are surrendered for it, the total circulation

remaining pretty much the same, and subsequently the gold coin returns. We are accustomed to attach much importance to such temporary withdrawals of gold coin from the Bank; in reality they are, on the part of the Bank, but assets surrendered against liabilities. For all this kind of business in sovereigns, and also silver coin, the Bank of England acts as the regulating and absorbing factor; it manages this matter, especially the control over the state of the coinage, most admirably. That the Bank of England cares for the coining of sovereigns through the Mint, we all know; but the gradual increase of our gold circulation, since 1850, of 40 millions, would just as well have taken place if the public itself dealt directly with the Mint, if the present preventative arrangement (contrary to the spirit of the coinage laws, but defensible I admit) did not make the sale of bar gold to the Bank more convenient.

In the supernatant constituent of the general circulation.

Now, since the Bank of England, as we all know, is the regulator of the gold and silver currency through the issue department, if the general circulation thus concentrates its possible variations in that department of the Bank, it is evident

The variations in the total circulation concentrate in the Issue Department of the Bank of England.

That the *circulation of the Bank of England notes is the barometer by which*

the greater or lesser steadiness of the whole circulation can be measured. Accordingly, *any variations which take place in the Bank of England note circulation not only indicate the greater or lesser amount of general circulation*, but *all the other* variations which take place in the exchange between Bank of England notes on the one, and coin and country notes on the other hand.

The table, which I now submit to you, contains the extreme variations in the circulation of Bank of

England notes from 1845 to 1871, in the respective quarters, from 1st of January each year.

TABLE 10.

Showing the Extreme Variations of the Bank of England Note Circulation in each Quarter (from 1st January) of the Years 1845 to 1871 (in millions £ sterling).

Years.	First Quarter.	Second Quarter.	Third Quarter.	Fourth Quarter.
1845	20—21	21—22	21—22	21—23
1846	20—22	20—21	20—21	20—22
1847*	20—21	21—19	19—18	19—21
1848	20—18	19—18	19—18	19—17
1849	19—18	20—18	20—18	19—19
1850	20—19	21—20	22—20	21—19
1851	21—19	20—19	21—20	21—20
1852	22—22	23—22	23—25	25—23
1853	25—23	25—23	25—23	24—21
1854	23—22	23—20	21—20	21—20
1855	21—20	20—21	22—20	21—19
1856	19—20	20—20	21—20	21—19
1857*	19—18	19—18	19—20	21—19
1858	19—19	20—19	20—21	20—19
1859	20—20	22—20	22—21	22—20
1860	21—20	21—23	21—22	21—19
1861	20—19	19—20	20—19	20—19
1862	20—20	20—21	22—20	21—19
1863	20—19	20—20	21—20	22—19
1864	20—19	21—20	21—20	21—19
1865	20—19	21—20	22—21	22—20
1866*	21—20	22—26*	25—23	23—22
1867	23—22	23—22	24—23	24—23
1868	24—23	24—23	24—23	24—22
1869	24—22	23—22	23—23	24—22
1870	23—22	23—22	24—23	24—22
1871	24—23	24—23	25—24	25—24

This table shows that the variations in the circulation within one quarter never exceeded 3 millions, with the exception of 1866, when it was 4 millions, and from 1845 to 1865 the range is pretty equal. In the crisis of 1847 the issue actually declined by 1 million; in 1857, the more severe of the crises, during which the Bank

* Years of crises and panic.

made 2 millions extra issue, the increase was but 1 million. From 1866 there is an average general rise of 6 millions, the variations on which are even less than 2 millions. The variation in 1866 of 4 millions (nearer $3\frac{1}{2}$), is due to the fact that the country bankers' issues declined by $1\frac{3}{4}$ millions, and herein lies part of the evil perpetrated by these issues on the Bank of England. If you make allowance for this, and for the probable hoarding of gold during the panic, for the facility with which the Bank (on the authority for an extra issue) suddenly parted with notes, and the quick decline shortly after, you may possibly come to the conclusion that this solitary instance of $3\frac{1}{2}$ millions of increase of note circulation was due to other causes than the direct demands of commerce.

A reference to the table on last page accordingly shows :—

In spite of all movements, failures, crises, and panics.

That although the Bank of England circulation is the regulator of all the divergences in the other constituents of our general circulation, which *concentrate their effects there* and express them by *proportionately greater divergences* in that portion of the circulation ;—

although there is at times *great scarcity* of money, at another time *great plethora ;*—

although the public are charged with overtrading, although losses and failures follow, with crises, panics, and a host of evils ;—

yet—

the Bank of England circulation remains pretty regular.

The public does not make away with money, or uses too much of it.

This cannot mean that the public makes an undue use of the circulation by overtrading, by losing or destroying money. The extent of the "accommodation" which the public requires from the Bank is precisely identical with the amount of notes which the public uses, all other matters are matters of clearing account, and as far as the so-called scarcity or plethora of money is concerned, you will see that they do not in any way affect the actual use of more or less money, and that the commerce of the country *cannot be charged either with destroying money or with using too much of it.* On the contrary, in spite of the panics and crises which are caused by the Bank's inability to hold bullion, the circulation remains firm. But what is more significant still, and shows clearly that the merit of this regularity is entirely due to the public, and not ascribable to the virtuous conduct of the Bank, the public resists every effort made by the Bank to cram more notes into use. Whenever the Bank is in that " safe state " of having ample bullion, say 23 millions on a circulation of 25 millions, leaving, say 13 millions of notes *in Reserve*, over and above what the circulation can possibly use, what does the Bank do but tempt the circulation by lowering the rate, for no other purpose than to invite the use of this Reserve? Nothing is more significant, in the whole of this enquiry, than the *absolute indifference* with which the commerce of this country *refuses* to have anything to do with these continual attempts to inflate the circulation.

On the contrary, it keeps what there is, and steadfastly resists all attempts at inflation.

Through the continual offer of the Bank's Reserve of idle notes.

No solution of this question of the Bank of England note issue is possible unless it be distinctly recognised *that the circulation is thus regular.* And one of the express objects of this treatise is that of bringing this matter into the prominence which it deserves. Understand, then, that the *circulating* mediums of this country consist of (at the present time) 105 millions of gold, 18 millions of silver and copper, 12 millions (4 in Reserve) of country notes,

The paramount importance of this fact.

being   135 millions, to which
must be added   26   ,,   of Bank of England notes ;

together   161 millions,

The
inexorable
firmness
of the
circulation.
which amount is subject only to gradual increase or decrease, but not to spasmodic additions and subtractions. Whatever divergences (excepting gradual increase or decrease) may take place, consist principally in the exchanging of sovereigns for notes, and *vice versa*, showing their effects in the *supernatant* bank-note circulation, and these effects themselves, as seen by the table on page 113, remain within such limited bounds that they cannot possibly have any serious and really legitimate influence on the rates of interest.

There is
practically
no scarcity
of money,
nor use for
any surplus.
All that concerns scarcity or surplus of money is disposed of by this simple and inexorable·fact; it is utterly idle to talk of practical scarcity when the supply is there, and it is utterly useless to maintain a surplus of money when such surplus cannot possibly be used.

The lessons
to be
derived
from this
fact.
Several important lessons can be derived from the fact of this inexorability of our circulation.

It shows, in the first place, that the circulation is not *elastic* in the sense of schemers who require what, in their meaning of the term, they call *elastic* currency. The elasticity of the circulation is confined to its gradual increase (and perhaps decrease also), and for

The misuse
of the term
elasticity.
It concerns
gradual
increase
only.
this purpose nothing stands in its way. The freedom with which gold flows into this country, the firmness and closeness of the prices at which gold is sold and bought (thus giving the merchant the exact point upon which he can reckon his profit), brings us this valuable international medium in abundant supply. The country may retain as much of this as it pleases, and through this freedom of choice the demand for, and use of money is capable of the highest development.

The free-
dom of
supply of
gold and de-
velopment
of the
demand.
The great rule of free supply, as that essentially necessary for the encouragement and development of the demand for gold coin, is operative here, and the total

thus accummulating in the country, or rather the balance used after cheques and clearing systems have modified it in their respective ways, is in full accord with the principles of valuation* on which our prices are held for the supremacy of our position in international commerce. Our industrial classes may suffer some injustice from the token system by which our silver coinage becomes so restricted—but the whole mass of gold money in the country stands, *and must stand*, in due numerical relationship to the number of commodities and their prices.

In accordance with the principles of international valuation.

All the talk about elasticity, " to correspond with the demand, with crises and difficulties," is mere twaddle. Still more absurd must now appear the proposal of schemes for all sorts of additional Bank note issues. Could 70 or 100 millions of " national currency" be crammed into our circulation, or, to notice the proposal of Mr. Anderson, made in Parliament, for the issue by certain banks on Government securities, what would be the effect if these banks did make an aggregate issue of 20 or 30 millions of such notes? The present merit of our system, as far as the term elasticity applies, lies in the fact that under the supply of gold (the fruits of our commerce with the world) we can continually increase the stock of coin by the most natural process. This, in the first instance, is done through the Bank of England stock of bullion, which will also bring about an increase of the notes in legitimate use. The tension thus at work would be utterly broken down if, by some act of the legislature, 10 or 20 or more millions of notes were suddenly brought out alongside of the 161 millions of money now in use, and tried to force

The absurdity of schemes for indefinite or definite supplies of Bank notes.

They would destroy the true elastic force of our currency.

---

* They would be still more so if the 15 millions of fixed issue were not in the way.

their way into circulation. Or, if it were proposed to dribble the amount into circulation at the rate of 1 million a year only, this would only weaken the true elastic power, viz. the gradual increase, and replace bullion to that amount. This elasticity and reciprocity between our trade and bullion are already weakened by the *fixed* issues of 15 millions of the Bank of England and the 16 millions of country issues. Every additional million would widen the gap, and in its endeavours to find a place in the circulation, would compete with, and keep away, so much bullion. And all other minor schemes, such as one lately proposed, viz., to give, in the event of crisis, the right of issue to the extent of 2 or 3 millions to certain banks in London, belong to the same category of error. All these suggestions, however moderate they may appear, originate in the minds of financial cooks, who are totally ignorant of the real state of the case, who fancy that the public has made away with money, that the "scarcity" can be restored by additional notes.

The same spirit at work in all such schemes, ignorant of and incapable of citing facts.

The most remarkable of the wise sayings current when a crisis sets in is uttered by certain defenders of the Bank's system, who whine away in this style :— " Why should the Bank of England be called upon to come to the assistance of speculators by coming forward with *large sums of ready money ?* Why should the Bank of England, any more than other banking institutions, be compelled to furnish the mercantile community with *more Bank notes*, to save it from ruin, and from the natural consequences of that imprudence, by which merchants have squandered away money entrusted to them for the carrying on of business, in spite of warnings and previous crises ?" That such is the current talk in times of crisis you will admit ; but if you refer to the facts here laid before you, you will clearly see the flagrant perversion of truth.

A current fallacy as regards the distress for money.

It is untrue to say the public has made away with money, and that it requires *additional sums of notes* to rescue it from ruin. The Bank is not called upon to furnish them, as the facts show. It is, on the contrary, the Bank of England which loses bullion, by its inability to protect and maintain its stock. This is the chief and only original difficulty, —all the others are but the accessory consequences. If, from what I have said respecting the conflict between the international rate *versus* the Bank rate, and the facts here shown as regards the comparative regularity of our circulation, you rightly understand this matter, you will be able to appreciate the degrees of "childishness" involved in the current saying quoted above, and in the present system of the Bank.

Its untruth and the real truth.

The true causes of that undefinable event, *a panic*, will also now clearly appear. I have stated before, that the circulation is firmly engaged in the business of the intercourse between individuals, that it is impossible suddenly to cram money into it, and equally impossible suddenly to curtail it, the Bank of England circulation forming the supernatant portion. Now, when at any time there are 21½ millions of Bank of England notes in circulation, as on 18th November 1857, and Bullion declines, as it did, to 6 millions, giving, with the fiduciary issue of 14½ millions, but 20½ of issue, there is consequently not only no reserve, but the circulation is actually attacked to the extent of 1 million. Hence, before the evening's accounts were closed, there would have been ruin, and an almost indescribable state of confusion and panic, if the Government had not stepped in and allowed 2 millions extra issue. You may often have heard that the "fate" of the Bank and others depended upon the few minutes which the Government had for decision. Since the circulation

The real cause of panic.

of the notes has increased to 25 and 26 millions, the panic points are necessarily shifted to 10 and 11 millions of bullion, together with the 15 millions of fixed issue.

A panic, then, means nothing less than a state of bullion so low that the issue no longer fits the circulation, and so giving a prospect of a general scramble for money. That this is entirely the fault of the Bank, and not that of the public, you will infer from what you have now learned. That under such circumstances the suspension of the Act for more notes allays the panic is quite true; but the restoration of matters beyond this, for which the three examples of crises are quoted, is not due to the issue of more notes, but to the very high tension of interest, which, concurrent with the permission to give out more notes, began to tell upon the return of bullion to us, and so restored the level required for circulation, through the force of a factor, which is otherwise opposed to, and made practically powerless through, the over-issue of notes.

THE AVAILABILITY OF THE RESERVE OF THE BANK OF ENGLAND.

The idea of the necessity to maintain "a large Reserve" is so much in accordance with what seems prudent and wise, and the recommendation to "keep Reserve" is so continually uttered, that any writer on this subject must well guard himself against the suspicion that he does *not* recognise the necessity of Reserve. This suspicion might arise if, in the course of my remarks, I criticise the requirements for, and the true character of, the *present* Reserve,

and recommend its abolition. I must accordingly guard myself by telling you that, in substitution for the *present system* of Reserve, I shall propose another, more effective and certain in its nature; but I postpone its explanation to Part II. of this book; for it is, above all, necessary that the ground should be cleared, and that you should first perceive the great errors which are inherent in the present system, so that, by way of contrast, the other better system may be easier understood.

The substitution of a better system, explained in Part II.

We have now ascertained—

Firstly. That the circulation of the country is regular by far within the range of the violent fluctuations to which the Bank of England total issue is subject.

Secondly. That it is capable of *gradual* increase, and that this is effected principally by the free supply of gold.

The connection between Circulation and Reserve.

The circulation being thus regular—say, at the present period amounting to 161 millions—neither sudden additions nor sudden withdrawals therefrom being in the nature of things possible—any *Reserve* of money above this (absolutely idle) must have a distinct purpose, a *raison d'être* for its existence which we can clearly understand. If by any system of issue, in addition to the stock of money in circulation, the whole amounts to, say, 170 or 175 millions, and if but 161 millions are actually used, neither more nor less, what is the extent of the " availability " of the 10 or 15 millions of Reserve?

The clear definition of the purposes of Reserve.

However laudable may appear the desire for a large Reserve, implying as it does the sense of accumulation and caution, you may probably admit that it is a subject which may nevertheless be quietly and coolly considered; that it can be measured by fair and reasonable standards of facts, and that when it is proven as not in accordance with such facts, we have the right for further search into its character.

The reasonable considerations by which the use of the Reserve can be measured.

For the sake of order, I propose then to commence with the usefulness of the Reserve on behalf of the Bank of England itself.

The requirements of the Bank of England.

The Bank of England requires Reserve :—

Firstly, For the accommodation of its customers (the public ?)

Secondly, For the safety of its own position, against liabilities.

Thirdly, For the purpose of set-off against withdrawals of Bullion in the Issue Department.

Firstly, Accommodation to the public. The investments made by the Bank, and the advances and discounts which the Bank grants to the public, *are measurable by the circulation,* that is to say, their sum total over and above capital, rest and deposit ——as far as it depends on the actual use of money—is in accord with the amount of Bank notes which the public use. The Issue Department and Bullion have nothing to do with this, for although the importer of gold receives notes, these are either brought into the Banking Department at once, or find their way there during the day. Increase or decrease of deposits, according to which the Bank invests in or disposes of Government or other securities, are but matters of account. The *numerical amount of the total circulation* remains the same, and the *Bank of England circulation* represents the transactions which have passed through the Bank by way of advances and discounts. The discounts made by the Bank vary considerably, but when they decline they are replaced by Government and other securities offered to the Bank, their owners discounting bills instead of the Bank. This involves but one form of accommodation for another, the sum total passing for them, and ultimately reaching the circulation, remains the same. *The question of accommodation generally of the public is therefore included in the returns of the*

The use of the Reserve for the accommodation of the public.

Is comprised in and identical with the circulation.:

circulation, so that the supposed usefulness of the " Reserve " for that purpose is thereby determined and settled.

It is of the utmost importance now, that this matter must be clearly understood. In whatever state the money market may be, however short other people may be of money, and however great the disturbances may be, the Bank's action in accommodating the public rests upon the numerical test of the circulation. It may be admitted that the most severe tests to which this could be put are the crises and panics which in 1847, 1857, and 1866, exceeded in violence all that ever happened in any country. And nothing less could be expected from the average of our gigantic trade, which, with its incoming and outgoing, but steadily increasing thousands of elements, is like a regular clockwork, producing an average whose firmness is evidenced by solid profits, no less than by the very fact of the regularity of the circulation itself, absorbing and equalising with comparative ease all that is charged against it, justly or unjustly, in the way of irregular trading. It is unnecessary then to tell you that any large Reserve at the Bank of England cannot possibly serve the purpose of additional accommodation.

You will see then that the sound commerce of this country, by the regularity of the *circulation*, which *includes* the *accommodation* required by it from the Bank, utterly refuses to have anything to do with the frequent 10 or 15 millions of Reserve, consisting of a surplus of fiduciary issue, which is virtually debarred from acting as money. And if you bear this fact in mind, and refer to the want of progress of the Bank, its insufficient participation in the discount business of the country (see pages 23 to 37), you may here perceive the indication of a reason for this remarkable state of things, for against this *useless issue* the Bank of England *cannot possibly obtain a proper equivalent.*

Second, The use of the Reserve for the safety of the Bank now requires attention. The Bank of England has liabilities, and, like any other banker, it must keep a cash Reserve in order to guard against any possible sudden withdrawals of deposits.

Having shown you before that the Bank of England need not keep a large Reserve for the circulation and accommodation therein comprised, the question narrows itself to the simple point : " *How much Reserve does the Bank require for protection against withdrawals of deposits ?*" Although the Directors of the Bank may tell you, "that is our affair and not yours," yet nothing can prevent you from searching into the matter, for the accounts are published. You will concede, in the first place, that a Reserve must bear some reasonable proportion to liabilities. Rough economy might say : keep 40 or 60 or 80 per cent. You will agree that such suggestions would put an end to all banking, and that we may as well look to the actual facts, and the reasonable standards which they afford.

The Bank of England holds, say at any given period, 25 millions of deposits, which it invests in securities of the first class. The value of the capital and rest of 18 millions (whether fully invested or not, their *value* is there), gives a total of security of 43 millions of assets, against 25 millions of deposit liabilities. Now when the subject of reserve held by other banks is spoken of, such banks holding say 20 millions of deposits on a capital and reserve of 1 or 2 millions only, the uppermost question is not that of enabling such banks to make further advances out of their larger or smaller reserve ; it is rather that of security, for if, by some means, the great mass of the assets held should suffer any serious depreciation, the amount of capital and rest might be deemed insufficient to cover the losses incurred. As far as the Bank of England is concerned, this danger need not be feared, for the capital and rest of the Bank of 18 millions, with 25 millions of the safest investments, are an overwhelming Reserve in account.

The question of realising this Reserve in account into currency in order to meet *gradual* withdrawals of deposits is often solved by other Banks, who do not possess the privilege of an issue as a stop-gap, and the natural liquidation of assets of 43 millions in first class realisable securities, against a gradual decline in 25 millions of liabilities, would probably be far in advance of withdrawals. Such a gradual decline of the bank's business in deposits presupposes loss of confidence, and a kind of demoralisation of the bank's affairs, which is probably the most remote of all contingences that, under its well-known management, can possibly be imagined.

The question of *sudden* withdrawals of deposits now arises. These may be caused, either by any imaginable further demoralisation of the bank's affairs, and this we may either entirely dismiss or lump in the absurd notion of a general smash, or they may be caused by the *capricious action of depositors*. An estimate of the nature of these deposits here becomes legitimate. Of the deposits of 25 millions, those made by the State and on behalf of quasi public interests, are not liable to such caprice. Let us assume however that one-half of the amount, $12\frac{1}{2}$ millions, might be subject to instantaneous claims, and that the Bank some day would be called upon to pay down 5 or 6 millions. It has indeed been suggested that the London bankers, who keep aggregate balances of from

6 to 9 millions at the Bank, might suddenly take it into their heads to withdraw 5 or 6 millions. In making this suggestion, let us ignore the fact that, by the arrangements of the Clearing House, the Bank of England is made the final liquidator, engaging all the interest of the bankers in its maintenance, that any capricious action against it must therefore break up the whole system, and a *preconcerted* substitute found. We may further ignore that both interest and honest dealing make such a caprice an almost punishable matter, punishable at all events by public opinion. Ignoring also, that public opinion in its turn would approve of any measure which the Bank might adopt without forfeiting the confidence of right-thinking men (for in the trust which the Bank undertakes in a business of this kind, which on account of this supposed liability to capricious withdrawals, is presumably not a paying one, and one which the Bank, but for the high public considerations involved, would otherwise do better to decline), what would be the effect of such a course of sudden withdrawals of deposits from the Bank by bankers and others?

The answer is simple enough. Upon the actual circulation such sudden withdrawals would have no effect, they would not enter into it, the money so withdrawn would be on the market seeking investment, and thus *give to the Bank* the *readiest means* for realising quickly its valuable assets, and for receiving back its notes. *Virtually a mere transfer of accounts would take place*, in no way relating to amount of currency at work. The Bank of England has frequently, at sudden emergencies, when depositors were short of money, realised several millions of assets, and you will perceive that when it actually hands back money to its depositors, these must in their turn find employment for it. The sudden creation of 5 or 6 or more millions of new securities is quite as impossible as it is to cram into, or to withhold from, circulation equal amounts of money, and the bankers could but take up the securities with which the Bank of England would part.

Considering now the severe tests which this matter of actual money in Reserve has undergone, there remains but one final suggestion—that of a general "smash" in the commerce of the country. The indefinite feeling that against such an event a Reserve is useful, is erroneous. It is hardly necessary to say that such a smash need not make us fear for the supremacy of the assets of the Bank of England and other Banks over their liabilities; what concerns us here is the amount of currency which might be required in addition to what we have. A general failure of business of this kind would have the simple result of converting the whole then existing claims into *matters of account*, to be liquidated officially or otherwise. The liquidators would give cheques in settlement, to be passed through the usual channels, and this expresses a view in accord with both the practical earnestness and the theoretical joke here involved. Not only would no additional currency be required, but the stoppage of business would free so much of what had been engaged, as to cause an almost immediate plethora of money. If hoarding were resumed, such hoarding would certainly not apply to the Bank of England note, for great as is our faith in its safety, when under the above supposed calamity it has ceased to be convertible, it would lose its legal tender value by law.

The far-fetched contingency alluded to in the above paragraph, and the improbable events discussed before that, can now be set against a practical fact which

The final suggestion of general bankruptcy

Such an event would lead to a plethora in the already existing supply.

The remarkable

fact of the
increase of
deposits in
times of
pressure.
deprives them, if not of their theoretical, at all events
of their practical basis : the supposed withdrawals of
deposits in the events of crisis and panic. For *when
pressure and crisis threaten*, when money is in demand,
when the depositors of the Bank might be supposed to
make withdrawals—we find that, *on the contrary*, there
is *a sensible increase in the deposits instead !* The
crises of 1847, 1857 and 1866 show this distinctly.
This remarkable fact covers and overlies the whole
subject of reserve. Although this feature of our
money market has created much surprise, it is never-
Demon-
strating the
real
strength of
the deposi-
tors.
theless a most natural thing, and so long as this
nation continues in its present state of moral strength,
we shall see the same phenomenon repeated as the
occasion arises.

The ex-
treme irre-
gularity of
the Reserve
shows its
failure.
Now, if you should still have some lingering
suspicion that the present reserve is useful for the
purposes enumerated, you will, at least, admit one
thing :—

For the purpose of guarding a bank by way of
Reserve it is requisite that the amount of the same
should be some regular per centage on the direct
liabilities or deposits. If the present Reserve is
supposed to be useful for this purpose, it ought to
have shown some such regular average at the disposal
of the bank—but what is the fact ? There have been
times when the Reserve of the Bank not only declined
to nothing, but when 2 millions extra issue had to be
made by the suspension of the Act—at other times the
Reserve exceeded 15 millions ! With such a reserve,
you will admit, it is impossible to satisfy legitimate
requirements, or to conform to the reasonable dictates
o business ideas—it defies and nullifies them all.

One last purpose for which the present Reserve of

the Bank might appear useful remains to be considered. If 160 millions of money are in regular circulation at any given time, and if, including the fixed note issue of 15 millions we have, say, 170 or 175 millions of money, or 10 or 15 millions of idle Reserve at the Bank, you may deem this amount useful for the *replacement of bullion which might be withdrawn.* For inasmuch as the amount of money in the Issue Department of the Bank depends on the presence of bullion and the 15 millions—if thus at one time there are, say, 20 millions of bullion, giving 35 millions of notes for a circulation of 25 (or 10 millions more), but if at another time there are but 10 millions of bullion on the same circulation, you would think that the 10 millions of Reserve would come in and supply the gap. This might seem most natural. Yet nothing can be more monstrous and fallacious than this idea. *It is the maintenance of this idle Reserve, which, long before it can perform the office of filling such gaps,* drives bullion away from this country, and causes almost all the difficulties under which we labour. It is this surplus of "Reserve" of legal tender money which gives to our money market the false appearance of strength and plethora, and forces the Bank to lower interest unduly, entailing all the consequences which I have illustrated, and leading to the conflict between the international value of money and the Bank and market rate. And, as you will have gathered, the principal object of this book is that of breaking through the network of error created by this false idea, and to suggest a remedy. For this purpose the following chapters will strengthen my case, and prepare the way for a reform.

The supposed purpose of the Reserve to replace withdrawals of Bullion.

Its seemingly natural application.

Its real mischievous action is the cause of all the difficulties.

To demonstrate this is the object of this Book.

FALSE SUGGESTIONS FOUNDED ON RESERVE.

The statements and remarks laid before you may enable you to come to the conclusion that the total amount of ready money required for the circulation—or indeed for all practical purposes—is a factor of some reliability, and in itself quite independent of Reserve. Whatever more or less Reserve we may hereafter keep must be considered as a matter resting on its own merits, and not in direct connection with the circulation and business generally.

These facts are also useful in order to dispel a number of suggestions with which the controversy is now embarrassed. Among these the most in vogue is that of attributing the difficulty we are in to the insufficiency of the Reserves held by Bankers throughout the country. Estimates are made of the total liabilities of Bankers in London and elsewhere;—they are roughly guessed at from 400 to 600 millions. With these their "own Reserves" and that of the Bank of England are compared. It is declared not only that Bankers' Reserves are quite "out of proportion" to the "over investments," but that Bankers have no right to call upon the Bank of England to keep Reserve for them at its own expense, &c., &c. In these suggestions it is entirely overlooked that the scarcity of money originates at the Bank of England—that this is a matter connected exclusively with international trade, and that the local trade has nothing whatever to do with it, save in suffering from the struggles of the Bank in trying to draw money from all quarters to replace the bullion it has lost. After what I

The remarks made before establish the reliability of the factor circulation.

False suggestions as regards Reserve.

False method of estimating Bankers' liabilities against cash Reserve.

have said before, it must be plain to you now that such talk is of no value in all that concerns the use of actual money. If these Banks did keep an aggregately larger Reserve in *cash*, they would do nothing more than hoard money, and as money cannot be permanently kept out of circulation, without being replaced from elsewhere, and cannot re-enter it at will, such Reserves could only serve as security to those who have claims upon Bankers, and against such claims the Banker may just as well hold Government securities. Without reference to circulation.

Altogether, this subject of over-trading and over-investment by Bankers in its relation to the currency is misunderstood. It is the character of the securities invested in that is in question; and the demand for cash reserves is made on the supposition that, in the event of such securities proving non-realisable, the Banker should have " money in hand " to pay with. It might be said, " A cash Reserve will make him more careful in his investments, for fear of losing it, he must not mind the profit forfeited." If thus the question of caution only arises, a Reserve in Government securities ought to be as safe an investment as can be desired. The fear of losing, either on cash or Government securities, is alike powerful; but if the banker held Government securities, which bring him in three per cent. interest, he would gain some equivalent, for the sake of which he might sacrifice the larger profits he is seeking in the supposed "over-investment" business—*i.e.* he would, and *could*, be more careful in regard to it. The real state of the case of Bankers' Reserves. Concerns the character of the investments made.

But you will say, " There may be failures, entailing loss of confidence, and all that sort of thing—money will be *missed*, and the banker may be in jeopardy, the country in danger!" Failures no doubt are disagreeable things to bankers, but they concern Failures and want of confidence result in matters of account only.

They do not
destroy
currency. *only the bankers' accounts.* They *do not destroy currency,*
or set it aside, or put it away, or fail in furnishing it.
To those who have claims on him it is immaterial
whether the banker obtains the currency from the
contracts which failed him, or from other securities;
and in this simple matter lies the key to the mystery
between failures, loss of confidence, and supposed
loss of "money." The latter is the just warning
"not to do it again;" and if a banker refuses to
continue the transaction in question—if, in other words,
a "stoppage of business" occurs—it has as little to
do with the amount of currency as the refusal to
clear a cheque has reference to the capacity of the
London Clearing House.

No
legislation
can stop
errors of
judgment
in banking. In other respects, no prescribed amount of Reserve,
no Bank Act, can induce Bankers to deal in " better "
securities, provided even the country did afford them.
In our country, whose manifest prosperity should make
us presuppose that the securities which have furthered
it must somehow have been respectable, the Bankers
cannot, on the average, go wrong; where they do go
wrong there are special demerits of omission and
commission which, like all matters of this kind,
ultimately require the services of a liquidator. If bad
Reliance on
express
Reserves
increases
liability to
commission
of greater
errors. judges of credit had a comfortable cash reserve to
rely on, they would probably enter into transactions
resulting in a still greater mess, and the ultimate losses
arising from engagements on the faith of it might
exceed the proportion of presumable extra dividend
from such cash Reserve.

The
supposed
insecurity
of contracts
should be
traced to its
real original
source. It is true, however, that the false system of the
Bank of England itself may contribute to speculation
and over-trading, inasmuch as it renders pernicious
the existence of, and the entrance into, contracts by
reason of the violent rates of interest which it is
obliged to make for the recovery of bullion; because,

for the sake of a few millions of gold, many hundreds, if not thousands, of millions of contracts are continually placed on an altered value of money. The unwary are caught by this, the chances of failure for those, whose deep experience has not taught them the necessary lessons are thereby enhanced. It is the secret fear, that among the mass of contracts running there are thus insecure ones, insecure as if by some undefinable fate rather than by actual error of contract, which makes certain economists anxious on behalf of some of the Bankers in the country and in London. Hence, " large cash Reserves" are recommended, and if these recommendations are not attended to, as they cannot be in the nature of things, the would-be moralist indulges in blaming the whole banking and mercantile world. It is so easy and costless a process to utter such warnings, or to recommend " Reserves" and " Measures," and then to abuse a whole community. It is more painful to investigate facts—and only by doing this can we bring about a reform, in accordance with the rights of the legitimate commerce of the country, thereby placing all illegitimate business in a more distinct and more recognisable category.

The term " Banking Reserve " has obtained currency, and most of the writers on the subject of the Bank Act make use of it. It is a pompous and "implying" sort of expression, but does it really imply anything practical? You may admit that, when the circulation is supplied, when banking has done all that it can do in order to establish or to equalise proportions between business and currency, it cannot in any way whatsoever make available the so-called " Banking Reserve." The expression, as we use it now in reference to the present Reserve, is in reality a meaningless term, which may hint at something, but is incapable of intelligent definition. The true Banking Reserve of a country is furnished by, and lies in, the strength and convertibility of its investments, and its claims on others, which, under a proper system of issue, become immediately available; whereas the present "Banking Reserve" is just that which prevents the realisation of the true Reserve.

Attempts to connect Liability and Reserve. Of all the attempts to solve this problem of the Bank of England Note Issue, those which endeavour to effect a combination between the direct liabilities and the Reserve of notes at the Bank are the most noteworthy. Several economists have of late entered upon this task, and flounder in the mire of its errors. The purposeless nature of these attempts will appear from the following :—If at any time the Bank held 25 millions of Deposits, the Reserve being 10 millions, the proportion would be 40 per cent. Of the Deposits, which the Bank invests in securities, an amount of—say 10 millions—belongs to Bankers and others, and it is perfectly immaterial whether this 10 millions be used by the Bank or through the Bankers themselves, our Money Market would be in precisely the same position whether the securities be held by the Bank or by others. Now if the 10 millions of Deposits be thus The purposeless nature of these estimates. set aside, the Bank being left with 15 millions and 10 millions of Reserve, the proportion would be 60 instead of 40 per cent., and we would "congratulate ourselves on the safer position," without the least change being effected in the market, or in the amount of money used.

The wide differences in the Bank's Reserve. Independently of all this the present actual practice of the Bank offers no principle upon which a rule could be enunciated. I have tested this matter in two different ways—*firstly*, by taking the proportion of Reserve to Liabilities at *each change of interest;* secondly, by taking the *highest and lowest* Reserve in

each half year ; and ranging these under the respective
rates of interest the following results appear :—

TABLE 11.

*Table showing the Highest and Lowest per centage of Reserve
(including Coin) to Liabilities (including 7 days Bills) of
the Bank of England for each rate of Interest.*

	(By Changes of Interest.			By Highest and Lowest Reserve in Half Year).			
Year.	Date.	Proportions of Reserve.	Rate.	Proportions of Reserve.	Date.		Year.
1852	April 24	64	2 %	65	Sept.	25	1852
1862	July 23	45		42	May	6	1868
1849	Nov. 24	68	2¼%	66	March 20		1852
1868	Nov. 18	40		43	June	14	1871
1848	Nov. 4	61	3 %	66	March 24		1849
1868	Dec. 2	39		38	Dec.	2	1868
1855	June 16	63	3½%	62	Aug.	5	1848
1865	July 26	33		26	Jan.	31	1846
1855	May 5	52	4 %	66	March 18		1848
1865	Aug. 2	31		33	Sept.	16	1863
1855	April 7	50	4½%	63	June	16	1855
1869	May 5	35		40	June	13	1860
1854	Aug. 2	50	5 %	54	Feb.	18	1854
1856	Oct. 4	23		23	April	17	1847
1857	July 18	42	5½%	42	Jan.	18	1865
1855	Oct. 6	31		33	May	6	1854
1864	Dec. 14	48	6 %	45	Dec.	18	1847
1856	Oct. 11	21		24	Oct.	11	1865
1856	Dec. 6	36	6½%	37	June	13	1857
1857	April 4	23		20	Oct.	18	1856
1866	Feb. 21	45	7 %	48	Dec.	14	1864
1865	Oct. 11	23		28	Aug.	8	1864
1864	Nov. 9	40	8 %	41	March 20		1861
1847	Oct. 23	14		11	Oct.	23	1847
1864	Sept. 7	35	9 %	35	Sept.	7	1864
1857	Nov. 4	15		15	Nov.	4	1857
1857	Nov. 11	7	10 %	3	May	30	1866
1866	May 16	5		20	Aug.	15	1866

This table, which gives varieties from two different
points of test, will show you how that no combination
between Reserve and Liabilities is possible.   In 1852

The impossibility of finding a guiding

the Reserve is 42 per cent., with interest at 2 per cent., and in 1864 it is 41 per cent. with interest at 8 per cent! Between the extreme limits here given there are all sorts of odd variations which makes the discovery of a principle impossible, and which prove conclusively that the question of liabilities of the Banking Department has little or no connection with that of Reserve. The economists who vainly endeavour to bring about such combination have discovered generally that Interest rises when the Reserve is small; what this amounts to, *for a rule*, the above figures will show. That the Reserve diminishes when the *Bullion is withdrawn* we know, and that is the sole and simple reason of the phenomenon. Under the present system of issue this only original cause would remain in force whether the liabilities of the Bank be 10, 20, 30, or 40 millions.

A writer,* who is a fair type of this class of "Reserve" economists, in his letters to the *Times*, in December 1873, says—

"I have called a reserve of 36 per cent. of the liabilities a point of full safety. Will any one challenge the assertion? One-third of the liabilities was long ago proclaimed to be the rule of sound banking."

This writer talks of analysis and science—where does he furnish the former? or, is the latter contained in assertions and proclamations made "long ago?" Of the circulation and its incapacity for absorbing Reserve, of the rate of interest and the office which it performs in reference to Bullion, as one of the constituents of the monetary system, and of the relationship between them, no notice is taken by this school of writers—all is "lumped" in the "Reserve." How this Reserve is

margin notes: principle in such proportions. | Example of the guess method, by Professor B. Price. | The vagueness of these guesses.

---

* Professor Bonamy Price.

to be maintained, by what it must be preceded, whether
that which it precedes has any force or not—of all this
we hear nothing. It will be found that when struggling
intellects of this class have succeeded in finally fixing a
per centage of " reserve," to " liabilities " of the Bank,
that as a further solvent they will suggest the "issue of a
certain amount of government paper money," and some
definite sum, 10, 20, 30 millions, is likely to be pitched
upon. I do not say that the writer of these letters
to the *Times* will be guilty of such coarse financial
alchemy, but it is just on the cards that the school
will resolve to adopt this expedient; that, forgetful of
the several factors whose rights must be considered,
they select one, succeed in combining it with the next,
but are unable to fit these first results with the
variations of the following factors, and then take
refuge in deliberate assertion and guesswork. I refer
to my remarks on the controversy in the preface of
this book, and the above quotation seems to verify the
prediction, for the question, " Will any one challenge
the assertion ? " tops the matter.

If, as I have endeavoured to show you before, the
action of the Bank in making bullion, or tantamount
decline of Reserve, guide the rate of interest, instead of
making interest guide bullion, resembles the putting of
the cart before the horse, this proceeding of making
Reserve guide both, is best designated as an attempt to
make the load drag both cart and horse. It must be
evident to you that in dealing with the circulation,
consisting of a definite amount of coin and Bank of
England notes, as the supernatant portion, the first
thing required is that the amount of bullion must be
kept up to its level. *When that is done*, all *is done* that
we want, the practical use of Reserve is then at an
end, or rather, if then we wish to keep a Reserve of
notes, we can indeed realise the agreeable proposition

Marginal notes: The attempt to lump all in one factorship. The hotch-potch resulting therefrom. The final refuge in more assertion. The ignoring of the first requirements as to bullion.

of keeping such a Reserve* at a continuously regular amount, for it need not be encroached upon, and might be laid by for a remote "rainy day," so as not to influence the rate of interest. I do not herewith wish to say that we should keep no Reserve, or one of a regular large amount, you will see hereafter what is the nature of the Reserve I have to propose. In calling your attention to this first requirement, viz., the keeping up the level of bullion to circulation of notes, I show

The clear result when this requirement is provided for. you the absolutely clear result which would follow, and upon which we can build a superstructure. And you may agree with me that the attention of our economists should be directed to this first point. Hence the fallacy of commencing with the superstructure of Reserve before there is a foundation. The, at present, fashionable method of attempts to solve the problem, by guess-work as to proportions between liabilities and Reserve, will soon see its day. It is to be hoped that the writer of the letters to *The Times* will succeed in finding more definite items for enquiry and reform; the circulation generally, the circulation of the Bank of England note, and the due proportion of bullion thereto must have precedence over Reserve.

THE DESTRUCTION OF BANKERS' AND OTHERS' SOLID CASH RESERVES BY THE PRESENT BANK OF ENGLAND RESERVE.

One climax in my charges against the present

The real destroyer of all Reserve. Reserve of the Bank of England system will now be reached, if I tell you that when times of crisis appear, the *Bank of England alone is in jeopardy.* It is the public which, instead of withdrawing money,

---

* Of 10, 15, 20, or more millions.

actually strengthens and helps the Bank by more
deposits, increasing its Reserves, *it is the Bank of
England which does not only use up its own large
Reserves, derivable from free deposits and the issue
of 15 millions, but which uses up the Reserves of
bankers and others* placed in its care, until, after having
drawn all into the vortex, it obtains for its relief a suspension of the Act, and *an extra allowance* of credit
issue ! It is not the public which has kept too little
reserve, or made away with that of the Bank; on the
contrary, I repeat, the public in times of crisis
actually increases its Deposits, and strengthens the
Bank—the *Bank absorbing all.*

Whoever has watched the controversy of the Bank
of England during the last two or three decades must
be aware of the assertion made, that the public does
not keep sufficient reserve; that if they did so, we
should get over our troubles. These assertions are
made either in laudation of, or in order to shield, the
Bank of England; not purposely perhaps, but because
there are few people prepared to believe that this
institution *can* be wrong. The strongest facts are
consequently required in order to break through this
prejudice and the injustice thereby committed.

For the full understanding of this matter it is not
necessary here to discuss the amount of Reserve which
Bankers should keep, nor whether, having reference to
the character of the currency, these Reserves should
be cash, or held in Consols. Nor is it necessary to
mention that (as a reference to the table on page 11 will
show) such bankers' Reserves have materially increased
with increase of commerce. What concerns us here
is the destruction by the Bank of England system
of Reserve, of the Cash Reserves of the country,
whether they are large, just sufficient, or too small,
or deposited at the Bank before, during, or after

Margin notes:
By using up her own and other people's Reserves.

The alleged insufficiency of Bankers' balances at the Bank of England.

Irrespective of the amounts prescribable.

The Bank's action in reference to these Reserves concerns us here.

the event. If the Reserves alluded to were small and insignificant, the Bank of England, with its enormous resources, ought to be all the more careful of their preservation. An analysis of the Bank of England accounts as they appear in ordinary times of prosperity, *with ample* Reserve, will show this matter by way of contrast with times *of crisis*.

The following *pro forma* of weekly statement represent such a case of *ordinary prosperity* :—

ISSUE DEPARTMENT.

Example of ordinary good account.

LIABILITIES.		ASSETS.	
Notes issued . . .	£36,000,000	Government Securities	£11,015,100
		Securities . . .	3,984,900
		Gold coin & bullion	21,000,000
	£36,000,000		£36,000,000

There being, say, 23 *millions of notes in circulation*, the difference of 13 millions passes into the Banking Department.

BANKING DEPARTMENT.

LIABILITIES.		ASSETS.	
Capital.	£14,500,000	Government Securities	£13,500,000
Rest	3,500,000	Other Securities .	15,000,000
Public deposits. .	8,000,000	Reserve Notes . .	13,000,000
Other deposits . .	15,500,000	Coin	500,000
Seven days' bills .	500,000		
	£42,000,000		£42,000,000

Analysing the account of the Banking Department, so as to show the proportion of Bankers' balances, bills discounted, and temporary advances, the following appears :—

ANALYSED ACCOUNT OF THE BANKING DEPARTMENT.

LIABILITIES.		ASSETS.	
Capital.	£14,500,000	Government secu-	
Rest	3,500,000	rities	£13,500,000
Public deposits . .	8,000,000	Other securities .	9,000,000
Other deposits. .	10,000,000	Bills discounted .	4,500,000
Bankers' balances.	5,500,000	Temporary ad-	
Seven days' bills .	500,000	vances . . .	1,500,000
		Reserve of Notes. .	13,000,000
		Coin	500,000
	£42,000,000		£42,000,000

Bank rate of discount 2½ per cent.

Analysed account.

Such a position would accordingly appear " safe," and of the two items here under consideration the *Reserve of the Bank* of 13 millions exceeds the *Bankers' balances* of 5½ millions by 7½ millions. *Supposed safe position.*

Watch now what occurs when this "safe" position, by way of large useless Reserve, begins to tell upon the export of bullion. When a few millions of bullion are withdrawn, and times of pressure arise in consequence, the Reserve being diminished to 6 or 7 millions, you would suggest *that at the least the Bank should keep intact the Bankers' 5½ millions !* But these you find are also attacked, the Reserve diminishing, *until the issue,* the deposits, *including bankers' Reserve,* and *all available resources,* are swallowed up ; the Bank of England being left, as in 1857 and 1866, with nothing, and forced to ask for the suspension of the Act for extra issue. Further, in the meantime, before this low stage is reached, the deposits and Bankers' balances *increase ;* nevertheless they do not stop the storm. The absolute Nothing and Minus which the Bank thus brings about are entirely owing to the previous large Reserves, the consequent unduly low rates, the enforced export of bullion, and the inability of the Bank to keep its stock. For even when the rate is raised at first on a moderate

Departure of bullion and utter disappearance of Issue, Bankers' Reserve and deposits in the vortex.

The absolute Nothing and Minus.

amount of Reserve, it is that Reserve of whatever amount which interferes with a just rate, and no bullion comes in until the very highest rates are reached.

At *such times of crisis* then the weekly statement of the Bank's affairs may be given as—

ISSUE DEPARTMENT.

<table>
<tr><td colspan="2" align="center">LIABILITIES.</td><td colspan="2" align="center">ASSETS.</td></tr>
<tr><td>Notes issued . . . £25,000,000</td><td></td><td>Government Secur. £11,015,100
Other Securities . . 3,984,900
Gold Coin & Bullion 10,000,000</td><td></td></tr>
<tr><td align="right">£25,000,000</td><td></td><td align="right">£25,000,000</td><td></td></tr>
</table>

Example of crisis and no Reserve.

The circulation, before 23 millions, having for the moment risen to 24½, the Reserve in Banking Department is reduced to ½ million.

The account of the Banking Department made up by items which experience confirms, *analysed* as before, would then appear as :—

BANKING DEPARTMENT.

Bankers' Reserves 8½ millions, Bank's Reserve ½ million.

LIABILITIES.		ASSETS.	
Capital £14,500,000		Government Secu-	
Rest 3,500,000		rities. £12,000,000	
Public deposits . . 9,000,000		Other Securities . 10,000,000	
Other deposits . 10,000,000		Bills discounted . 18,000,000	
Bankers' balances. 8,500,000		Temporary ad-	
Seven days' bills . 500,000		vances . . . 5,000,000	
		Reserve of Notes . 500,000	
		Coin 500,000	
£46,000,000		£46,000,000	

Rate of interest, 10 per cent.

You will see, by this account, that whereas the *Banker's Reserves* entrusted to the Bank of England are 8½ millions, the Bank's *total Reserve* is but half a million.

Can you deny that the Bank has swallowed up the Issue, the deposits, the Bankers' Balances, the increased deposits, and extra issue? Is it not a matter of absolute fact as well as of account? You will find that the crises of 1857 and 1866 represent the features of this case, with the difference that in 1857 circulation was 20 millions, and Bullion could fall as low as 6 millions, whilst in 1866 the circulation was 26 millions, and Bullion fell to 11 millions.

Next to the disturbances, the crises and panics to which such a state of the Bank's account gives rise, the most striking feature has always been the almost instantaneous increase in the Bank's investments, rising in the above accounts, from 29½ to 45 millions, followed by a rapid decline. A reference to pages 10, 11 and 27 of this book will show you that in 1857 the Bank's bills under discount suddenly rose from 8 to 17 millions, with temporary advances included to 20 millions, whereas three months before both amounted to but 7 millions, and a month before to 10 millions, the rise being nearly 14 millions. Again in 1866, whereas in February the total of bills discounted and advances were 8 millions, they rose during the crisis to 24 millions, besides 1 million increase in Government securities! *The sudden increase in the Bank securities.*

The current explanation of this action on the part of the Bank is this: " In times of crisis, when other people have made money, the Bank of England alone can help the public—because it has money!" whereas the truth of the matter is this: " It is not the public which has made away with the money, for the circulation remains regular. It is the Bank itself which has lost Bullion (the basis of its issue). It is the Bank which, having lost its Reserve, *then attacks* and makes use of the *Deposits and Reserves of Bankers* held in trust, and increases its investments by additional deposits." And yet, although these additional deposits plainly prove that the public and the Bankers have not only not made away with *The erroneous current explanation of this fact.* *The Bank of England losses, bullion and Reserves.*

money, but actually furnish more, it is said, " The Bank is the only factor in our market which knows how to keep Reserve !"

In reality then the Bank of England, after losing Reserve and Bullion, which it is its own business to maintain, replaces these losses by the deposits belonging to the public, and engages these, Bankers' balances and fresh deposits, to the last farthing, requiring extra issue besides. The danger to which this exposes the real solid Reserves of the country belonging to the depositors would long ago have manifested itself, were it not for the large capital and rest of the Bank,

under the shadow of which this proceeding goes on. And should an honest Government refuse again to suspend the Act, should, through decline of bullion below panic point, the Bank of England note remain once unpaid (and thereby lose its legal tender rights), a state of confusion would arise, in which the solid elements of deposits might have to bear the brunt. Remote as this may be, large as may be the Bank's capital, there comes the higher consideration as to

just treatment of these deposits, and their equitable employment. In all that concerns the Bank of England's sorry discount business you will here discern reasons which may explain to you the nervous state of the institution, for the deposits appear to be destined to serve only as a refuge, to take the place of bullion, when the much vaunted Reserve of notes has destroyed bullion, and disappeared itself with this performance.

Imagine now what would take place if, instead of an increase of deposits, a decrease took place. The deposits being free, it is immaterial, as far as supply of money is concerned, whether *the Bank* uses them for advances, or the *depositors themselves* do so. If at such times of crisis, when, under the extremest pressure only, bullion just turns back—the depositors withdrew their deposits to discount bills with them, the mercantile community would be just as well served, there would be the same supply of money—no alteration in the currency—but the Bank of England would certainly be unable to meet its engagements. This extreme contingency may never occur, but the gigantic misconception which maintains that the Bank is safe and others are unsafe, which, whilst theory and practice prove that the Bank's inability to hold bullion causes the mischief, nevertheless accuses the public, involves a shortcoming of intelligence that should be protested against as immoral and undignified.

The charge of over-trading at such times accordingly lies at the door of the Bank of England. This will appear to you, if you bear in mind that any ordinary Banker whose right to invest capital first is not disputed, is called upon to keep free out of, say 12 millions of deposits, 2 millions of cash, investing but 10. The Bank of England, on a presumed note Reserve of 9 millions, with deposits of 25 millions, would make investment of 45 millions, but whereas the private Bankers' Reserve consists of actual cash, the Bank of England Reserve consists of paper money—of a *cash value in proportion only to the bullion held on* the whole issue—a kind of Reserve which, moreover, ruins itself by operating against bullion.

The Bank of England is liable to the charge of over investment.

But it is not in times of crisis alone that this over-trading on the part of the Bank manifests itself, these only just show the utmost possible point, to which, short of an absolute minus, such over-trading can possibly be stretched. At other times similar encroachments upon Bankers' Reserves take place. The following table will illustrate this. It gives the total of the Bank's Reserve and Bankers' balances, the differences showing the result :—

At other occasions than crises, the Bank encroaches upon the Bankers' Reserves.

TABLE 12.

Table showing the Reserves of Notes at the Bank, selected from each half-year, with Bankers' Balances as included therein, and consequent Bank Reserve without them.

(In Millions and Decimals.   00,000 omitted.)

Year.	Total Reserve of Bank.	Bankers' Balances.	Bank's Reserve.	Year.	Total Reserve of Bank.	Bankers' Balances.	Bank's Reserve.
1845, Mar. 22	9·6	0·8	8·8	1859, Mar. 23	13·3	3·3	10·0
Nov. 1	5·2	1·5	3·7	Oct. 19	8·3	3·6	4·7
1846, Jan. 24	5·4	4·6	0·8	1860, April 11	4·9	4·2	0·7
Oct. 10	8·3	0·9	7·4	Oct. 24	6·7	5·6	1·2
1847, Mar. 6	5·7	1·0	4·7	1861, July 17	7·4	3·7	3·7
Oct. 30	1·1	1·9	†0·8	Dec. 25	10·0	3·7	6·3
1848, Mar. 25	10·9	1·7	9·2	1862, Mar. 26	10·3	3·9	6·4
Oct. 28	8·0	3·3	4·7	Oct. 29	8·3	5·9	2·4
1849, Mar. 25	10·9	1·0	9·9	1863, Mar. 25	9·1	4·0	5·1
Dec. 22	12·4	1·4	11·0	Nov. 11	6·0	4·7	1·3
1850, Mar. 30	11·8	1·6	10·2	1864, Mar. 23	8·4	2·8	5·6
Sept. 21	10·3	1·3	10·0	Nov. 16	7·5	6·8	0·7
1851, Mar. 22	9·2	1·1	8·1	1865, Mar. 22	9·5	4·5	5·0
Dec. 20	12·1	1·5	10·6	Oct. 25	5·2	4·7	0·5
1852, Mar. 20	13·1	2·7	10·4	1866, May 30	0·4	7·8	†7·4
June 26	14·2	2·4	11·8	Dec. 26	11·3	6·5	4·8
1853, Mar. 19	11·1	1·8	9·3	1867, Mar. 20	11·5	5·3	6·2
Oct. 22	4·2	3·0	1·2	Sept. 11	14·4	6·8	7·6
1854, Mar. 18	7·2	2·0	5·2	1868, Mar. 18	11·9	5·5	6·4
Oct. 21	5·9	3·9	2·0	Nov. 4	8·9	5·7	3·2
1855, Jan. 23	11·8	3·1	8·6	1869, April 7	7·2	7·0	0·2
Oct. 13	4·5	3·4	1·1	Sept. 22	11·1	5·6	5·5
1856, Mar. 15	5·8	2·8	3·0	1870, June 22	13·0	5·6	7·4
Oct. 18	2·5	3·1	†0·6	Dec. 14	14·1	6·4	7·7
1857, Sept. 12	6·1	2·4	3·7	1871, June 21	17·8	7·1	10·9
Nov. 11	0·9	4·6	†3·7	Oct. 25	10·8	12·1	†1·3
1858, Mar. 24	13·0	4·1	8·9	1872, Mar. 20	13·0	6·8	6·2
July 14	9·9	5·4	4·4	July 13	10·0	13·0	3·0

The fixed issues to 1855 was	14,000,000.
From 1855 to 1861 was	14,475,000.
„ 1861 to 1866 „	14,650,000.
„ 1866 to 1872 „	15,000,000.
Extra issue in 1867 „	2,000,000.

Also cancelled in 1844 and 1866.

The items with a † denote the times when the Bank thus encroached upon the Bankers' Reserves, entirely absorbing in 1857, 3·4 millions out of 4·6 millions, and in 1866 7·4 millions out of 7·8 millions. The "differences" in Reserve generally show how variable are the Bank of England's own Reserves when those of the Bankers are set apart.

Setting aside Bankers' Balances as definitely belonging to bankers, the 56 instances given in this table show that the Bank over-exceeded its investment, so as to stand there

					Showing the frequent minus and variability of the Bank's Reserve.
In 1 instance with a minus of 7·8 millions					
1	,,	,,	,,	3·7 ,,	
1	,,	,,	,,	1·3 ,,	
2	,,	,,	,,	under a million	
5	,,	,,	plus	less than a million	
6	,,	,,	,,	1 to 2 millions	
11	,,	,,	,,	3 to 4 ,,	
10	,,	,,	,,	5 to 6 ,,	
11	,,	,,	,,	7 to 9 ,,	
8	,,	,,	,,	10 to 11 ,,	

If you should be of the opinion not only that the Bankers' balances ought to be kept intact, but that besides this the Bank ought to keep a Reserve of its own of no less than 7 millions, you will see that out of the 56 instances quoted there were 32 under the mark, excluding the 5 of absolute "minus."

It may now be surmised that when these rare and extraordinary occasions occur, the Bank of England makes good profits. They are indeed good harvest times!

The heavy spasmodic profits made by the Bank.

The following are the sums of *gross* interest earned from the 15 millions of fixed issue, calculated in accordance with the proportion actually used, and the respective rates of interest :—

	£		£		£
1845	167,000	1854	379,000	1863	310,000
1846	204,000	1855	300,000	1864	576,000
†1847	485,000	1856	549,000	1865	347,000
1848	188,000	†1857	675,000	†1866	690,000
1849	121,000	1858	103,000	1867	88,000
1850	86,000	1859	113,000	1868	92,000
1851	166,000	1860	285,000	1869	186,000
1852	38,000	1861	426,000	1870	111,000
1853	222,000	1862	138,000	1871	59,000

The average of 24 of the 27 years is £222,000, the remaining three, the years of crisis of 1847, 1857 and 1866, stand with respectively £485,000, £675,000 and £690,000, and you must bear in mind that the actual high pressure and duration of crisis lasted but a few weeks in each of these years.

But it would scarcely seem necessary to give figures—the inference is too natural, and *we know* that at such times of crises the Bank makes sudden starts in discounting largely. We accordingly find, *that when* the Bank of England *is unable* to check the *egress of bullion* by poising the rate (as it can do, without hindrance or fetter), when consequently it has lost bullion, used up its own reserve and that of the Bankers, and subjects the industry and commerce of this country *to losses and excitement*, and by *its attempted encroachments* upon the circulation to *panic*—then is the time for the Bank to do *a roaring business !*

The harvest of the Bank when it has caused crisis and panic.

Business men will agree with me that such a thing is not in accord with reason, even if the Bank of England profited by the distress of the country without participating in its cause at all, if it were but laying in wait, so to speak, for these good roaring times. A business man would shake his head as much at their sudden increase as at their equally rapid

Contrary to fair business ideas.

decline. But when the Bank is not only a participator in the trouble, but as far as bullion is concerned, the first and principal instigator of the mischief, the thing becomes serious; finally, when the Bank is enabled to perform this feat of unusual discounting with other people's money, and still obtains more, all rhyme and reason appear to be lost!

Submitting, as we seem to do, to such anomalies, I may here be told, "This is all very true and bad—but we suppose the Bank cannot help it—circumstances are in its favour, and we have overtraded!" I deny that circumstances force the Bank to this course, for on several occasions, when interest was high, under the very same conditions, the Bank followed a different policy. The most noteworthy of these cases occurred in December 1863, when the Bank preserved 13 millions of bullion and $8\frac{1}{2}$ millions of note Reserve with 8 per cent., and kept its discounts at the level of 8 millions. Again in 1872 the rate rose to 7 per cent. to protect 19 millions of bullion and 11 millions of notes, the discounts being 7 millions. Although, in both cases the interest rose to nearly crisis points, the Bank parted with no more money, the circulation remained unaltered, and yet trade went on, simply for the reason that the regular balances coming in were just as available for the business of the country direct through the hands of bankers and depositors, as if they had passed through the Bank of England. And you will understand this reasoning: "If the Bank of England is losing bullion because people present notes to the Issue Department, so as to withdraw bullion, why does the Bank part with more notes against discounts, so that more bullion may be withdrawn?"

You may now ask still: "Is this action of the Bank of England, as regards sudden varying discounts, deli-

Denial that this is the unavoidable consequence of circumstances.

Examples of contrary action.

Why the Bank is able

to do this will be shown in next chapter.

berate and malicious, or what is its cause? I have stated before that the high character of the Directors, and their public spirit, does not admit of any such suggestion. Nevertheless the Directors have the undoubted right to do the best for their proprietors, and any plainly offered chance for gaining money, especially when, although falsely, it takes the form for relief to commerce, must not be refused by them; it may be but *a consequence of the system*. That is the case; and there is a distinct minor cause which, occasionally, enables the Bank to obtain a momentary hold on the market. This cause is rare, and in itself unimportant, but inasmuch as an explanation of the relationship between the Money Market and the Bank Reserve is required for its appreciation, I postpone its consideration to the next chapter.

The inheritant destructiveness of the present note Reserve illustrated by example.

So far however I have shown you the fact that the present Bank's note Reserve destroys the true Reserves of this country. Nor can it be otherwise, for this is an inherent characteristic of the system, which I can illustrate to you in the following way: Supposing the Bank of England's Reserve fell to 6 millions, and interest stood at 10 per cent. Supposing that at this juncture the London Bankers made up their minds to strengthen the Bank by a deposit of *gold of* 10 *millions*. This 10 millions they would not, and could not, withdraw from the circulation, for reasons already given, they would have to *import* it from abroad, by realising foreign stocks and other claims; a task not difficult, for we as a nation hold perhaps more than 1,000 millions of claims, and 1 per cent. from that is not much for turning the exchanges in our favour. The Bankers would accordingly deposit the 10 millions of bullion at the Bank, increasing their balances from, say 5 to 15 millions. *Very soon after the importation of this* 10 *millions of gold, the Bank of England would drive them* out of the country again, with *almost mathematical force.* For under the present issue system, when these 10 millions had passed from the banking to the issue department, there would be a "Reserve of notes" of 16 millions, and the rate of interest would go down from 10 to 2 per cent. Hence the artificially cheap market would lead again to the almost immediate export of bullion by the arbitration of exchanges and to engagements by speculation of the false surplus of money. The Bank itself would obtain securities as assets against the increased Bankers' balances, *i.e.* home securities which their holders would sell for the use of re-investment in foreign securities, and so the gold would go back again. The Bank would do 10 millions worth more business with 10 millions more of Bankers' property, that would be all the result. The bullion difficulty would remain as before, the same process would be repeated. Indeed, by collecting this Reserve of gold and giving it to the Bank under the present system of maintenance of the fixed fiduciary issue of 15 millions the catastrophe would be hastened!

The fixed issue would annul every attempt to secure a Bullion reserve or a level of Bullion.

I ask you to ponder over this, in order to show you the destructive force of the present Reserve of notes, and the impossibility of our obtaining a bullion Reserve, so long as the fixed fiduciary issue exists. Not that a positive clear idle bullion Reserve is either desirable or maintainable, but what is in question here is the *level of bullion* for which the Bank struggles, and which it can never reach, as long as the 15 millions of fixed issue remain. Be the extra importation of bullion 5, 10, or 20 millions, be the sacrifice which the public makes to "strengthen" the Bank ever so great, it is all useless and futile, the present system of issue will drive away such Reserves and counteract every effort in this direction with something almost like contempt. But if the fiduciary

The mathematical force of this acts with something like contempt for the sacrifice made.

Reserve were reduced when bullion comes in, it is obvious that bullion would be retained in the precise measure of such reduction. You understand, of course, that I am only speaking of temporary reduction (and not of the abolition of fiduciary issue), and that it may increase again; and what I have said respecting such Reserve, holds good in showing the absurdity of all schemes as to more issue by other Banks, or by the State. The true Reserve must arise from a practice the reverse of the present system.

THE MONEY MARKET AND ITS SPECIAL PHASES APART FROM BULLION WITHDRAWALS AT THE BANK.

Although the movements of bullion at the Bank are the principal disturbers of the value of money in our market, yet, as we have seen, they do not affect the circulation, nor consequently the actual supply of money, until the panic point is reached. It nevertheless frequently happens that we hear there was a " strong demand for money to-day," or " there was no demand for discount to-day;" and these indications of apparently varying supply and demand occur when there is no abstraction of bullion going on, when there are no failures or disturbances by foreign loans—when all is quiet and fair. Even the 4th of the month (the due date of many bills) can be excepted, for it is usually specially provided for; the above phases of seeming scarcity or supply appear quite independent in their character. To-day there is scarcity or strong demand, to-morrow or the day after, no demand; occasionally the former lasts a week or longer, to be followed by an equal period of flatness.

These phases you find noticed in the daily reports, and although they seem to be but transitory, and

<aside>Certain phases in the money market.</aside>

<aside>Which appear to be independent of the question of bullion.</aside>

therefore not of great importance, yet they give you the idea that there is something else, besides Bullion, which causes certain contingencies in the money market. The full appreciation of this matter will be much facilitated by clearly defining the points which show the relationship between our money market and the currency. You hear of Stock Exchange transactions, foreign loans, financial enterprises, companies being formed, of discounts, exports and imports, our engagements, the circulation, the Bankers' Clearing House, and all the great mechanism by which our commercial and social intercourse is carried on. In what manner are they connected with the currency of which we make use, and on the supply of which we are made dependent?

It will first be necessary to separate from this mass of business all matters of *international relationship*, which find their final settlement, not in the instant abstraction or addition of actual currency, but in the *stock of Bullion at the Bank of England*. Foreign loans, railways, banks and other establishments abroad, for which we find the money or incur engagements, include their effects in *the balances of trade* and consequent rates of exchange, which upon the great international arbitration and clearing system to which they give rise, involve the shipment of actual Bullion for any balance of account which may remain, and this principle carries any transaction to completeness, whether it is an instantaneous one, or contracted for by "our engagements." Hence the great transactions in loans, of 10 of 15 millions at a time, making a large aggregate during a year, for which many persons expect that we should part with equivalent sums in gold, are carried out with great facility. The *annual balances of trade in our favour* (the balances between imports and exports, shipping, &c., which the accumulated income

What is their nature and influence.

International contracts separated from local contracts.

from previous investments continually enlarge) cover

whatever we do in regard to foreign loans or foreign enterprises, their immediate or prospective results concern the bullion at the Bank only, when the entire set-off of accounts and exchanges including gold and silver passing through our market, is finally balanced for or against us. The contracts concluded on behalf of matters of that kind, by way of calls or bills, may be lighter or heavier, but any gap or space for more is soon filled by those who watch the market, and have new loans and enterprises waiting their turn, so that on the whole these engagements are of a more or less regular character. For any great specific loan (such as the late French loans), we can always modify its spasmodic effect by selling a proportion of other securities on foreign " Bourses." In other respects, our " engagements " for international purposes of this kind, amalgamate with the great business of exchange and bills of exchange, which as I have described on pages 87 and 90, are held by foreign Bankers when interest here is high, or sent in for

discount when it is low. The amount of currency of the country remains unaffected by these movements; the scarcity of supply, or the state of plethora of money (as part of the considerations on the money market, arising when foreign business or engagements are under discussion) *concerns* the amount of *Bullion in the Bank exclusively*, and all and everything that relates to foreign business, you can regard as entirely separate from the actual amount of currency in the hands of the public. The acceptances which we have undertaken for foreign business, *as soon as they are sent here*, become converted into, and form part of the mass *of local contracts*.

The " local " contracts remain then as the constituent with which the mass of current money has to deal. The transactions of a *local nature*, which do not *definitely absorb currency for their settlement*, include Local contracts not affecting the currency. Stock Exchange business (through which the Clearing House returns are so enlarged on settling days), all kinds of payments in the special markets for goods on "prompt" days, and a variety of other matters for which the use of the banking and cheque system has been adopted. So much of the currency as may occasionally be used for these purposes, finds its way back to the Bank; the extent to which it is thus used Loans and discounts. lies much within the variations which take place in the note circulation. As far as advances, loans, or discounts are concerned, it is immaterial whether these are made on securities, acceptances, or open credits. They are the factors of demand *versus* those of supply of money, all other transactions are capable of exchanging themselves, even when the network of the due payment of advances and discount has been disturbed. Of the money required for advances and discounts, a very large proportion is also "cleared" in account, or for money's worth, but that which comes *into direct contact with actual money*, involves a question between *units* or numbers, independently of all considerations as to capital, money's worth, cheques, and clearing.

(It is impracticable, therefore, to estimate the amount of actual money furnished day by day, or used day by day, by the Clearing House returns, because small actual differences in money are often settled by the exchange of very large cheques and discount accounts).

The *actual source* of supply is accordingly derived The current source of supply. from *the money* coming in every day, from *time bills and contracts falling due every day.*

And this, as the *source of supply,*

The current demand.

Is met by the *daily offer for the incurring of fresh sets of contracts, as the demand.*

You must not confound with this a *fresh* supply of money, such as from gold mines, or from other sources which also arise in connection with international trade, and are partly exported, partly retained by the Bank; their incorporation into the circulation is a gradual process. *The supply here spoken of is that arising from the stock of money actually on hand as, day by day, payments are made.*

The differences in daily supply and demand constitute the special phases.

The *special phases* now which arise in our money market (to which allusion is made in last chapter) are due to—

The *want* of *agreement between* the sums of money *discharged* from contracts (loans and discounts) every day, and the *amount* of fresh contracts *offering* for its re-employment.

The matter must be narrowed to the contracts in direct connection with actual money.

For the better understanding of this matter, it is necessary again to separate all supposed effects on the money market caused by failures, loss of confidence, and all the dark mysteries presumed to exist in connection therewith. I have already stated that failures and loss of confidence are matters of account, causing no difference in the currency, for the bankers must come forward with other securities if they want to obtain currency for the discharge of claims, or the incurring of fresh business. I can quite understand that you will have some suspicion as to such mysterious connection, because so very large a portion of business is settled by clearing, and the amount of currency does not seem large enough for all. Bear in mind, then, that whether we used 300 or 500 millions of actual money, instead of the 160 now in the country, the question of non-agreement between the daily supply and demand, is not a *pro rata* or per centage matter, but concerns a definite amount of difference in the

money market and its range. Finally, in order to
enable you entirely to separate the question of
failures, loss of confidence and other mysteries, let
me remind you that the phases in question occur
principally in ordinary quiet and seemingly prosperous
times.

According to Mr. Palgrave's "Notes on Banking," the bills in which we deal amount to 1,100
millions per annum, or to averages of 300 to 350
millions in existence at any one time, running at a
mean time of 90 days, giving 3 to 4 millions per day
in bills alone. To this must be added a large amount
of business not carried on by bills, and if the daily
average total is taken at from 6 to 8 millions, it may
possibly be found to agree with the business the nation
does for international account, and for the production
and consumption of commodities throughout the
country itself.*

The presumable clear average amount of these movements per day.

It is immaterial whether this average amount is
strictly correct or not, but it must now be further
modified so as to show how much of this is connected
with actual money. The true office performed by these
instruments of contract and exchange is that of
drawing in, and sending forth again, smaller mediums
of actual money into the great industrial and commercial channels. So much of the bills and loans as
are connected with orders from abroad or from home,
whether they are contracted for *post facto*, or on the
cash basis, or on credit for future delivery, must leave
an aggregate of Bank notes, gold and silver coin, to go
into the country for continuous payments on account
of the business contracted for. In due time, having done

Their actual connection with cash.

---

* Bills between tradesmen and customers, and many other
transactions, may be designated as *subsidiary*, made on commodities
which have passed on the larger contract before.

its office, it returns through the channels of home trade to collect again in Bankers' hands—to be sent forth again on its round, thus connecting the money market with its supply. This connection does not involve the actual sending forth by railway of all the money coming in, the greater portion is arranged for in account with country bankers, but it is well known that in certain of our great industrial districts the Bankers require a regular weekly supply from London, and in special cases large amounts are sent.

The actual sum of cash thus involved, not in forwarding from London alone, but in the accounts concerned, may amount to from 2 or 3 millions per day, or some such sum, which, when allowance is made for the wages funds present on the various spots, is required afresh for replenishing it. On the whole, when not disturbed by war, or by some other cause of mischief, the regularity and the gradual increase of this office of the currency in connection with industry and home trade, in a country like ours, is a matter of course. The great process of production is not liable to extensive spasmodic movements. The production, whether by agriculture or industry, of all kinds, is a matter of growth, and in its million-fold constituents presents an aggregate in which the utmost possible stimulation that can be responded to, or exceeded, in one or more special branches, enhances the whole mass by but a small per centage. No contingency can enforce large deviations in the course of a day. In the same way the demand is of far greater regularity than the extreme fluctuations in the rate of interest in our market would lead us to suppose. It also rests on a gigantic system of average, and the stimulation coming from certain special quarters is but fractional as regards the whole. The gold discoveries of California and Australia, for instance,

Comparative regularity of production and regular growth.

Degrees of regularity of demand and its gradual increase.

offered inducements for large shipments of goods, but after deducting the speculation which took place during these contingencies, the solid equivalent balanced the account, and brought production to its level. The experience which we have made with our circulation, not only as regards its regularity, but also its increase contemporary with general prosperity, fully bears out this unshakable, though expanding, character of our trade, even in face of the attempts which the Bank of England make against it by long periods of offer of idle Reserve, and the terrible and short assaults, when it has lost the proper proportion of bullion.

The principal cause of the agreement or non-agreement between the daily incoming and outgoing currency will now appear. It may so happen, that when the commerce of the country is flourishing, when there are plenty of *long orders* on hand, that the *currency sent* from the money market *remains longer in the industrial districts*, showing that it is kept there, by serving *a larger range of local contract business;* a sign of greater prosperity.* As a set-off against this it follows that the aggregate of contracts (loans and discounts) incurred on behalf of this business is of a *longer date than* usual, and that there are consequently days or short periods, when the average of *bills falling due is less than usual*, when the regular current supply falls somewhat short of the requirements for fresh business, and so the announcements of temporary "demand for money" or "abundance of money" changing from day to day will be understood by you.

On the supposed requirements of from 2 to 3 millions a day, there may, accordingly, on certain days,

The retention of currency in our industrial districts a source of satisfaction.

The consequently longer contracts and smaller average of due dates.

* It is just this continued tension of increasing trade which has brought about an increase of 40 to 50 millions in the circulation of sovereigns within the last 20 years.

be say £100,000, £200,000, or £500,000 short supply, and money be in demand in corresponding degrees.

That the variations are not in excess of this we know, for a demand of £500,000 on the Bank is an unusual thing, and if it lasted three or four days, would be regarded as a serious matter. The nervousness under which the market labours now, as regards these comparatively small requirements, is shown by the close attention paid by the Press to every £100,000 going in and out of the accounts at the Bank. We are also aware that these extra temporary demands often change, the next day even, to extra temporary over supply, when there is *abundance of money*, although the range of such abundance may not exceed a hundred thousand or two. I must again impress upon you that matters of account or any vague supposition as to the fitness and willingness of the factors of supply and demand in the money market generally are not concerned in this. The divergences here before us have reference solely to the actual bodily presence of *cash*, gold, or notes, and all the surmises and anticipations formed, turn on nothing but actual money, our attention being centred even on what, in a powerful market like ours, would seem to be but insignificant sums.

On such occasions then the discount market comes

to the Bank for money. The amounts so required, as stated before, may be but from £100,000 to £500,000. And here the true *availability* of the Reserve of Bank notes shows its range. The differences which I have pointed out to you (see page 113) in the Bank note circulation, as confined within 1 or 2 millions, are owing to this cause. The range of perfect legitimacy, as well as the true office, of fiduciary issue, are also here made apparent; for if, with this continuously moderate advance in demand for money, the circulation was so supplied by fiduciary issue—whilst, at the same time, the rate of interest was poised so as to retain so much bullion in the country for regular absorption, by improved home trade, — the accord between the factors would become evident and regular.

But what does the Bank of England do? In its nervous state, not able to draw a distinction, and fixing its attention solely on the Reserve as the guide for the rate of interest, the Bank is alarmed at the temporary withdrawal of a few hundred thousands of sovereigns for the country, or an equivalent increase of circulation. A demand on its resources of half-a-million is a very serious item, and up goes the rate! Discussions as " to what will be the rate " arise ; Bankers take precaution *by increasing their Reserves.* At first, certain discount brokers, in anticipation of the rise, require advances on bills, and apparently increase the demand; a further rise may follow, until, when the turn comes, when Bankers have so much enlarged their Reserves at the Bank that the Bank begins to do a pleasant business with them, the thing collapses again, and the discount brokers are caught. Whoever studies our money market will admit that the play and speculation on the rate of interest often has this result.

The present nervous-ness of the market.

You may agree with me that this nervousness of the market, caused by such temporary requirements, should not exist. We are so rich, our investments abroad are so enormous, that any serious discussion as to £100,000 or £200,000 within one day, appears an almost ridiculous matter. If, in addition to this, you bear in mind that these temporary requirements are chiefly connected with increasing trade and circulation, the inimical action and uncertain policy respecting them, will strike you all the more.

This should not be so.

In these remarks on the money market, I trust I
have succeeded in showing what are the special phases
and causes of disturbances apart from the bullion
question. Beyond these special phases there is *nothing
whatever that can* create upsets or difficulties, excepting
internal revolutions, war, or bad Government schemes.
This does not only hold true for England, but for any
other fairly prosperous nation. The currency present
in the country performs the office here described, viz.
that part of it, which is not in the purses of private
people, travels through the hands of workers, until it
concentrates again through retail and wholesale trade
into the main channels. There it is taken up by fresh
contracts which send it out again, and all this takes
place over and above the clearing and banking systems.
It is in the nature of things, and you will find this confirmed not only by the known character of these phases,
but by the practical figures of the total circulation,
that they should not be spasmodic or violent, though
that circulation may be subject to gradual increase
caused by the profits realised in international trade.
Here the true office of the Bank note circulation, which
can be made pending the coining and distributing of
gold, as well as that of the fiduciary Bank note for the
equalisation of the valuation, may become evident to
you. It may also strike you that such temporary or
regularly increasing requirements might be met by
a regular equalising system.

In any case you will now recognise what these
phases are, and mark *their complete distinction* from
the incapacity of the Bank of England to keep bullion,
which as I have shown you is a matter resting entirely
upon the *international* valuation, determined solely by
the rate of interest which the Bank adopts. The effects
of the error which cause this incapacity *are the real
terrible* disturbers of our money market. They may

The legiti-
macy of
these
phases in
the money
market.

Their
moderation,
and the
easy way
with which
they should
be
equalised.

The great
contrast of
the effects
of with-
drawals of
bullion.

be said to be the *only cause*. That the fearful deception and convulsions to which they lead, disorganise
all other interests, intensify the phases above described,
and tend to tear asunder many regular connections, to
the loss of one and advantage to the other, you may be
able to infer.

The confirmation of this fact will be found on reference to the last chapter, where, on page 150, I refer to
these special phases in our money market in connection
with the spasmodic discount business of the Bank. For
although, as shown, these contingences mostly take
place in prosperous times, they are not only occasionally matters of accidental disagreement, but when the
weight of idle Reserve has led to low interest and
speculative contracts, there is, shortly before crisis, a
state of deception as to prosperity which requires that
more currency should be given out. When, *coincident*
with this, there is also *a rapid withdrawal of bullion*,
when there are high rates of interest, when failures
occur, and Bankers not only hesitate to realise other
securities at a possible loss, but in view of the generally uncertain anticipations, increase their Reserves;
then is the time for the Bank of England to do the
roaring trade I have spoken of in the last chapter, to
use up its capital, rest, issue and all the deposits—
and to do business with the *increasing* Bankers' Reserves
itself! Hardly has the crisis been thus completed,
when the sudden collapse of business at the Bank, to
the usual low level, sets in, almost giving the impression
that these roaring times were but a " frightful vision."
The connection between this subject and the over-
trading by the Bank, as exhibited before, is thereby
established.

The coincidence between requirements of this kind and bullion withdrawals.

The misuse of the fiduciary issue for sudden business at the Bank.

THE COMPETITION BETWEEN THE BANK OF ENGLAND'S NOTE RESERVES AND THE DAILY SUPPLY OF THE MARKET.

It must now be shown to you what are the mischievous effects of the surplus of heavy note Reserves at the Bank of England in the money market generally. What need is there for keeping at the Bank 10, 12, or 15 millions of notes—clear above all possible requirements of the demand for notes! waiting there, day by day, in competition with the current supply?

The general competition of natural supply with the note Reserve arising from the fixed issue.

That the heavy surplus so arising is in continual competition with the current supply, the lowering of the rate of interest proves—the Bank endeavouring to hold out inducements for the use of the Reserve by the public. This would be right and fair, if the Bank did succeed so to place the Reserve but (as a reference to the returns show) that will continue for many months at a time without moving. The contradiction and the enigma here involved will appear clear to you, if you reflect upon the position of the Bankers *versus* the Bank. The Bankers come into possession of the current resupply day by day, and if it were not for the unduly large Bank of England Reserve, they would be able to re-invest this resupply at whatever rate of interest *they might deem proper*. Not that they could ask any high rate they pleased, for the natural countercheck of decline of demand, and the supply from arbitration of Exchanges from abroad would effectually prevent any capricious action; but you may admit that they would be able to take an independent stand in asking a fair rate.

Its continual competition with the sufficient current supply.

But along with the 2 or 3 millions daily available there stands the Bank of England with 10, 12, or 15 millions of money, claiming its share, so that there are

The uselessness and unfairness

16 to 21 millions of money offering for the supply of of this competi- tion. the 2 or 3 millions actually required. Can anything like a fair competition be expected, or a proper adjustment of the rate of interest?

The market rate of interest, which, according to what we have discussed on page 91, should be in The submission of the market rate enforced. accord with the international rate, here becomes utterly powerless. When the idle note Reserve at the Bank reaches a certain figure, down goes the Bank rate, under the supposition that the circulation will make use of it. The Bankers must follow this first attempt at competition and lower their rates, so as to retain their business in hand. The Bank, finding that the The consequent rapid and extreme decline in the rate of interest. Reserve does not move, goes lower still, the Bankers again follow. Yet the Bank obtains nothing for a long period, however low the rate may be placed, however rapid may be its decline. The reason for this is obvious. If the Bankers allow the Bank to obtain bills to invest part of its idle Reserve, say 5 millions, and clear the market for the day — it *is they*, the Bankers, who are left in *the lurch* with *their current-supply*—which, in that case, is added to their Reserve, and paid into the Bank of England as additional deposit and additional means for investment by that institution.

"But," it will be said, "it is not always the Bank of England which commences lowering the rate; it is, The market is obliged to be before-hand with the Bank Reserve. on the contrary, the market rate which begins, and leaves the Bank no option but to follow." Here the whole mischievous influence of the idle Reserve beyond the concerns of the Bank will be made manifest to you. The above remark would lead to the supposition that the market had means of supplying itself with *fresh* money, apart from that comprised in the range of general operation of the circulation. That cannot be the case, for if such fresh money were imported by way of sovereigns or bullion, the Bank of England's store of gold and the Reserve would be increased: such gold could not be *forced* into circulation without replacing notes. The Bankers have no right of issuing notes, and cannot "create" money apart from the method described, and this good feature of our valuation remains intact. The whole of the supposed greater supply in the hands of the Bankers can only arise from within the range of the present circulation (in which the cash in Bankers' tills is included), and this temporary *plus*, as I have shown to you, cannot be large or permanent. But just inasmuch as the peculiar phase of *minus* in the market described in the last chapter, when concurrent with withdrawals of bullion, gives the Bank the chance of fastening on the discount market, so does the phase of temporary *plus* in the market, together with the accumulation of bullion, utterly deprive the Bank of discount business (excepting the small portion done with regular account current customers), and *leaves it with the large Reserve.*

The competition for first-class bills is as keen, if not keener, than rivalry in other trades; and knowing how large the supply of money is at the Bank, the discounters *must* be beforehand in lowering the rate, or else they will have idle Reserve instead of the Bank. Not only must they be beforehand day by day, but they must be in advance for any future lower change. It is not the Bank alone which is guided by the state of this idle Reserve—the public can just as well, and perhaps better, appreciate the situation; and, knowing what is the practice of the Bank, take time by the forelock. The destructive force of the false system of supply, not only as regards bullion but also as regards the rate of interest, will appear on reference to the Bank's accounts in January 1874, The Bank of England, then holding $11\frac{1}{2}$ millions of

The "reverse" phase of the market.

The sharp competition in anticipation of practice.

Such practice being well known in the market, and cannot be departed from.

idle notes—a state of Reserve which by previous
practice and inexorable rules made interest $2\frac{1}{2}$ to 3 per
cent.—then endeavoured to keep the rate at 4 per
cent., a thing most desirable on account of the pending
claims for gold from Germany and the generally higher
state of international interest. But it was useless to
do so: the market was at $3\frac{1}{2}$ and 3 per cent.; and so
the Bank was obliged also to lower its rate. You will
see by this that the idle Reserve does not only involve
the Bank of England, but that, as legal tender money
pressing on the market in overwhelming excess of requirements, it ruins and destroys equitable adjustments.

The impos-
sibility on
the part of
the Bank to
hold a rate
higher than
the practice
of the
present
Reserve
dictates.

Hence, without the slightest disturbance in the
amount of circulation, there are here the elements of
a wantonly destructive conflict. The purposeless
destruction of the basis of money value, which is
thus almost continually going on, is not only damaging
to the interests of the Bankers, but it is *absolutely
useless to the Bank*, for no effort of the Bank can force
this Reserve into circulation.

The
wantonly
destructive
but useless
conflict.

These matters form a theme worthy of the closest
attention of our Bankers. Indeed, the suggestion has
already been started that Bankers should form some
central establishment of their own for guarding their
Reserves. Such suggestions are impracticable; the
Bank of England has the note issue, the control of the
gold coinage, and any opposition to it is not only
mischievous to all interests, but contrary to economical necessities. Moreover, the Bank of England
is a great convenience to Bankers themselves, as the
centre of the Clearing House system. Many Bankers,
no doubt, will say " the Bank has answered our purpose," and that is all we want. If by that is meant
that the ups and downs of interest are beneficial to
them, they are in error. Not only do the generally
lower rates of interest absorb the spasmodic profits made

These
matters
cannot
answer the
purpose of
Bankers.

Their
interests
demand
a reform.

at other times, but, when the Bank of England loses its bullion, and Bankers, for no tangible fault of their own, but on account of the alarm, increase their Reserves, they are virtually forced to surrender their own resources, which enable the Bank to deprive them, for the time being, of discount business. When, as here shown, the interests of the Bankers, their Reserves, their want of control over the market rates, with all the mischief wide and far, are so completely subject to the vagaries of a vicious system, the plea of "answering the purpose," made for want of contemporary comparison, should not prevent a reform which can be made without disturbing the convenience of the mechanical arrangements now in force.

Such reform will only enhance the convenience of the mechanical arrangements.

THE INFLUENCE OF THE IDLE NOTE RE-SERVES ON SPECULATION AND MER-CANTILE MORALITY.

It is now fit that the well-known dogma uttered by the admirers of the Act whenever a crisis occurs, and to which I have made allusions in the first chapter of this book, *viz.* that " Speculation is the cause of all this, the Bank is free from all blame;—it is the Bank which holds things together, and if people *will* speculate they must *suffer* the consequences ; it serves them right ! "—should receive consideration.

The dogma regarding speculation.

It must firstly be clearly understood that I do not undertake to defend speculation, but that, like every individual acquainted with commerce, I recognise the existence of a speculative tendency as almost a matter of course. I admit further that any seemingly too rapid development in investments, be it in financial undertakings, in the shipping of goods, or other enterprises, is subject to the suspicion of being specu-

The tendency to speculation unlimited ; but the sweeping charge must meet with protests.

lative ; that prudent financiers are right in their conservatism as regards this matter.

But when you are told that that which is in question here concerns *one immaculate establishment* against a whole community, you acquire the right of protesting against such a dogma. For if you bear in mind what a crisis (such as those of 1857 and 1866) really means, you may probably be struck with what may be called their *wide-spread* and *general* effect, leading one to suppose that, with the exception of those excessively prudent, the whole British trading community is thoroughly demoralised. If the failures happening were confined to speculators whose wrongdoings and over-trading are evident, or to improvident merchants, we might be satisfied with the result; but not only does the ruin affect small, honest, and industrious concerns, with moderate means, bringing great losses to wealthy commercial houses, but it seriously interferes with our industrial power, and finally throws thousands of people and ten thousands of workmen into pauperism. The whole conflict between the Bank, with its dogma of its own purity, against the trading community and its speculation, involves a charge against the character of the British people, its industrial and mercantile pursuits, to which, as matters now stand, we seem to bow with resignation and meekness, accepting, as a matter of fate, the decree of the wise men who tell us their system is immaculate, not only above all considerations of morality, but that it is a just and wholesome corrective by way of smash and ruin and crisis.

What can be said to weaken the force of this dogma ? The British public can say : " We have been prosperous, we have fourfolded our business—You, the Bank of England, have made but little progress, you stand now nearly as you were twenty-five years

The morality of the whole trading community in question.

With the immaculacy of one establishment.

Against this charge the British public can defend itself with sound reasoning.

ago—the same agitation as to the good or evil effects of your system, goes on. This shows we know our business—you, the Bank, do not know yours so well."

Should the admirers of the present system attach no value to this common sense view of the thing, the British public can go farther, and say :—" Agreed that you, the Bank, need not make any progress, that this is a matter not concerning us, why should you be unable to guard yourself against the effects of speculation ? Why should you, in the event of crisis, not only be unable to keep your own assets, among them principally Bullion, not only use up the whole of your powers of Reserve conferred upon you by the privilege of the note issue; but swallow into the bargain the deposits, including the Bankers' reserves whose keeping you undertake, and require suspension of the Act, and more issue to crown all ! "   The British public might further say :—" The business of banking, as far as its machinery, account keeping, calculations of interest and other mechanical matters are concerned, is plain enough—the *art of Banking* consists of the faculty of keeping *your own*, that is the *very least* of what might be expected of that powerful institution of the most wealthy powerful nation, the Bank of England, leaving altogether aside the question of its general progress in accord with the nation's progress, and that of the world at large. You, the Bank of England, fail miserably in both requirements, and if you turn round upon us, and say that we have brought you to this by speculation, you must either be weak in your management or, admitting that wise and earnest men govern you, you must labour under *a bad system*."

Take now the most general view of the case :—

Admit that a certain degree of speculation is

The Bank cannot hold its own assets, but uses up the Reserves belonging to others.

The art of Banking consists of knowing how to guard assets.

inherent in any mercantile community, that to a The Bank of England's supposed legitimate influence in controlling speculation. certain extent it is the consequence of prosperity, that it involves the "never venture, never won," which, fairly conducted, enforces progress. Recognise, nevertheless, that an institution like the Bank of England should not only stand aloof from all connection with it, but that by its own action it should exercise a beneficent influence against its excesses—when, knowing that the only means for exer- By its power to regulate the value of money. cising this influence is the rate at which money is offered and obtained, that the Bank of England, by the presumed automaton action of its present arrangements, is supposed to be directed by the plainest rules of supply and demand—you would probably imagine that but little intelligence be required so as to exercise this natural beneficent control.

The system, you might think—

should be able to counteract the effects of speculative tendency, so as to limit *its effects*, in fair proportions, to its original force. In imagining this you would say : this must be done by the *Art of Banking*, Entirely nullified by practice of the present system. but finding, as we do, that the Bank has no such influence, you would expect, at least—that speculation should be left to take its own course, and *grow by itself*, to its own ruin, and *without* involving others, especially the Bank of England.

And you may now be more or less surprised to hear, when I assert: *That the Bank of England system is* On the contrary the present system deliberately encourages speculation. *not only powerless to exercise this controlling influence, utterly unable to guard itself against the inroads of speculation, but that it is the principal cause why speculation flourishes and thrives* to a degree with which the cropping weed would thrive when, instead of lopping its growth, it is, on the contrary, tenderly nursed and manured in the most liberal manner. And all that the Bank can do is, that when this growth has reached a certain stage of height and visible corruption, along with legitimate business, and brought the establishment itself low, *is to break down violently and desperately the whole sound growth of our commerce,* in the anticipation that the foul trees among them will be destroyed. Unfortunately the roots remain, and when all is down, when sound trade has been weakened—which is always the case after the desperate struggle of crisis,--our "Reserve" again manures the vicious roots, with quicker results perhaps than before, as the whole periodical return of the same events seem to demonstrate.

Measuring the scope of this matter by figures, if speculation has an original force of 1, which by the reasonable and natural art of banking might be reduced to $\frac{1}{2}$, or at least left as 1, the Bank of England system encourages the growth of its power threefold or more, so that three-fourths of the charge of immorality hurled against the speculative portion of the British public should properly be placed to the account of the present system of the Bank. If you bear in mind what I have said in previous chapters, the fact of the regularity of the circulation and all that the Bank does, you may, if you do not fully agree with me in the above estimate of proportion, see some show of reason in favour of this view of the case.

But without these previous reasons your common sense will be able to deal with the facts, that whereas our money market depends upon the regular incoming and outgoing of money, of say 2 to 4 millions a day, there is at the same time offering the reserve of the Bank of 8, 10, 12 or 15 millions of money. It has equal rights with all the legal tender money in circulation, and the fact of its being perfectly superfluous for circulation intensifies the might with which it forces itself against outlets less firm and callous than the circulation. What is the consequence? When that reserve reaches say 12 or 14 millions, merchants and others are deliberately told there is an "abundance" of money on the market. Bankers tell you "The Bank is exceptionally strong." The force of this deception, with the offer of 2 per cent. interest, cannot have any other effect than that of lulling people into false security, and making them undertake matters with resources already in hand, without at first involving the actual use of the Reserve. But after the Reserve itself has thus been relied upon, when it is called upon to show its availability in practice, it disappears, substance and shadow, proving a veritable snare of the worst character, and leaving nought behind but wise sayings and mutual recriminations.

The disappearance by itself of the surplus of idle note Reserve.

Besides the general effect here described, the natural laws of valuation ruling commerce are thereby violated. Before this, I have illustrated to you in what manner the unduly low rates of interest caused by the false plethora of money affect the exchanges—how, by the law of arbitrations, the 15 millions fixed issue keep bullion from the market in a certain permanent way—and how the whole action, adverse, to us, takes place, as dependent on simple natural laws of arithmetic. The *same principle prevails in all dealings in commodities, whether such* commodities are bonds, shares, or produce and manufactures,—the *inducement of profit* turns upon the terms upon which the moving material, money, can be obtained in advance or by discount. The same law of arbitration becomes effective, with this difference only, that whereas in exchanges the operation is purely mechanical, resting on fixed rates, and instantaneous, there remain, in regard to commodities, the questions of price, of estimate, of shipping time, of credit, and

The law of valuation here acts in mercantile matters.

By a similar process arbitration as in exchange of money.

several other considerations which a merchant must take into account, and through which the contracts made, between their commencement and ending, absorb a longer period in their general liquidation. The *price of money remains the principal basis of these contracts*, and whatever field for moralising there may be in warning merchants and others against contingences of price, false estimates of supply, in enjoining them to be prudent—it is upon this contract basis of money, that the whole matter, including prices, finds its *raison d'être*.

Watch now what occurs! Whenever a crisis with high rates has swept the market—when the rapid regaining of bullion throws the fixed issue into Reserve—down tumbles the rate of interest to $2\frac{1}{2}$ and 2 per cent. For six months or a year it so remains, too many links are broken, and commerce is too depressed to exhibit demand. The plethora continues, and capitalists obtain but small returns. Gradually foreign enterprises are offered, *money being so cheap* in England—domestic schemes are started. At first the public is shy of these matters, the calculations do not seem to leave enough margin for a crisis, the cry to "preserve margin for the future" still ringing in their ears. The plethora continues, and as other people have begun to realise actual profits on the transactions proposed, one after the other capitalist takes part in them, until the "securities" thus at first rejected become familiar, obtain a market value, and actually find their way—as legitimate subjects to advance upon—into the hands of Bankers, and perchance the Bank of England itself. The history of the Atlantic and Great Western Railway matters, the London, Chatham and Dover dividends, and other similar securities, plainly prove this.

In the same manner the general industry and commerce of the country are affected. The manufacturer abstains for a time from making engagements The general commerce based on abnormally cheap money. in the purchase of raw material, for there is not margin enough, but one of his neighbours commences—makes profit—and the other must follow, or be idle. Tell the merchant in Calcutta, or some other port, not to ship goods unless he sees a certain per centage of profit. He is a good, honest and clever man, with a moderate capital, and abstains for a time. Others commence, he follows, and when the rate of interest is flung upwards, down go margins and prices to boot, and he is ruined. Nor is this necessarily the merchant's fault. He himself may have secured his margin, but the Indian or intercolonial Banker, who calculates his profit on the rate of discount at which he disposes of the six months' bill, cannot afford to remain without business until the rate rises—he is bound to follow the market, and give a better exchange.

Moralise now as much as you like about these matters, blame competition and the desire to get rich The economical law involved in all this is independent of morality. to your hearts' content, but you must and cannot deny that the cheapness or dearness of money influence prices, that they give the true and legitimate ground for calculating profits, that you cannot demand that merchants should operate without reference to them, and then ask yourself the question whether the abnormally low and high rates which prevail in our market are the consequence of the ordinary legitimate contingences of commerce, or whether they are due to the inability of the Bank to maintain bullion. Rates of interest must vary, and merchants must guard themselves accordingly; but if you agree with me as to the real cause of the extreme variations in our rates, you cannot help the conclusion that the Bank of England, by the plethora, largely contributes to the encouragement *of speculation*, nourishes and raises it so to speak, in order to stifle and destroy it at another! It is the refinement of profits in commerce, based upon our own firm gold valuation, which has contributed to our supremacy in competition; railways and telegraphs have advanced this immeasurably, and if, in following these dictates, the charge of speculation or of immorality is levied against the mercantile community by the admirers of the Bank Act, you may well turn round and ask them whether their own assumptions as to the fixed issue of 15 millions does not involve a far greater charge of untruth, of disorganised intelligence and morality.

The time allowed for the final break down of contracts on money unduly cheap.

The contracts concluded upon such unduly cheap basis of interest are capable of passing through a seemingly prosperous period before they fall into the stage of more or less definite decay. In enterprises of all kinds, such as railways, the time of construction, delays, the *dénouement* of false calculation, and hopes of development, encourage and frequently justify extended advances, which, but for the intervening smash, would be perfectly legitimate and prove their legitimacy thereafter. In mercantile and shipping matters it is not the settlement of the first transaction which brings ruin, time is taken by shipments, hopes are held out that the next season will be better, only a portion of the capital is lost, more credit is asked for and given, until the hole is too large for further hopes of filling it up. Now, although all this is mixed with all sorts of considerations, degrees of speculation, from the more modest venture, to the reckless dealing of the inexperienced or fraudulent, and although rich and experienced houses, from better experience, keep aloof, the same principle of fictitious contract basis underlies them all. It contributes to the false prosperity of a few years, and entails their contrary, the years of dearness of money and final

break down.   In this general struggle the honest
small man has long ceased to find a place, the business
centres in a few hands, but among the larger houses
even there are victims.   Trace the history and rates
of interest between the crises of 1847, 1857 and 1866
through their course, and you will find that the *dénouement* corresponds with the description here given.

That this system of encouraging and stifling enter-
prise and commerce, in so violent and spasmodic a
fashion, has its counter effects upon the original tendency to speculate, by rendering variations more
frequent, and *chances* more available, is evident.
Hence there are people who can profit by these events;
hence there are phases in our manufacturing districts,
when speculation naturally interferes with what are
but plain mechanically profitable doings.   Hence also
more complications arise in international as well as
local matters; the great system of deception extends
its corruption to quarters where it would scarcely be
expected; hence, amongst other things, the case of
Overend, Gurney & Co., was *not the cause* of the crisis
of 1866, *but the consequence* of the whole play of anomalies and untruths which encouraged and upheld the
faults committed for a long period before the final crash.

[margin note: The enhancement of speculation by way of reaction.]

I trust I have now succeeded in showing the
separate causes and effects on our money market, and
you will bear in mind the points clearly established.
The chief disturbing effect, the withdrawal of Bullion
does not concern circulation nor speculation, but the
Bank itself—bullion being attracted or repelled by
high and low interest *alone*, viz. that being the only
remedy.   Its application is entirely in the Bank's
hands, and the failure of the Bank in maintaining its
stock can be due to no other cause than that the Bank
applies the remedy of higher rate too late, or allows

[margin note: The clear causes and effects.]

interest to fall low too soon. Whatever the cause may be it does not concern this plain fact, and you should strongly refuse to listen to any twaddle which endeavours to mix other matters with this want of mechanical adjustment. Consider now all that happens in a crisis besides this—how the bullion is reduced—how this endangers the circulation—leading to panic—how the fearfully high rates destroy both sound and unsound contracts—how failures, deserved or undeserved, occur, entailing ruin and poverty, and watch with what placidity and bold assurance the admirers of the Act will tell you it is all the fault of speculation. The other feature, that of the plight of the Bank itself, which in spite of the limited influence of the Bank in the active life of the country, exhibits the institution as stripped of its bullion, with its Reserve of notes gone, with its deposits, the solid wealth of the country, including the reserves of the bankers kept up by their prudence, swallowed in the vortex, and endangered with an appeal *ad misericordiam* for more deposits or more issue.

The economist need not be told that in questions of supply and demand of this kind, any grievous fault in the system of supply multiplies its effect day by day, by incessant repetition and recurrence, and although but 15 millions are concerned here, they represent a unit, whose evil effects must be multiplied until it reaches the total represented by the thousands of millions transactions, in the determination and valuation of which it plays so overwhelming a part.

For the consideration of economists.

THE DIRECT LOSS TO THE BANK ON THE ISSUE.

The validity of the rule, that in legitimate commerce and in progress nothing is done without profit or loss to all parties concerned, will appear now when you enquire what is the advantage which the Bank gains by the issue. You no doubt think that the Bank of England must make a large profit thereby. The validity of the rule of mutuality.

The arrangement which exists is as follows:—The Bank, in its issue department, holds invested 15 millions of securities, on which it receives an annual interest of say 3 per cent., or £450,000. After deducting the expenses of the issue and the share of so-called profit which the State receives, there remains a certain balance to the profit of the issue department. Besides this, then, the Bank receives back its investment (to use this expression) in the shape of 15 millions of fiduciary notes, which it can use as money; and you probably imagine that by this process of investing money twice over—of killing two birds with one stone—double profits must be made. Yet I am prepared to show that the Bank loses a sum by it, which on the average is equal to £100,000 per annum. The supposed double profit on the issue.

In order to make this clear to you, you must bear in mind the fact that the sum of notes issued on bullion brings no profit whatever to the Bank of England, although there is a slight profit from the purchase and sale of that material. As far as interest or profit on its use as portion of the issue is concerned, it is immaterial whether the amount in bullion be 5 or 25 millions, or any other sum; indeed it may be said that the Bank, for the convenience of the public, entirely bears the general charges which fall No profit on bullion.

on the issue against bullion for the benefit of the public.

The whole merit of the case of profit and loss rests on the 15 millions of fiduciary notes, the use of which as money is supposed to cover the expenses on the total issue, and to leave a profit besides. It is absolutely necessary that you should agree to this as a matter of account; and thus bear in mind the purpose of the 15 millions, not because I seem to you to be opposed to these 15 millions, but because this method of stating the case is the only true one. Before ascertaining this profit, we must first consider what are the expenses attached to the issue department.

In a Parliamentary paper (Bank of England, 7th February 1861, No. 12, page 13), the Committee makes the following report in reference to the issue :—

" ISSUE DEPARTMENT.

" The expenses of the issue department of the Bank of England have been returned to ns as follows :—

	£
Wages	89,731
Pensions	8,063
Rent	25,600
Repairs	8,568
Directors' allowance	2,926
Rates and taxes	2,300
Stationery	1,811
General charges	6,790
Bank note paper	11,623
Interest on cost of machinery	1,500
Compensation paid to bankers	20,493
Totals	£179,405

Besides these actual expenses, Clause 2 of the Act of 1844 provides that the Bank of England shall pay £180,000 per annum to the State, viz. :—£60,000 for stamp dues and £120,000 for share of profits. The Parliamentary statement then goes on :—

Account furnished to Parliament.

" The profits of the issue department for the year have been returned to us as follows :—

	£
Interest on fixed securities	445,117
Gain on foreign coin and bullion . . .	10,811
	455,928
Deduct expenses as above . . .	179,405
Profit	276,523

Of this sum the public receives from the Bank—

1st. Composition in lieu of stamps	£60,000	
2nd. For share of profits of the } circulation department . }	128,078	
		188,078
Net profit		£88,445

The variations according to changes in the fixed amount of issue.

I must further state that this return refers to a year when the issue stood at £14,475,000. No returns of expenses were published when the issue stood at £14,000,000, or when, in 1861, it was raised to £14,650,000, and finally, in 1866, to 15 millions. I am obliged, therefore, to determine the expenses of these other years according to the amount of issue; and when it is borne in mind that during recent years bankers' compensation has increased, and rent or other charges have risen, the proceeding would seem fair, and serve as a set-off against any miscalculation of previous years. I accordingly returned the expenses:—

		£
From 1845 to 1855	. . . . .	173,511
„ '55 „ '61	. . . . .	179,405
„ '61 „ '66	. . . . .	181,574
„ '66	. . . .	185,912

Besides the actual expenditure on the issue, the Bank pays to the State the above-mentioned sum. in composition of stamp duty and so-called profits on the issue, which in the first period,

				£
From 1845 amounted to	.	. . . .	180,000
,,	'55	,,	. . . .	188,078
,,	'61	,,	. . . .	192,480
,,	'66	,,	. . . .	195,078

So that the total expenditure may be given,

			£
Since 1845	. . . .	358,511
,,	'55	. . . .	367,483
,,	'61	. . . .	374,054
,,	'66	. . . .	381,000

On the other hand, the investment of the " fixed securities," which at the above return were £14,475,000, yielded £445,117 ; calculated at the same *pro rata* manner—

£		£
14,000,000 would have brought	.	430,510
14,475,000	,,	. 445,117
14,650,000	,,	. 450,495
15,000,000	,,	. 461,261

The profit on bullion is apart from this.

In the return submitted there also appears the item, " gain on foreign coin and bullion, £10,811," as profit on the issue. I leave this item (which is sometimes larger) out here, for it has no immediate reference to the issue of the 15 millions of notes. It arises solely in connection with the portion issued on bullion, and the Bank can deal in that article without the fiduciary issue. In this view I am confirmed by one of the Directors of the Bank of England, who at the Bank inquiry of 1857 (see Report 220, Sess. 2, p 36, No. 360), said, " The profit upon bullion and coin is entirely irrespective of the issue of notes, and, though it comes to the profit of the same department, it is in reality not a profit contingent upon the issue of notes."

This gives the result that the investment of the 14 millions—(increased now to 15 millions) at the interest here set forth, less expenses—yields an annual balance in favour of the issue department of—

		£
From 1845.		76,999
„ '55.		77,634
„ '61.		76,441
„ '66.		80,261

That is to say, the Bank, having parted with 15 millions of money by way of investment in certain advances to the State and on other securities, receives, when the expenses are deducted, an annual profit of £80,261, equal to a rate of interest of $\frac{8}{15}$, or a little more than one-half per cent. per annum on the money laid out. The net profit of the issue department.

Clearly understand then: So far the Bank has advanced money to the State (11 millions*) and bought (4 millions of) other securities for the issue department, laying out a total of 15 millions of money at interest of 3 per cent., which, deducting expenses, leaves the above profit of £80,000 per annum. This then is *one of the sources* of profit.

The *other source of profit* now arises from the use of 15 millions of Bank notes acquired by the *Banking Department* (see clause 2 of the Act). If the whole 15 millions were thus employed at, say, $4\frac{1}{4}$ per cent. (the average rate of interest), the Bank would make, including the £80,261, a total profit of £717,761 per annum. The supposed profit of the 15 millions in the banking department.

A reference to the state of the Reserves will show

---

* I here repeat that it is an error to say the Bank has lent its capital to the Bank for notes, because the amount of capital rises above that of the issue. It is immaterial how the Bank originally parted with the 11 millions of money to the State whether from capital or means, or whether the amount so authorised for issue is supposed to form the Bank's capital. Equally immaterial is the fact that the State owes the debt in account, it might just as well be converted into Consols, or other negotiable securities of equal value.

The heavy
Reserves
show that
this profit
cannot be
made.
you that this is impossible, for these 15 millions of notes instead of being employed in circulation are mostly held in Reserve, entering into use only at a total average of about 6 millions (the circulation of 10 millions indicating danger, and that of the whole meaning crisis and panic).

Calculation
of these
profits.
I have calculated the total interest which the Bank thus receives from the employment of that portion of the fiduciary issue which it has been able to use, or, if you like it better, of that portion of the total issue, which, after deducting bullion, is put into circulation. In doing so I have taken the Bank rates of discount as they stood from week to week, and although the Bank makes certain advances below that rate, in which the employed proportion has a share, I have—seeing that on rare occasions it makes a higher charge for long bills*—adhered to the current rate.

TABLE 13.—*Total of Interest Earned by the Bank on the Notes in Circulation above the Amounts of Bullion held.*

	£			£
1845	167,207		1860	285,300
'46	204,769		'61	426,930
'47	485,567		'62	138,584
'48	188,003		'63	310,108
'49	121,351		'64	576,180
1850	86,791		1865	347,814
'51	166,005		'66	690,177
'52	38,460		'67	88,984
'53	222,956		'68	92,986
'54	379,351		'69	186,611
1855	300,721		1870	111,566
'56	519,672		'71	59,053
'57	675,227			
'58	103,864			7,118,148
'59	113,902			

The total for the twenty-seven years gives an average of £263,635, and if you add thereto the so-called

---

* I am aware that the Bank has of late years taken to the practice of charging higher rates than it declares, notably in 1873—but these roaring times, happily, are short.

profit of the issue department at the respective rates (according to issue), an average of £77,641, you obtain £343,276, which, on the average amount of the issues, gives a return of interest of 2·346 per cent. per annum, or a little over 2⅓ per cent. That is to say, *the investment of the 14 to 15 millions at 3 per cent.* (or a trifle more), after *allowing for expenses*, together *with the profit* which the Bank makes on the 14 *to* 15 *millions of notes*—the two birds killed with one stone—the *whole business* yields but 2⅓ per cent., equal to an annual loss of £100,000 on the supposed first investment of the money at 3 per cent. The profit from both sources leaves a loss of £100,000 per annum.

But the question has no great special reference to the investment of the 15 millions in the first instance. That investment is an accomplished fact, yielding, at 3 per cent., £450,000 per annum, and standing as a mere security, the issue might go on, say under some other form of guarantee, without taking into account the rate of interest derived from the investment. Indeed, if that were made a question, I have the good right to say : the Bank might use this money in commerce, at a free rate of interest, varying on the average of 4¼ per cent., without being encumbered by the rate of interest imposed by the issue and the expenses attached thereto. In that case the loss per annum might be stated at £287,500, a matter for the consideration of the proprietors. The interest on securities on the issue is a separate matter.

The question may be narrowed simply to the expenses of the issue on the one hand, and the profits of its productive element on the other hand, and then according to the average expenditure of £263,635 per annum, against the annual expenditure of £365,688, the average loss per annum is £102,000, showing about the same result. Putting together the annual expenditure as against the annual produce of interest, the following profit and loss account can be made out :— The question lies between expenses and profits on the 15 millions.

TABLE 14.—*Showing the Annual Charge on the Issue, the Annual Interest, and consequent Profit and Loss per Annum.*[*]

Years.	Annual Total Charge.	Annual Interest Earned.	Profit.	Loss.
	£	£	£	£
1845		167,207	—	186,304
'46		204,769	—	148,742
'47		485,567	182,056	—
'48		188,003	—	165,508
'49	353,511	121,351	—	232,160
'50		86,791	—	266,720
'51		166,005	—	187,506
'52		38,460	—	315,051
'53		222,965	—	130,546
'54		379,351	25,840	—
1855		300,721	—	66,762
'56		549,672	182,189	—
'57	367,483	675,227	307,744	—
'58		103,864	—	263,619
'59		113,902	—	253,581
'60		285,300	—	182,183
1861		426,930	52,876	—
'62		138,584	—	235,470
'63	374,054	310,108	—	63,946
'64		576,180	202,126	—
'65		347,814	—	26,240
1866		690,177	309,177	—
'67		88,984	—	292,016
'68	381,000	92,986	—	288,014
'69		186,611	—	194,389
'70		111,556	—	269,434
'71		59,053	—	321,947

One of the remarkable facts shown by this table is that the three years when large profits were made were 1847, 1857, and 1866—the years of panic and crises; and I invite you to refer to page 147 of this book, where this matter and the extra profits made on increased deposits are discussed. A considerable portion of the profits of the Bank during crisis are thus owing to increased deposits, *i.e.* from assistance entirely apart from the issue.

The large profits only made in years of panic and crisis.

---

[*] The Bank also loses about £30,000 per annum in the Reserve of Coin. This Reserve of Coin is not included in the Table.

THE FALSITY OF THE SUPPOSED AUTO-MATON OPERATION OF THE ISSUE AND THE UNNATURAL ACCUMULATION OF RESERVE IN THE BANKING DEPART-MENT.

I have now furnished you with material sufficient to enable me to dispose of one of the main errors by which the method of defending the present system is principally conducted. The admirers of the Act will tell you two things :— *The principal allegations made.*

Firstly. The issue department of the Bank is a purely independent matter; it acts like an automaton machine. The banking department has nothing whatever to do with it; just as little as any other banker. The latter has its own independent account. *The assertion as to the purely automaton character of the issue.*

Secondly. The accumulation of the large Reserves is quite a natural thing, over which the Bank has no control. It results from the free operation of supply and demand. The same accumulations would take place if the note issue were entirely removed, and replaced, say, by gold coin (or as the favourite expression goes, "if" the Government paid the debt to the Bank, or undertook to pay the notes *for* the Bank). *The invocation of the laws of supply and demand.*

When such formidable words as "automaton" action, "and the laws of supply and demand," are invoked by persons of authority, you begin to feel small, and, finally, you give in when you are shown the weekly statement, of which, *pro forma*, the following is a representation :— *The formidable character of these pleas.*

ISSUE DEPARTMENT.

LIABILITIES.	£	ASSETS.	£
Notes issued . . .	38,000,000	Government debt .	11,015,100
		Other securities .	3,984,900
		Bullion	23,000,000 .
	£38,000,000		£38,000,000

BANKING DEPARTMENT.

	£		£
Proprietors' capital	14,553,000	Government secu-	
Rest	3,447,000	rities	14,000,000
Public deposits. .	8,000,000	Other securities .	17,500,000
Other deposits . .	17,500,000	Reserve of notes .	12,000,000
Seven days' bills .	500,000	Coin	500,000
	£44,000,000		£44,000,000

Not only does this balance nicely, but you will be
Apparently backed by the weekly Bank statement.' told that "should you have any doubt in your mind
about the Bank's having given up, or somehow sacri-
ficed, capital and resources on behalf of the issue
department, *look* at the statement *of the banking
department*, where you will *find the capital and rest
and the deposits in full* numbers balancing with the
assets." After this you feel inclined to give in;
and, in truth, most economists are thus dismayed and
deceived.

Yet nothing can be more false and deceptive than
But nothing can be more false than this method of showing the case. this method of stating the case. Clause 2 of the Act
distinctly provides that the notes from the issue de-
partment shall pass into the banking department, and
thereby absolves the issue department from the
liability of holding notes which the circulation cannot
make use of, throwing the whole onus of the Reserve
of idle notes on the Banking Department. You may
admit that this is contrary to an "automaton" action.
It may also strike you as natural that when any
system of issue is supposed to be automaton and inde-

pendent, it should within itself contain the power of re-gulating its status; and so the Issue Department ought to be able to supply itself with Bullion—*i.e.* bring into action the motive power to attract Bullion. But this is an office which the Banking Department performs for it also. It is utterly idle to maintain the plea: the public can bring Bullion, or exchange Bullion for notes, and *vice versa.* That which is in question here is the *actual force* to be exercised for the importation of Bullion, and that force is entirely in the hands of the Banking Department, which, by raising or lowering the rate, causes the issue to be thus supplied. The automaton character of the issue thus resembles the celebrated Chinese steamboat, which, perfect in all its parts, only wanted provision for steam in order to move, and had to be towed by another ship.

The pretence that the Issue Department has this in-dependent character would best be shown if, as it has often been suggested, the Department was transferred to the State, to be carried on at Somerset House. If the State there held say 22 millions against a total issue of, say 37 millions, and on a circulation of 25 millions, it could not maintain Bullion unless it had the power of establishing a rate of interest, and trade would care very little for the mere declaration of a rate. The State might " consult " the Bank, but even the Bank need not care for Government rates, as soon as it has got rid of the present liability on the issue. The State would be compelled to open a Banking Department of its own and turn Banker, so as to gain the practical means of influencing the issue, or the latter would speedily come to an untimely end.

The transfer of the issue to the State could not compel the Bank of England to hold large Reserves. The Bank would then stand with its Capital, Rest, and Deposits, and the whole and sole question of Reserve

The lifeless character of the Issue Department.

The Banking Department is the moving force.

The impossibility of transferring the Issue Department to the State.

Without the State becoming also the Banker of the Nation.

Freed of the issue the Bank would require but a moderate regular Reserve.

would have reference to possible withdrawals of Deposits. Knowing that these do not, in case of pressure, decline, but rather increase, the Bank of England might say : we will keep 4 or 5 or 6 millions of Reserve, or more or less, and keep whatever per centage we deem proper at a regular figure. As to keeping 15 or 16 millions of Reserve against 26 millions of Deposits, secured moreover by an additional 18 millions of Capital and Rest, the Bank of England would be unable to do so, and it would for the future avoid the falling of its cash Reserve below the regular per centage determined upon.

The Issue Department is carried on at the charge of the Reserves in the Banking Department.

Any excessive Reserve then, arising from the present system of issue, falls on the Banking Department, and lessens its power of doing business to the extent of such excess. It has often been said " the Bank has surrendered its Capital to the issue. If this Capital were returned, or the State Debt paid off, matters would be settled." I have before this stated that this paying off of the State Debt makes no difference in the Issue (unless 11 millions of credit notes were abolished), and that the fact of the Bank's Capital being $14\frac{1}{2}$ millions and the Issue 15 millions is more or less accidental. Nevertheless, it is true that the Bank's Capital, upon which the Dividends must be paid, bears the brunt of the anomaly, and, as the guarantor of the Deposits, any discrepancy would fall upon Capital. The admirers of the present system are unwilling to admit this. They will persist in telling you " (1) the issue is self acting; (2) the Bank's capital and rest are quite intact, and invested against best securities ; (3) the banking and deposit business of the Bank of England is a matter standing entirely on its own merits, we can pay these off at any time, and show the Bank's capital fully invested."

The following is a *pro forma* statement with 23

millions Bullion in the Issue, and 26 millions in circulation, putting Deposits at 26 millions, total securities at 32 millions, and Reserve of 12 millions in the Banking Departmeut :—

Supposed case of liquidation of Deposits.

ISSUE DEPARTMENT.

Notes issued . . £38,000,000	Government debt .£11,015,100	
	Other securities . . 3,984,900	
	Bullion. 23,000,000	
£38,000,000	£38,000,000	
Notes in the hands of the public 26,000,000		

Statement showing the effect on the Bank's Capital.

BANKING DEPARTMENT.

Capital £14,553,000	Gov.& other securts. £32,000,000
Rest 3,447,000	Reserve of notes . . 12,000,000
Deposits (Public and Private) . . . 26,000,000	
£44,000,000	£44,000,000

If, now, according to the above hint, the Bank paid off its Depositors, how would the case stand ? The Bank would first use the 12 millions of Reserve of Notes ; but *as these cannot be incorporated with* the circulation, they would *instantly return to the Reserve.* The Bank would simply loose the securities obtained against the Deposits, and this is the legitimate way in which all Deposits find their orderly liquidation. The account would then stand :

BANKING DEPARTMENT.

LIABILITIES.	ASSETS.	
Capital £14,553,000	Gov.& other securts. £6,000,000	
Rest 3,447,000	Reserve of notes . 12,000,000	
£18,000,000	£18,000,000	

The asset of idle Reserve of notes left.

Bear in mind that 12 millions of Reserve are frequently on hand ; but if there were but 7 or 8 millions the Capital would still be laid idle to that extent.

The strength of this position is undeniable, but where is the Bank's profit ?

Showing the great loss to the Bank by the issue.

There would be the £80,000 profit in the issue, and . . . . . 180,000 at 3 per cent. on the 6 millions of Government and other securities,

or £260,000 gross

out of which the Bank would have to pay its banking staff and expenses (probably equal to the whole sum) before it could make a dividend on the capital.

With any given amount of Reserve.

I have here taken 12 millions as idle note Reserve, but if that Reserve, either by decrease of circulation, or by increase in bullion, was augmented by 3 millions— a thing that has happened frequently—the above small *gross* profit would be diminished accordingly. And, as on one occasion (1871), the Reserve amounted to more than 17 millions, and may with the increased bullion (not to speak of the cry for more Reserve uttered by certain economists) some day amount to 18 millions, the statement of the Department might be—

BANKING DEPARTMENT.

Proprietor's capital £14,553,000		Goverment securities	———0
Rest 3,447,000		Other ,,	———0
		Reserve of notes	£18,000,000*
	£18,000,000		£18,000,000

The enforced incompetence of the Bank's capital by the Reserve.

That is to say, in order to hold such a note Reserve, the Bank would be obliged to sell *all* the securities which it holds against the 18 millions of capital and rest for the sake of holding a Reserve of 18 millions of notes coming from the Issue Department—absolutely useless for the purposes of circulation—debarred from all connection with the commerce of the country. You will admit that whether we bring deposits and securities back into this account, the effect, so far as idleness of resources is concerned, will remain the same.

This reasoning must prove to you that the Issue Department is really carried on at the charge of the Bank's capital.

Let me suggest that if in the weekly statements of the Banking Department the following slight tranposition had taken place, upon the supposition that there were, accidentally, 14½ millions Reserve, viz.—

BANKING DEPARTMENT.

Dr.		Cr.	
Proprietors' capital .	£14,500,000	Reserve of notes . .	£14,500,000
Rest	3,500,000	Government securi-	
Public deposits . .	8,000,000	ties	14,000,000
Other deposits . .	17,500,000	Other securities . .	15,000,000
7 days' bills . . .	500,000	Coin	500,000
	£44,000,000		£44,000,000

the common sense of the proprietors would have discovered the economical hocus pocus played with their capital before this.

I need hardly carry the case of the large desirable (?) Reserve to 20 or 22 millions ! What would the Bank do with a bullion Reserve over and above circulation ? *The ludicrous aspect of this matter.* is a suggestion frequently made. The Bank would be quite unable to receive it; it could only ask Parliament to increase its capital, in order that such capital should stand, *pro forma*, against a larger reserve of notes and gold, perfectly useless. The ludicrous position here arising is equalled only by its counterpart, viz., when the low state of the stock of bullion threatens the circulation, and causes that indescribable state—a panic ! (See pages 119-120.)

The true appreciation of these plain matters will now show you that, by a diminution of the Reserve, the *The Reduction of Reserve brings the capital into use.* Bank regains the power and profit on its capital and rest. For if that Reserve, from 15 or 12 millions

13

be reduced to 5 or 6, it follows that the securities at the Bank must increase in precisely the same ratio as the Reserve decreases, and thus free the Bank's capital from the odious obligation of being represented by a useless and idle surplus of mere paper money.

What I here submit to you, you may deem confirmtory of all that I have said in this book respecting the want of progress of the Bank, its moderate dividends, and its insufficient participation in the real business of the country. Saddled with the unhappy reserves of this nature, which the circulation cannot absorb, in exchange for which its capital is bartered away and rendered useless (or such equivalent of deposits, if, as proprietors, you should give preference to your capital over deposits), you cannot expect that the resources of the establishment should be properly used, or that the Bank should be able to hold its own without gigantic struggles, resulting in its remaining behind the prosperity of the nation.

THE VIOLATION OF THE RULES OF SUPPLY AND DEMAND, AND CONCLUSION OF PART I.

The evidence which I have been able to lay before you on the whole case will enable you to dispose of one of the main difficulties in the way of this enquiry, viz. the tenacity with which the admirers of the Act assert that the rules of supply and demand are effective under the present system. Whenever these large Reserves are spoken of they will tell you " that their accumulation rests upon the operation of the natural laws of supply and demand, and that the same accumulation of Reserve would take place, if the fiduciary issue were replaced by gold coin.

The allegation that, if the fiduciary issue were

abolished and replaced by gold coin, the same accumulations would take place, is refuted by the fact that gold has an international value; that any surplus of it will find its way abroad against the return of full equivalents in commodities and securities deliberately chosen. In order to narrow this to the case of the Bank of England, with a presumed surplus stock of, say 14 or 16 millions of gold coin, and deducting therefrom 6 or 7 millions, which the Bank would keep for its own purposes of Reserve (or any greater or lesser amount), the surplus offering would go abroad against foreign securities to be held by bankers and merchants, who, in their turn, would sell to the Bank such home securities as that establishment is in the habit of taking. This exchange of accounts would be continuously in operation, and modify every extreme, the Bank being guided solely by the level of Reserve of cash which it might deem proper to maintain as a regular per centage on liabilities. It is just for the reason that the Reserve of notes itself is not available for export, that it thus accumulates, and thereby causes the overwhelming and unnatural export of bullion itself.

The undue accumulation of gold coin would be prevented by its international value.

In all that concerns supply and demand it is unquestionably true that, where the constituents are left to their free operation, they must bring about a natural adjustment and an intelligible result, clearly traceable and applicable. But when the factors operating together are not free and pliable, either partly or on the whole, when distinct characteristics can be shown that they have an admixture of limit, or are subject to limits arising from distinct outside causes, the rules of supply and demand must fail in their presumed inexorable agreement, just for the reason that the outside influences are also undeniable and inexorable facts.

Freedom of factors of supply and demand.

Arbitrary partial limits and characteristics depending on other factors interfere in their agreement.

This element of restriction is present, in the first

place, in the supply, as represented by the Bank of
England's note issue; the *fixed limit* of 15 millions
at once disturbs the legitimate operation, for its want
of assimilation to other matters and rights prevents
the true balancing of the factor supply within its own
sphere.

The other element—the circulation—is almost
wholly of a firm character, excepting only as far as
gradual increase or decrease is concerned. But, as
has been suffiently shown, it cannot be moved at
will, and refuses to answer the appeals on behalf of
supply. And this characteristic is not loosely inherent
in it, it is the consequence of separate factorships,
which connects the circulation with the production
and consumption of commodities, and which require
to be led back to other original considerations. The
intelligent consideration of these matters is absolutely
necessary before any adjustment can take place, before
the whole system can be left to itself, before it practically realises the idea of inexorably true balance,
which must be accepted with all its consequences.

*Before such an adjustment, or even an approach to it,
can take place, it must be* recognised *that this* 15 *millions of fixed issue* is the cause of all *the mischief and
the sorry misfit between supply and demand.*

In the course of this book I have shown you:—

1. The want of progress of the Bank of
England, compared to the great progress in all
other directions.

2. The insufficient dividends of the Bank
in juxtaposition to the profits realised by all
other participators in the development of commerce during the last thirty years.

3. The comparatively insignificant and unsatisfactory share of the Bank in the active life of commerce and discount business.

Compare the fivefold progress in all other directions with the figures concerning the Bank of England. Make every allowance for the conservative tendency of the latter for competition and other causes; say that the Bank need only have increased twofold, or, go lower still, say it need only have doubled its affairs; but you will find that it has made no advance whatever. The only increase that has taken place concerns 3 millions of circulation since 1866, and an equal amount of *Bankers' Balances*, *i.e.* an accession of strength by the competitors of the Bank who have been abused for not keeping sufficient "Reserve." No fairly intelligent and candid enquirer can avoid the suspicion that this result is unnatural, and that it forms *prima facie* evidence of a state of things which ought not to be, even were the matter but one of theory. But when the periodical returns of crisis and distress set in, when the utmost mischief is done, we find evils brought before us which cannot practically be greater, unless they culminated in utter destruction.

I have shown you further

4. That the seat of the error must be in the Issue Department, and have explained

5. The state of the controversy, &c.

6. The origin and main principles of the Act of 1844.

7. The demerits of the fixed issue as to its computation.

8. The demerits of the idle note Reserve arising therefrom.

9. The effect of the fixed issue on bullion and exchanges.

10. The conflict between the Bank rates of interest and the international rates.

The evidence laid before you, as regards these frequent changes in the rate, proves their unnatural character; it cannot lead to any other conclusion than the recognition of the undue influence on interest by the superfluous note Reserve, and the consequent violent rebounding of the rate,—such rebounds being, after all, scarcely effective.

11. The general circulation and that of the Bank of England note, showing their comparative regularity.

12. The consequent non-availability of the Bank's idle Reserve.

13. The false suggestions made in reference to it, and to proportions between deposits and Reserve.

14. The destruction of the real Reserves of the country by the Bank of England system, as proven not only by the crises, but by many ordinary positions of affairs.

15. The money market and its special phases, explaining certain contingences.

16. The competition between the money market and the Bank of England Reserve, and the dangerous, useless and wanton conflict thus brought about between the Bank and bankers.

17. The influence of the Reserve on speculation, showing that it is the idle Reserve, and the artificial low rate of interest which foster and encourage speculation, and disorganise legitimate business.

18. The direct loss made by the Bank on the Issue, in spite of the supposed double source of profit from the arrangement.

19. The falsity of the supposed automaton action of the Issue Department, the Banking Department bearing its charge, and surrendering its resources to the fiction of the Reserve.

20. The violation of the rules of supply and demand therein involved.

And the succession of the evidence, thus laid before you, forms a chain which possibly leads you to perceive that all these anomalies are due to the great error pointed out.

If now you reflect upon what the Bank of England really is, the magnificence of its proportion, the vastness and strength of the field it occupies, the manifest solid prosperity there present, the evident good managership, you cannot but come to the conclusion that there must *be some strange and singular error* which disorganises the concurrence between this wealth and strength and wisdom. That error I trust you will now recognise. To one who for many years has watched the struggles under which our commerce suffers, who has studied other countries labouring under anomalies in monetary matters, and their economical relation to valuation, to industry and social life generally, *this error appears a most glaring one.* Here he sees the wealthiest and most industrious nation of the world, constantly progressing and adding wealth. One establishment only, the central financial one, remains behind hand; but beyond this he sees that because this establishment cannot perform a certain task entirely its own, there are breaks in the progress of prosperity, which bring ruin and distress not only to the mercantile community but to the industrial classes, and, consequently, drawbacks to the nation at large.

General reflection on the Bank's strength and splendid condition.

During the bitter controversies ensuing upon these disturbances, one party appears which deems this all proper, right and natural, and refuses to admit enquiry. Another party is violently opposed to the system, accusing it of doing great harm to the prosperity of the country, and pointing to the actual strife and conflict as the best proof of the justice of its complaints. This latter party he sees engaged *in vain endeavours to bring about amendment*—for none of the reformers appear to have the suspicion *that the error here pointed out is the real and sole cause of all the mischief*. Simple as the point has now become, it will yet be admitted that its subtlety required the consistent and elaborate treatment here given to it, in order to bring it into light, and in Part II., where suggestions for the reform of the present system will be developed, the simplicity of the remedy will be shown.

The small effort required for the recognition of the error and the remedy.

The subtlety, yet simplicity of the matter.

PART II.

THE PRINCIPLE OF TIMELY REDUCTION OF THE FIDUCIARY ISSUE.

THE facts and reasons given in the first part of this book might lead to the natural inference that we ought to reduce the mischievous *fixed* issue of 15 millions whenever it reaches a state of surplus hurtful to bullion, the money market, and the Bank's resources. You may have formed the conclusion that although the Bank can serve itself first from the vast stream of bullion passing through our market, yet it is not only unable to do so, by reason of the very low rates of interest which it adopts, but it cannot even hold that which it already possesses. It is evident then that the unduly *low* rates of interest are at the bottom of this difficulty, and these, in their turn, are due to the accumulation of a Reserve of idle notes, which, as I have shown to you, is much in excess of all possible wants. In determining the rates of interest, the Bank of England is guided principally by the amount of Reserve. But it is not only the Bank which watches the Reserve, the general public, and "the outside market," are just as able to judge interest by the state of the Reserve, and to act in accordance with, or in anticipation of it. This must be clearly understood, so that the reaction of the market rate upon the Bank rate is placed in the proper light. It frequently happens that the "market" is lower than the "Bank," so that the impression, as if the latter were dependent on the former, is created. Yet—and so the facts show—there is "no more money" in the "market;" any surplus there arising would at once find its way to

The facts given might lead to the natural inference.

That the plethora rate of interest of some years is the direct cause of extreme scarcity and high rates in others.

The Bank is guided by the state of the Reserve.

the Bank and its Reserve (see pp 165-166.)   Under the system as it now works, the Bank may *try to hold interest higher*, but the outside market is aware what are the customary rates with certain amounts of Reserve, and necessarily anticipates and defeats the Bank, by going lower. The Bank cannot hold interest at say 10 per cent. when the market is at 4 or 5 per cent., *but this much* is certain, that differences of ½ to 1 per cent. are entirely at the option of the Bank; that within the limits of the concurrence between the Bank and market, the Bank is absolutely free to make whatever rate it pleases.   Hence the Reserve guides both Bank and market, giving to the former the real initiative.

It has the initiative.

For the purpose of ascertaining the proportions between Reserve and interest, by which the Bank of England is guided, I have prepared a series of tables (too extensive for insertion here) showing the amount of Reserve, first and last, during each separate period of interest, and the average; which, after making due allowances for the three changes in the amount of the issue, show the following results :—

Amounts of Reserve and corresponding rates of interest.

Result of tables showing the ranges of Reserve with the corresponding rates of interest.

Minimum Rates.		*Range of Reserve.*			
10 per cent.	-	minus to		5 millions	
9 ,,	-	1	,,	6	,,
8 ,,	-	2	,,	7	,,
7 ,,	-	3	,,	8	,,
6 ,,	-	4	,,	8	,,
5½ ,,	-	4	,,	9	,,
5 ,,	-	5	,,	9	,,
4½ ,,	-	6	,,	9	,,
4 ,,	-	6	,,	10	,,
3½ ,,	-	7	,,	11	,,
3 ,,	-	8	,,	12	,,
2½ ,,	-	9	,,	14	,,
2 ,,	-	11	,,	16	,,

The difference arising here in the ranges of the Reserve as against the corresponding rates of interest are due partly to the regard which the Bank of

England has to the state of "other securities"
(although that is entirely lost in crisis), partly to
presumable error,* partly to changes of policy—for
whereas before 1847 the Bank was more liberal, it
has during recent years been more severe. But the
whole ranges do not differ by more than 5 millions,
which is the amount I have before this (see page 113)
accounted for as that within which the circulation and
the general business of the Bank finds ample play. It
also appears that during recent years the Bank has
kept a slightly increased Reserve, so as to protect
bullion against German demands. The variations in
deposits have no distinct influence, and a reference to
pages 134 and 135 will show why all calculations as to
proportion between Liabilities and Reserve are useless.
The above table exhibits the principle of progressive
decrease of interest with progressive increase of Reserve; and whether we take the lower as for previous,
or the higher figure, or their average, for present
practice, the result is pretty much the same. Since
the circulation has now increased a few millions, and
the Bank is not likely to allow the the Reserve to
fall as low as 5 millions without making the rate
at once 10 per cent., the higher range is the more
appropriate. This appears accordingly, and for the
purpose of illustration may be given, as :—

Interest.			Reserve.
10 per cent.	-	-	5 millions.
9 ,,	-	-	6 ,,
8 ,,	-	-	7 ,,
7 ,,	-	-	8 ,,
6 ,,	-	-	8 ,,
5 ,,	-	-	9 ,,
4 ,,	-	-	10 ,,
3 ,,	-	-	12 ,,
2 ,,	-	-	15 ,,

Definite
proportions
of Reserve
and interest
by way of
illustration.

* Of such presumable errors, for instance, may be quoted—
August 1865, when with 6 millions Reserve, the Bank held the

The common sense of the reader must now be appealed to in the following question:—What amount of Reserve ought the Bank of England to keep in order to represent that fair state of business which is deemed desirable? In answering this question, all the various suggestions made, that there should *always be* 15 or 16 millions of Reserve, or that there should be 35 or 50, or any other per centage against liabilities, may be set aside. What we must ascertain here should be taken from reasonable practice, and if, for argument's sake, I assume a Reserve of 10 millions, with interest at 4 per cent., I presume that a great many financiers would say:—" Such a Reserve, with interest at 4 per cent., appears to indicate a healthy and fair position; the amount is large enough to answer requirements, and we need not be alarmed when we have so much!" They may add: " Perhaps it is better that there should not be more than 10 millions."

Experience as to a fairly satisfactory state of Reserve, say of 10 millions and 4 per cent.

Now if at any time the Reserve in hand should be 15 millions, and interest lowered to 2 per cent., both being unnecessary and quite in excess, the dullest intellect might suggest that we should reduce the Reserve to 10 millions, so as to be able to keep the rate at 4 per cent. This setting aside of 5 millions of the fiduciary issue, at least for a time, need not imply any alteration in the present limit of the Act, the 5 millions thus temporarily withdrawn might be brought forth again, if at any time they were wanted; but their removal, when there is sufficient bullion, would unquestionably have the effect of enabling the Bank to retain 5 millions of bullion in their stead.

The plain principle of reducing surplus of reserve to some such level.

The secret of our present difficulties, and that of the

---

rate at only 3 per cent., and a few weeks later, with the same Reserve, at 7 per cent.; and 1873, when in September the rate was 3½, and in November 9 per cent.

absolutely unfailing remedy, are thereby laid open to you; and if this fails to meet with recognition, the amendment of the present Act is impossible, whatever other experiment may be tried. I have chosen the respective sums of 15 and 10 millions of Reserve and 4 and 2 per cent. interest, for the sake of illustration; the *principle itself* will verify itself with any other amount of Reserve or rate of interest that lies within range. And it must be distinctly understood that this matter is not one of account, the Reserve consists of surplus money, of bank notes, which have the full weight and right of legal tender currency, and which, as such, are offered and held ready for use at any given moment. The denial, or an attempted modification of this force of legal tender rights, would be a denial of all the anticipations and calculations by which we are now guided.

The whole secret of the difficulty, and the remedy involved in timely reduction.

Of the surplus of legal tender notes.

The timely reduction in the issue would accordingly lead to a more steady and less abnormally low rate of interest, and this, *prima facie*, would prevent bullion from leaving the Bank. The *status quo* would be maintained with greater regularity, and whereas of the three stages, 1st, of maintaining the *status quo*; 2nd, of replenishing it from current supply; 3rd, of forcibly restoring it by violent rises in the rate, the Bank is now totally unable to respond even to the first and able only to act "forcibly" for the purpose of the third; it would be enabled by the timely temporary reduction to cover at once the first and second stage, and the third necessity might never occur again, although recourse to it could still be had.

The maintenance of the status quo thereby made easy.

The natural law of compensation involved in this action will not only determine a suitable, or what may be called a normal rate, kept *in accord with the value of money in the outer world*, but will render the *departures from that rate less violent and less frequent*. The

The law of compensation involved in the reduction or increase of issue.

market rate will consequently maintain itself, without being dragged down by the Bank rate, but both will be able to act in concert, influencing each other by the legitimate indications of real supply and demand. At the same time the fiduciary issue will regulate itself in such a way, that that which is withdrawn at one time can, when necessity demands it, be added at another with perfect safety, leading to a system of Reserve of a more regular nature, under which bullion can be protected and attracted by means with which the weight of fiduciary Reserve will not interfere. By thus " saving " in time the fiduciary issue, we would not only save bullion in the first instance, but the notes set aside would become the *real Reserve*, laid aside in accord with what prosperous times are supposed to do for the benefit of less favourable periods. The system of fiduciary issue will thus enter into its proper and only true use, and when so used, its first effect will be that of regulating and modifying all the present difficulties, so that extreme necessities are not likely to arise again. The reduction and increase of the issue will accordingly carry its own Reserve power, and instead of the Reserve now varying between below zero and 15 or 17 millions, the amount will remain near a range, both moderate and ample, but much within the present extremes.

Among the great variety of the controversialists on the Bank of England question, the vast majority of our leading writers on the money market (notably the *Times*, as well as experienced bankers and merchants), is thoroughly conservative, strongly objecting to any increase of issue, or any suggestion as to more or less discriminate issue by Bankers and others. If not quite content with the results of the present Bank Act, this party defends at all events the principle of strict limit as absolute bar against excess. These prudent authorities must recognise that the timely reduction

of the present limit is of a still more conservative
nature, and if they would carefully investigate the
proposal here made, bearing in mind at the same time
the three occasions when the present limit of 15
millions was exceeded, they might come to the conclusion that timely reduction would have prevented
these events, and that this proposal would consequently remain all the better *within* the limit allowed
by law.

THE PRINCIPLE OF DECREASE AND IN-
CREASE OF FIDUCIARY ISSUE, AND
THE LATE PROPOSALS FOR INCREASE
ONLY IN TIMES OF CRISIS.

On reference to pages 45 and 49 of this book you
will find that the practical ground on which the controversy rests is occupied by the proposals made
during the Parliamentary session of 1873 for *an
increase only of* the issue in times of crisis, and by the
proposal here made, which recommends *both decrease
and increase.** *The
contrast
between
these
proposals.*

The nature of the proposal as to *increase of issue*
only is to this effect :— *The nature
and origin
of the
proposal for
increase of
issue.*

The present limit of 15 millions of fixed issue is to
be maintained ; but when crises occur, and when
interest is at 10 per cent,† the Bank shall be authorised
temporarily to issue more notes.

---

* I have already stated that Mr. Lowe's Bill, withdrawn by
Mr. Gladstone later in the session, and Sir John Lubbock's amend-
ment, were essentially of the same nature as the proposal made by
Mr. Forster.

† Mr. Lowe's Bill actually proposed that the rate should be
12 per cent., and that the "foreign exchanges should be in our
favour" before the extra issue should take place !

And the origin of the suggestion must be led back to the well-known fact that at previous crises (1847, 1857, 1866) the Bank Act was suspended, more issue allowed, when as the argument goes :

The suspension of the Act, the mere announcement that more issue could be had, "restored confidence, bullion returning to the Bank."

Anything more perverting of logic and real causes cannot well be imagined. In the first place, the object of contemplated reform in the Bank Act must be that of *preventing crises and panic, and the rise of the rate to* 10 *per cent.*, as far as legislation is able to do so, by the application of a timely remedy ; but in the proposal made, the *very crisis itself and the rate of* 10 *per cent.* must first take place, before the remedy is to be applied. The case of the stolen steed and the stable door would seem a natural proceeding alongside of this method of curing an evil. That the extra issue has the tendency of replacing and preventing bullion to come in, will be admitted.

The perversion of the facts betrays an equally flagrant state of false appreciation. The three suspensions of the Act took place at a time when the very highest tension of interest and state of alarm began to bring bullion back in a copious measure, and it would so have returned without extra issue. The so far accidental characters of these coincidences, of return of Bullion and suspension of the Act, is shown by the fact, that in 1857 only a portion of the extra issue was used, and that in 1866 the rate continued at 10 per cent. for a number of weeks without any extra issue being required, the return of confidence being owing entirely to the fact that the turning point in the return of bullion was coincidental with the permission to make the extra issue. And as to the loss of confidence, I trust I have made it clear to you that it is caused by

The perversion of logic and causes here made manifest.

The perversion of actual facts.

Their accidental nature.

The restoration of confidence.

mercantile failures, that it does not do away with currency, nor alters materially the circulation at one moment.

We may disregard this curious mixture of false logic, the confounding of coincidences, absurd expedients and general indistinct phraseology, in order seriously to consider what the result would be, if the present fixed issue, whilst remaining in force, were to be *extended only* when crisis sets in, without the set-off of previous reduction in times of plethora. Instead of curing the evils from which we now suffer, viz., the heavy withdrawals of bullion, the temporary increase of the issue would only enhance them, and in a measure probably, against which the present difficulties are but child's play. If, as I may have succeeded in showing you, the present fixed issue is the cause why the Bank of England cannot maintain a stock of bullion, there still lurks in the system, at all events, that apparent sense of caution which says, "You shall not go farther, for when you have gone so far you *must* make every effort to obtain bullion, at whatever sacrifice may be necessary for the purpose." This is a distinct declaration as to our valuation, which, although erroneous, so far binds all matters of international exchange within limits to which they must shape themselves, and to which they must respond by the mere force of arithmetical law. A reference to what I have laid before you on page 89 will show you how with what unfailing exactitude these demands are responded to. But if, when these demands for bullion are made, we at the same time make it a practice to create extra issue in its stead, the connection is rendered practically useless, and we shall fail in obtaining bullion. Already, during the crisis of 1866 (the third suspension of the Act),

The real nature of this one-sided increase of issue.

The laxity in the valuation thereby established.

International exchanges would cease to respond to our demands for bullion.

14

the French holders of English bills preferred to deal at once at the exchange for England of full 10 per cent. (although money in Paris was at 4 per cent.), and sent bills for discount here, rather than submit to the contingency of rapid declines from 10 to 3 per cent., as in 1857. These and other matters, which concern the *return* of bullion to us, the proposers of the scheme appear unable to grasp.

The overwhelming withdrawals of bullion.

Whilst bullion would thus be debarred from returning to us, it would, in the first instance, leave us with greater facility. The new valuation, for such it would actually be, could have no other effect than increasing the action of certain floating operations (see page 87), which, when culminating so suddenly, tell upon the Bank's bullion. These operations would be extended to ranges which need not involve the rate of 10 per cent., but float as near to lesser rates as expediency suggests, when at the cumulating point the withdrawal of bullion would become overwhelming.

The greater nervousness of the money market.

We should then witness the spectacle of still more sudden rises in the rate, and our money market would become far more desperate and changing than it is now. Periods would happen in which the Bank would frequently go to 10 per cent., only to drop down again as suddenly. If you bear in mind all that I have said to you respecting the conflict between the country's real resources, the deposits, &c., and the evident temporary advantages which the Bank derives from such a state of confusion, you may estimate to what a

And reversal of present experience.

degree uncertainty would prevail. That all this will upset our previous "experiences of crises and the suspension of the Act," as a supposed foundation for a remedy, every one but the proposers of the scheme will admit.

The money article of the *Times*, and other economists, object to the increase because they see in it the danger of encouraging overtrading. The common sense or rough method of expressing this danger is this :—" The present limit of 15 millions of fixed issue, at all events, has the merit of compelling people not to exceed bounds, to be prudent; if they are imprudent now, in spite of this warning, they will be still more imprudent when they know that more money will still be afforded to them. This change in the contract basis will be taken advantage of "for more dangerous speculations." This common sense view of the matter is perfectly correct, and in accordance with all the experience made and the ordinary instincts of mercantile prudence. *(margin: Effect on speculation and over-trading.)* *(margin: The common sense objection.)*

In my opinion nothing more dangerous could be invented than such a scheme, and that it has been started and admitted into Parliament is a sign of the demoralisation of true intelligence, into which the leaders of the English people have drifted in regard to this matter. Rather than admit so one-sided, dangerous, and ill-conceived an expedient, it would be better to listen to the wild schemers who want to create " 70 millions of national currency," or, who, like Mr. Anderson, wish to enable bankers to " issue more notes on the deposit of Government securities." For in that case the Glasgow bankers, as well as the Bank of England and others throughout the country, could maintain over investments, and in the general scramble which would inevitably follow, everybody would have an equal chance.* *(margin: The proposal as to increase of issue only, is a sign of the demoralisation of enquiry into the question.)* *(margin: It would be better to prepare for a general scramble.)*

---

* Among the host of suggestions, one has lately been made that, in the event of a panic, the Joint Stock Banks of London should acquire the right of making issues of legal tender notes of a few millions. All this shows the want of true appreciation of facts and principles under which " financial alchemy " of this kind

The
proposal
as to
temporary
increase
have
however
broken the
ground for
enquiry.

The introduction of these proposals into Parliament for a temporary increase of the fixed issue has nevertheless produced important results; it has *broken the ground* for inquiry, and advanced the question itself to within a small turn for satisfactory solution. The infallibility of the present form of issue has hitherto been fiercely upheld, in spite of the recurring disasters; but during the last Session several of the defenders of the Act, including Directors of the Bank, have conceded the necessity of reform. The dictates of economical intelligence and honour demand that they should not recede from this acknowledgment. Yet another advantage

The
acknow-
ledgment
of the
necessity
of reform.

has been gained thereby, as to the possibility of framing legislative enactments suitable to the case. Under the feeling of ultra-conservatism, which the whole subtle subject has created, people have gone so far as to believe that the 15 millions once fixed by law could not be altered, excepting by a continuous direct action, or by special resolutions, of Parliament. Among those who suspected the unsuitability of the present fixed issue, there were one or two who, in forming their first crude notions as to a remedy, suggested that Parliament should from time to time determine the amount of issue. Apart from the impossibility of gathering evidence for proper Parliamentary discussion, and the dissensions likely to arise in questions of momentary

---

produces so many short-lived but utterly sterile blossoms, in the beauty of which the authors expect others to revel. Another suggestion is that, during a crisis, "Exchequer Bills" should be created and declared legal tender! This suggestion comes from one of the leading Directors of the Bank. It is to be hoped that the high intellect of the gentleman will perceive the *real* causes of the withdrawals of bullion and the consequent crisis.

or rapidly changing situations, Parliament does not sit all the year, and the *trouble* of thus regulating money matters could not be undertaken by any such assembly.

The proposals of Mr. Lowe, of Mr. Fowler, and Sir John Lubbock, now distinctly prove *that a clause* can be introduced into the Act, to the effect that upon certain contingences, viz. : *the rise of the rate of interest to 10 per cent.*, there shall be a *temporary increase* of the issue; it is therefore equally practicable to *provide a clause* determining that upon 2½ per cent., or any other rate of interest, there shall be a *temporary decrease* of the issue. The close relationship between the proposals for a temporary increase only of the issue above 15 millions, and that for a temporary decrease below 15 millions, by way of compensation, is thereby shown. In many questions of this kind, the final decision may either lead to an increase of the mischief, or to a proper settlement. So in this case, if the *extension* only is admitted, the speed for further ruin of the interests concerned is only increased, but if in addition to *extension* the *reduction* is made to precede, the whole subject *is at once placed on the way of its absolutely satisfactory conclusion.*

They admit the possibility of regulating the matter by clauses of the Act.

And you will now perceive how all that I have said, respecting the *small subtle* error at the bottom of the mischief, has become verified in the closeness of the position between the two practically contending proposals, *temporary increase only* against *temporary reduction and increase.* It is merely necessary that the promoters of the former, instead of awaiting until the issue is gone, and interest at 10 per cent., looking backwards only, should endeavour to turn the other way for a moment, and take the wise precaution of *diminishing the issue* when not wanted, in the same way as

The subtle point of the whole controversy.

they propose to *diminish* the extra issue above 15 millions when it has done its office. The whole secret of the difficulty, and the simplicity of the solution may then be revealed to them; the practicability of the adjustment resting upon precisely the same grounds which they have adopted for their own scheme. As in the case of the error shown in Part I. of this book, so is the application of the remedy now brought to a head, or fine point, where the slightest turn to economical intelligence or awakening of common sense is required to turn the scale from still much greater evil to definite good. In the next chapter it will be shown to you that the present Act contains the principle here advocated, and why it has not been available.

The slightest turn of economical thought will provide the remedy.

THE TEMPORARY DECREASE AND INCREASE OF THE FIDUCIARY ISSUE PROVIDED FOR IN THE PRESENT ACT, AND WHY IT COULD NOT BE PUT IN PRACTICE.

The practicability of a reform of the Act in accordance with what has been said before, and the validity of the statements made will be made more evident to you by a reference to the present Act. Clause II. of that Act establishes the great principle of the issue, and is worded as follows, the sentences in italics referring to the temporary diminution of the issue :—

Clause 2 of the Act distinctly provides for a diminution of the issue.

Clause II.—And be it enacted that, upon the 31st day of August 1844, there shall be transferred, appropriated and set

Wording of
the clause.

apart by the said Governor and Company to the Issue Department of the Bank of England, securities to the value of £14,000,000,
whereof the debt due by the public to the said Governor and
Company shall be and be deemed a part; and there shall also, at the
same time, be transferred, appropriated and set apart by the said
Governor and Company to the said Issue Department, so much
of the gold coin and gold and silver bullion then held by the Bank
of England as shall not be required by the Banking Department
thereof; and thereupon there shall be delivered out of the said Issue
Department into the said Banking Department of the Bank of
England such an amount of Bank of England notes as, together
with the Bank of England notes then in circulation, shall be
equal to the aggregate amount of the securities, coin and bullion
so transferred to the said Issue Department of the Bank of
England; and the whole amount of Bank of England notes then
in circulation, including those delivered to the Banking Department of the Bank of England as aforesaid, shall be deemed to be
issued on the credit of such securities, coin and bullion so appropriated and set apart to the said Issue Department; and from
thenceforth it shall not be lawful for the said Governor and Company to increase the amount of securities for the time being in
the said Issue Department, save as hereinafter is mentioned; *but
it shall be lawful for the said Governor and Company to diminish
the amount of such securities, and again to increase the same to
any sum not exceeding in the whole the sum of* £14,000,000,[*] Distinct
provision
for a
diminution
of the issue.
and so *from time to time as they shall see* occasion; and
from and after such transfer and appropriation to the said Issue
Department as aforesaid, it shall not be lawful for the said Governor
and Company to issue Bank of England notes, either into the
Banking Department of the Bank of England, or to any persons or
person whatsoever, save in exchange for other Bank of England notes,
or for gold coin or for gold or silver bullion received or purchased
for the said Issue Department under the provisions of this Act, or
in exchange for securities acquired and taken in the said Issue
Department under the provisions herein contained: provided
always, that it shall be lawful for the said Governor and Company
in their Banking Department to issue all such Bank of England
notes as they shall at any time receive from the said ·Issue Department or otherwise in the same manner in all respects as such issue
would be lawful to any other person or persons."

---

[*] Since increased to 15 millions.

Although the above terms as to diminution of the issue form an integral part of this important clause, yet in the thousands of pamphlets and articles written on the controversy, you will find no allusion to them, and many of the readers here, of which several may have themselves written on the subject, will acknowledge that they were not aware of, or have paid no attention to this special part of the clause.

But here it is clearly and distinctly stated that it shall be lawful to diminish "*from time to time*," and "*again to increase*," in exact accordance with the spirit of the views expressed by the author.

Such diminution to be "from time to time," and "again to increase."

What was the object of Sir Robert Peel in introducing this provision?

Why has it not been acted upon?

That the above sentence is not an idle one, that it has not crept in by accident, will be admitted. There can be no doubt that Sir Robert Peel had a distinct object in view by placing it there. The suspicion may have arisen in his mind that by the combination of the fixed issue with bullion, it might at times be expedient to reduce the former for the sake of the latter. In the heat of the discussion however, under the novelty of the strict limit, in which rough economy delighted, the further consideration of this point has been overlooked; and Sir Robert Peel himself, under the impression that the issue of 14 millions would actually be used, according to the previous average (see pages 59 to 64, and table 4, page 62), to the extent of 11 millions, leaving but 3 millions margin, may have attached less importance to the matter. This is confirmed also by the fact that the 11 millions of Government debt were left as a debt in account, and not represented by Consols or negotiable bonds of the State, whereas the 3 millions were to consist of "other

Reasons why the sentence in question did not meet with sufficient consideration.

securities " at the option of the Bank. Again, Sir Sir Robert Peel would now acknowledge the importance of this matter.
Robert Peel expressed, from the commencement, the
opinion that the Act should be tested, and be made
subject to repeal or amendment within a year (see
clause 27); hence—if he was now alive, and the test
reapplied—there can be little doubt but that this
matter of timely reduction would now appear to him
as a *cardinal principle* of the Act, the only one wanting
to render *his work perfect.*

Why has the Bank of England not acted, or rather The inability of the Bank to act in accordance with this part of the clause.
why has it been unable to act upon the thus expressed
intention of the Act itself? The reason will become
manifest to you, when you bear in mind that, under
the Act of 1844, the Bank of England has virtually
entered into a contract with the State, in which the
latter takes a large share of the profits by a regular
annual payment, as clause 8 of the Act prescribes :—

Clause 8.—And be it enacted, that from and after the said 31st Clause 8 of the Act. Providing for a regular share of profit to the State.
day of August 1844, the payment or deduction of the annual sum
of £120,000, made by the said Governor and Company under the
provisions of the said Act passed in the fourth year of the reign of
his late Majesty King William IV. out of the sums payable to them
for the charges of management of the public unredeemed debt shall
cease, and in lieu thereof the said Governor and Company, in consideration of the privileges of exclusive banking, and the exemption
from stamp duties given to them by this Act, shall, during the con-
tinuance of such privileges and such exemption respectively, but no
longer, deduct and allow to the public from the sums now payable
by law to the said Governor and Company, for the charges of
management of the public unredeemed debt, the annual sum of
£180,000, anything in any Act or Acts of Parliament, or in any
agreement to the contrary, notwithstanding : Provided always, that
such deduction shall in no respect prejudice or affect the rights of
the said Governor and Company to be paid for the management of
the public debt at the rate and according to the terms provided in
an Act passed in the forty-eighth year of the reign of his late
Majesty King George III., intituled "An Act to authorise the
advancing for the Public Service, upon certain conditions, a propor-

tion of the Balance remaining in the Bank of England for the payment of Unclaimed Dividends, Annuities, and Lottery Prizes, and for regulating the Allowances to be made for the Management of the National Debt."

This annual payment of £180,000 to the State has since increased to £195,000 a year (in consequence of the additional 1 million). In the return given (see page 181) the sum of £60,000 is stated as composition in lieu of stamp duty, the balance being described as "For share of profits of the circulation department."

On pages 179 to 186 I have demonstrated the actual results of this arrangement as far as the Bank of England's profit is concerned, and the figures there given show that the actual profit made *on the circulation* of the fiduciary issue (after deducting that of notes founded on bullion), is not sufficient to cover the technical expenses of the issue, together with this regular annual share of profit which the State receives, the yearly average loss to the Bank being £100,000. A reference to these pages may probably lead to the inference that this so-called profit of the issue is not fairly divided, that the State obtains too much. There can be no doubt that the sum of £180,000 annual share was computed upon the assumption that a regular circulation of 11 millions of fiduciary issue would be maintained, and if that had been the case, the charge, equal to 1½ per cent. per annum, would not be an extravagant one, for the State is entitled to share in the profit made by such issues.

But when, as experience shows, the fiduciary issues vary from nothing to 15 or more millions, with the most incongruous sums at other times, when for years at a time 9, 11, and 14 millions are in Reserve, *i.e.* *not used* in circulation, when, further, the use of 11 millions reduces the Reserve to 4 millions, creating alarm and foreshadowing danger, you may probably admit that this regular payment of "profits" to the State is not in accordance with facts. In all matters which are thus compounded for in a rough anticipatory manner, one of the parties must suffer an injustice, and this injustice becomes increased when the future does not verify the anticipations, or produces new features. Where such large public interests are concerned, and in a money market so delicate as ours, this rough and uncouth method of compounding is a most unfair thing, and although, as far as direct profit and loss are concerned, the Bank of England bears the first brunt, yet as the nucleus of our monetary system it is influenced thereby, and in its turn influences the interests connected with it.

The unfairness of the regular charge.

Further—when this nucleus, as one of the two contracting parties, is bound at the same time to have regard to the interests of its own proprietors—it cannot, in spite of the desire to act in a public-spirited manner, make sacrifices of money or principle beyond a certain range. There must be some *inducement*, some *mutual* advantage, before any extra voluntary action can be fairly expected. Hence, *if instead of insisting upon the* regular payment of £195,000 *per annum*, the State had consented, *from time to time*, to receive less, when the fiduciary circulation was low, and more again when it was high, the Bank might have reduced the overweight of issue in accordance with the words "as it should see occasion" in clause 2.

The Bank has no inducement to reduce the issue.

The Bank of England already bears the high technical charges attendant upon the issue, and must recover these, as well as the annual payment, from the use to be made of the 15 millions of issue. The matter will again be made clear to you if you review the position. The Bank has placed 15 millions of securities in the Issue Department, for which it

It already bears the high technical charges.

receives 3 per cent. per annum. These securities have absorbed 15 millions of money, whether this be taken from capital or from resources, or in exchange of bullion. The Issue Department, in its turn, obtains the 3 per cent. on the 11 millions of State debt and the 4 millions of other securities, it being immaterial whether the debit or credit pass first to the Banking Department or not, both departments belonging to the same institution. So far, then, the account is balanced. In considering this matter, you must not allow yourselves to be confused by the Parliamentary account, which *credits* the Issue Department with the interest derived from the securities bought with the

resources of the Banking Department, and thus shows a fictitious profit. Nor must you allow this matter to be mixed up with the Reserve arising in the Banking Department in consequence of the inability of the Issue Department to pass the surplus into circulation. The best method for disabusing your minds from the hocus pocus here involved, is that you should imagine there was no Issue Department attached to the Bank, or that it were conducted by some other concern. In that case you must decide whether the Bank of England, instead of investing the 15 millions in the Issue Department, would not do better by holding securities in the Banking Department—say 10 millions in Government stock and 5 millions in cash reserve—rather than submit to the holding of Reserves of from less than nothing up to 15 and 17 millions.

Next comes the produce of the 15 millions as employed in circulation, from which must be deducted, firstly, "the expenses," leaving the balance available for "division of profits." The net produce and expenses are as follows :—

TABLE 15.—*Showing the Gross Produce of the Fixed Issue, less Technical Expenses, and the Supposed Balance of Profit for Division between State and Bank, and Loss.*

Years.		Gross Profits.	Technical Expenses.		Balance remaining for Division between State and Bank.	
1845		£167,207	£173,511		£5,304	Loss.
1846		204,769	,,		31,258	Profit.
1847		485,567	,,		312,056	,,
1848		188,003	,,		14,492	,,
1849		121,351	,,		52,160	Loss.
1850		86,791	,,		86,720	,,
1851		166,005	,,		7,506	,,
1852		38,460	,,		135,051	,,
1853		222,956	,,		49,445	Profit.
1854	...	379,351	,,		205,840	,,
1855	...	300,721	179,405	...	121,316	,,
1856	...	549,672	,,	...	370,267	,,
1857	...	675,227	,,	...	495,822	° ,,
1858	...	103,864	,,	...	75,541	Loss.
1859		113,902	...	,,	...	65,503	,,
1860	...	285,300	...	,,	...	105,895	Profit.
1861	...	426,930	...	181,574	...	245,356	,,
1862	...	138,584	...	,,	...	42,990	Loss.
1863	...	310,108	...	,,	...	128,534	Profit.
1864	...	576,180	...	,,	...	394,606	,,
1865	...	347,814	...	,,	...	165,240	,,
1866	...	690,177	...	183,912	...	506,603	,,
1867	...	88,984	...	,,	...	92,590	Loss.
1868	...	92,986	...	,,	...	88,588	,,
1869	...	186,611	...	,,	...	5,037	Profit.
1870	...	111,566	...	,,	...	70,003	Loss.
1871	...	59,053	...	,,	...	122,521	,,

Whether there be a loss or profit on the year, *the State enacts a regular annual sum, now amounting to £195,000*—designated as "its share"—and it has thus received, since 1845, a sum of no less than £2,900,000 *in excess* of the balances between actual profit and loss from the issue.[*] You may admit that

---

[*] It will of course be said: The Bank gains £450,000 per annum on the 15 millions of securities. This investment is a matter standing on its own merits, and if the above excess to the State be deducted, the whole arrangement, investment and note issue, still leaves a loss of more than £100,000 to the Bank (see page 185).

this method of drawing profit on the part of the State is utterly wrong and indefensible in principle, and cannot but act as an odious tax on prosperity.

This will now show you why the Bank has no inducement for a timely reduction of the issue, why rather, considering this heavy charge, it is only natural that the Bank should obtain as much from the use of the fiduciary notes as it can. This does not mean that the Bank deliberately sets aside dictates of prudence and pits its interest against the public weal, but the force of circumstances and the arrangement itself cannot have any other tendency. The whole effect of the anomaly concentrates itself upon cheapening interest, driving bullion away, and leading to all the extraordinary results and conflicts which I have set forth in the first part of this book.

The remedy to be applied can easily be inferred. The State *should take its share of profit in accordance* with the *real principles upon which profit is divided* periodically. This may occasionally give less, at other times more, per annum, and therewith the matter reduces itself to the consideration whether the Budget of this mighty nation can afford to substitute for a trifling *fixed* income one that, like other estimated incomes, may vary. Indeed, considering the gigantic interests at stake, and the subtlety of the matter, the question might well be asked, " Why should the State not give up altogether the £195,000 per annum ? Much larger sums are deliberately spent for purposes of infinitely less importance, and in this case the advantage to the welfare of our commerce, would much enhance the taxable power of the country, recouping the Budget manifold ! " But this is not asked for, because a share of profits in bank note issues legitimately belongs to the State ; all that is required here is that the share should be real, and when this principle

The forces of bad arrangements here operate together against sound practice.

The State should take the share of actual profits.

Which with the reform might become fairly regular, if not larger than at present.

comes into action, the whole business will be regulated so that the gross profits themselves will be more regular and larger, perhaps, than they are now.

THE PRACTICAL SOLUTION OF THE QUESTION CONTAINED IN THE AMENDMENT OF CLAUSE 8 OF THE PRESENT ACT.

From the foregoing remarks you may now be able to perceive that clause 8 of the Act, which in itself is but a subsidiary provision, seemingly distinct from the great features of the case, is the real obstacle to the immediately practicable reform of the Act, such reform being foreshadowed in clause 2 itself. If you have carefully followed the course of matters as I have opened it before you, you will not only see the coincidental agreement between the views I advocate and the simple ground here prepared for you by the Act itself, but you may admit that the method which I have adopted for guiding you out of the labyrinth of darkness to the appreciation of this point was necessary. Simple as this matter now seems to become, it is just such simple considerations, which in subjects surrounded with so much mystery and controversy are most difficult to bring to the surface, excepting by the most consecutive course of ample analysis.

The subject reduced to its simplest form.

You will then see that the solution of the matter is entirely dependent on clause 8, and that is the only amendment required in the whole Act as far as it concerns the Bank of England issue.* The problem before the legislature is therefore one that can be disposed of by a very short Act only, little expenditure of violent dis-

The amendment of clause 8 gives the practical solution.

---

* The clauses concerning the country bankers' issues may be subjected to a reform hereafter (see page 282).

cussion, and without mutual accusations and conflicts between vested interests.

All other clauses respecting the Bank of England *may* remain absolutely intact, and require no alteration whatsoever; *the great determining clause* 2 need not be altered at all, unless it be for the conversion of the State debt of account into a negotiable form. But even this is not absolutely necessary—the transfer from the issue to banking department, and *vice versa*, is a matter which Bank and State may settle. If but a portion of the State debt were converted into Consols, sufficient to respond to any possible or experienced reduction in the Government securities of the banking department, for immediate negotiation if need be, the Bank of England might transfer Consols from the banking to the issue, and take the State debt into the former department.

The great main points in this contemplated reform, which should not only satisfy the admirers of the strict limit of 15 millions, but also the advocates of large Reserves, are these;

The limit of 15 millions as determined by clause 2, the *bar to overtrading*, may remain in force nominally. The only difference in its availability concerns a *temporary timely reduction*, and the *extra* conservative nature of this proposal might be approved of without further question. The "regulating" forces, thus set to work, will not only definitely oppose the accumulation of too much "offer" of money, but *per contra*, prevent the reaction for excessive absorption of bullion, and as this excessive absorption to 15 millions has only happened three times (1847, 1857, and 1866) it is reasonable to infer that with a better regulation it will not occur again, and that the fiduciary circulation will fluctuate less in either direction, giving an average *within* the 15 millions. If at any future time more should be wanted,

All other clauses on the Bank of England may remain absolutely intact.

The maintenance of the limit and Reserve satisfied.

The limit of 15 millions can remain as a nominal one.

the matter can be considered. It will be found however that it is immaterial whether the nominal limit be made 15 or 20 or 25 millions, so long as effective precautions are taken against the undue accumulation of au actually offering, but otherwise *idle surplus*, of issue, and that can only be done by changing the *fixed actual issue* of 15 millions into a *nominal limit*.

The admirers of large heavy reserves might also be satisfied. For it is not proposed here absolutely to abolish the 15 millions of fiduciary issue which are supposed to assist (?) us in maintaining Reserve; all that is proposed is, that for the moment they should be set aside, to be just as available again the next. The only change thus made is that these Reserves should no longer serve as an inducement for overtrading, or for pressing down the rate of interest, and driving away bullion. *The attempt to satisfy the requirements of the circulation*, and the proper *proportion of bullion* must be made without our being obliged to take the *Reserves* into calculation. If that succeeds, *i.e.* if the action of the rate of interest by the Bank of England is amended so as to maintain bullion fairly in accord with requirements of circulation and our international relationship, we may contemplate the existence of a large Reserve with satisfaction. It will then *float*, so to speak, over the substrata of circulation, without weighing upon, or influencing the factors which regulate the market. As long as it does not do any mischief we may choose to increase it even beyond what we are accustomed to see now, for there is no harm in the further creation of fiduciary Reserve, provided it *does not enter the market*, *i.e.* provided that no necessity for its use arises. *That necessity cannot arise* when the circulation and its connection with bullion, lying below it, are effectually adjusted by proper rates of interest.

The Reserve would be equally maintainable.

If the adjustment of the circulation and bullion stock took place without reference to it.

It would "float" over the substrata and continue to do so without harm.

15

The full truth and satire of what all this means in reality will be manifest to those who can appreciate the habits and errors into which we have fallen as regards Reserves arising out of the present system.

The availability of the Reserve thus made subject to temporary reduction and corresponding increase, as well as the advantages which the Bank would acquire in the recovery for the banking department of its real resources, will appear from the following, in juxta-position to what I have shown on p 191. In order to appreciate this, we must first agree as to the amount of Reserve actually required by the Bank for sudden contingences. I have shown you before that there are no sudden contingences of circulation, because the circulation cannot be suddenly augmented or decreased, it is regular, and increases but gradually. I have also shown you that the Bank, instead of suffering from withdrawals of deposits in times of pressure, rather finds them increase. These contingences of both departments are consequently of a nature requiring but small Reserves. Nevertheless, let us say, "The Bank must keep at least 5 millions of regular Reserve for these purposes — you don't know what may happen!" Assume, now, that the Bank had 14 millions of Reserve, and that we set aside 9 of these, reducing it to 5 millions. But bear in mind, if this sum should seem insufficient to you, that we merely *set aside* for the moment the 9 millions; the 5 millions Reserve are therefore but a go-between, for at any moment we can call again upon the 9 millions kept apart.

Comparing, then, the position of 14 millions of Reserve, *without reduction* of the total issue by 9 millions, with that of 5 millions of Reserve *after* reduction of the total issue (assuming that there are

22 millions of bullion and 23 millions in circulation), the two accounts of the issue and banking departments would appear as follows :—

1. Without reduction of total issue—

ISSUE DEPARTMENT.

Liabilities.		Assets.	
Notes issued	£37,000,000	Government Debt	£11,015,100
		Other Securities	3,984,900
		Bullion	22,000,000
	£37,000,000		£37,000,000

Actual circulation ... £23,000,000.

BANKING DEPARTMENT.

Liabilities.		Assets.	
Capital	£14,533,000	Gov'ment Securities	£15,000,000
Rest	3,467,000	Other Securities	14,500,000
Public Deposits } Private ,, }	25,500,000	Notes in Reserve	14,000,000
Seven Days' Bills	500,000	Coin	500,000
	£44,000,000		£44,000,000

2. With the reduction of the total issue by 9 millions—

ISSUE DEPARTMENT.

Liabilities.		Assets.	
Notes issued	£28,000,000	Government Debt	£6,000,000
		Bullion	22,000,000
	£28,000,000		£28,000,000

BANKING DEPARTMENT.

Liabilities.		Assets.	
Capital	£14,533,000	Government Secu- rities and Debt	£20,015,100
Rest	3,467,000	Other Securities	18,484,900
Public Deposits } Private ,, }	25,500,000	Notes in Reserve	5,000,000
Seven Days' Bills	500,000	Coin	500,000
	£44,000,000		£44,000,000

The difference in the two sets of accounts would accordingly be this :—

Through the temporary reduction of the fiduciary issue by 9 millions :

1. The liabilities of the *issue department* would be reduced from 37 to 28 millions, and bullion remaining at 22 millions in both cases, the convertibility of the note would thereby be improved.

2. No change would occur in the amount of liabilities and assets of the banking department, but in lieu of the 9 millions of idle Reserve withdrawn, the Bank would receive back from the issue, say £5,015,100 Government debt, and £3,984,900 other securities, so that these items in the banking account would be increased by 9 millions, giving to the banking department, at 3 per cent., £270,000 more income.

3. The Reserve in the Banking Department would be reduced to 5 millions, *but at any time*, by a retransfer of the 9 millions withdrawn, or a portion thereof, that Reserve would be replenished or enlarged, and the spirit of clause 2 of the present Act carried out.

In representing the matter to you by these simple examples, bear in mind that this improvement cannot be carried out, so long as clause 8 of the Act remains in force, for the sum of £195,000 enacted by the State is equal, at 3 per cent., to the use of $6\frac{1}{2}$ millions of margin, the technical expenses of £185,000 to another 6 millions, together $12\frac{1}{2}$ millions, and it is perfectly indifferent to the Bank whether this margin is kept in the issue or included in the present Reserve.

On behalf of the vast interests concerned, the author ventures to suggest the following arrangement :—

The first 5 millions of the fiduciary issue should be considered as requisite to cover the technical expenses of the issue. These now amount to £185,000, but they may be capable of a reduction which will enable

The larger profit made by the Bank.

Suggestion as to arrangement.

the Bank of England to accept the advantage of the use of 5 millions by way of set-off against them.

On all the rest of fiduciary issue above 5 millions, the interest earned should be set aside as clear profit to be divided between State and Bank every year.

It might be left to the option of the Bank to place this 5 millions into the Banking Department as Reserve. In that case the Bank would be enabled to take full advantage of its deposits and 18 millions of its capital and rest, and at the same time satisfy the public consideration for the existence of such Reserve; or the whole produce of the fiduciary issue might be credited year by year to an account, out of which the Bank's expenses should be paid, and profits divided.

THE CONTROL OF INTEREST REGAINED BY THE REDUCTION OF LARGE RESERVE TO A TEMPORARY SMALL INDICATING RESERVE.

The advantages which the timely reductions of a large Reserve would confer on the Issue Department, and on the better use in the Banking Department of the Bank's real resources, are exceeded in importance by the effect which they would have on the rates of interest, on which the maintenance of the stock of bullion depends. I have before described to you (see pages 79 and 97), how these heavy Reserves drag down the rate much below the average of international interest, how, in the determination of the rates, the Bank is guided by their amounts (see page 203). It will now be evident to you that as the temporary removal of a large surplus can be accomplished not by destroying it, but by merely setting it aside for a time, and if consequently the indicator can be reduced

The principal advantage given by reduction of the idle Reserve of Notes.

to give correspondingly higher rates, *all danger of unduly* low interest, and its effects upon undue withdrawals of bullion is set aside therewith.

That is to say, the Bank will regain full liberty to uphold whatever rate of interest it likes, subject only to the influence of the market rate, which, in its turn, is connected with the international rate of interest. The Bank *need not take the initiative* in lowering the rate, thus spoiling the market rate to no purpose. The market rate will accordingly be that with which the Bank will remain in accord. Not only will this bring

in more business to the Bank, but it will do away with the useless competition between the Bank's Reserve and that of Bankers, through which the latter must submit to any low rate which the Bank may determine, without being able to employ the Reserve so offered (see pages 164, &c.).

This then removes, *prima facie*, the principal and almost only cause of disturbances in our money market, the undue withdrawals of bullion, for whatever bullion may after that be withdrawn, it must be taken by full equivalents in exchange, or can only be a positive surplus in our possession, to be disposed of by the natural laws which rule the price of money and determine the value of commodities.

The door for undue withdrawals being thus stopped, what are we to do when the attraction of bullion nevertheless becomes a necessity? The question is appropriate, because it involves that of: By what rules shall the Bank be guided in raising the rate? For, if the Bank regains full liberty of action, it would seem almost that it had such liberty under the old Act, or that

it would assume a position similar to that of the Bank of France and Prussia! Under the old Act (see page 52), the Bank of England did not make the mistake of letting interest go too low, but it allowed too much fiduciary issue without raising the rate high enough, and lost bullion subsequently; whereas, under the present Act, it deliberately drives away bullion, and then makes great efforts to recover it. Under the old Act, errors of *omission*, under the present Act, errors of *commission* took place. But under the old errors of omission were committed.

And recollect that the banks of France and Prussia do not suffer from heavy withdrawals of bullion like we do, because they never go so low in the rate (see pages 98 to 100). They need not go so low, for they do not include a large idle Reserve (useless for the purposes of circulation), in their accounts of money on hand, *but allow the fiduciary surplus to go back* in the same measure as bullion has refilled any gap in what is proper for the circulation ! From this it does not follow that the systems of the Banks of France and Prussia are perfect, for they leave much to discretion, whilst we, in England, endeavour to work by rules which leave as little room as possible to errors of discretion. The Banks of France and Prussia do better, but have no perfect system.

I may now succeed in showing you what were probably Sir R. Peel's intentions, when in his endeavour to effect a combination between limit, increase, and reduction, as prescribed by clause 2, he imagined that some fairly correct automaton arrangement would be the result. The reading of clause 2 will bring out the fact that, by the proviso for reduction, Sir Robert Peel had no other object in view than that of regulating the matter in accordance with circumstances. The strict limit of 15 millions, to cover both circulation and Reserve, must have arisen from the thought that the country should provide itself with bullion, and that the 15 millions should form a standard, by which the liberty of the Bank should be restricted, in the first place. In the second place, this standard should serve as the basis of calculation in favour of higher rates of Sir Robert Peel's endeavour to create automaton action. By increase and decrease of the issue.]

interest, for the maintenance of the circulation and *regular Reserve*, and such regular Reserve would become the true indicator. Hence, to make the regularity of the Reserve possible, *reduction and increase* were provided for within the limit of the 15 millions allowed. If the maintenance of a regular Reserve by these simple means had been accomplished, the natural result would have been a proportionate higher level of bullion—the strict maintenance of the average would have enforced a system of interest in which that average would have to be taken as a *negative* element, as a Reserve first to be cared for, and the rates would have been *anticipatory*.

Instead of this, the Reserve has not been taken as something to be *first secured* and held intact, but it has served as a *positive* element, additional to supply, and so engendered the practice not only of unduly low rates, as the first stage, but the tardy or *post facto* action as the second stage—the insufficiency of both to be corrected by the final effort.

Now, if in future the principle of reduction and increase effects the maintenance of a fairly moderate Reserve, it will be evident to you that any movement in the market will tell with greater proportionate effect upon 5 millions than on 15 millions, hence the indicator will be much quicker in its action. This does not mean that changes in the rate will be more frequent—on the contrary, they will be much less, but more *consistent* in their durance. The strict maintenance of the moderate Reserve, you must recollect, will do away entirely with the low extremes, and what we have to look to in reference to the inviolability of such Reserve concerns only *higher* rates.

The essential difference between the present practice, the old Act, and the arrangement foreshadowed in Clause 2 of the Act, will now be seen; the former

(marginal notes)
To create a standard of Reserve.

In favour of anticipatory action.

The action was changed into *post facto* with both extremes.

The regular Reserve protects Bullion and serves only as indicator for higher rates.

Clause 2 gives liberty of action together with indicator.

compels the Bank to lower the rates unduly, and, *per contra*, enforces measures increasing in violence as the Reserve progressively diminishes; both the others give the Bank full liberty to uphold rates, unencumbered with Reserve, but the old Act entirely failed in giving a guide for higher rates, thus disorganizing, by the reaction, the fair liberty to moderate rates. Clause 2 of the present Act however, affords this standard for guiding the rates, and little doubt need be entertained but that Sir Robert Peel, if alive, would now so construe that clause, and give effect to the reduction.

The necessity of affording standards and figures in preference to a mere haphazard liberty, need not be discussed here. Without them no regular action is possible in the construction of any system. And when we have ascertained that our monetary affairs are composed of certain factors, viz., the circulation, the Bank of England issue, the proportion of bullion and the rate of interest, all definable by figures, affording proportions in somewhat like mechanical relationship to each other, the necessity to measure and control them by a numerical agency is obvious. And when true principles are adopted for this purpose, the discretion of wise and experienced men cannot go wrong. The Bank of England is now guided by the Reserves arising from the misapprehension of, or from the inability of carrying out the spirit of Clause 2; and the endless muddle and strife into which this throws the whole practice and controversy, its defiance to almost all the efforts of experience and discretion, I have described to you before. But if Clause 2 is made effective, as it ought to be, a natural indicator will be found to arise from the practice, with which the directors of the Bank of England can deal, with a clearness of purpose and unfailing certainty, " as they may see occasion," in the words of Clause 2 itself.

A true indicator cannot fail to guide discretion rightly.

Its clearness and certainty.

I repeat, therefore, that in the whole of this question of the Reform of the Bank of England, little more is required than the amendment of Clause 8, so as to give effect to Clause 2, which may remain unaltered, and when that is done the whole problem is solved, as far as *the pressing necessity for doing so is concerned.* Further improvements are subject to separate consideration.

The problem solved by the amendment of Clause 8 of the present Act.

THE SYSTEM OF COMPENSATING INTEREST AND INCREASING RESERVE.

Although the amendment to the Act spoken of last will furnish the *practical* solution of the question, yet it may be worth while to consider whether a more certain system, founded on the principles enunciated, can be established, without involving any more essential disturbance of the Act. The idea, that from the factors in operation in this matter some automaton action is deducible, prevails in the minds of economists, and several attempts have been made in this direction. Some of these seek an adjustment of the issue upon a general notion of elasticity, unaware of the distinction between elasticity and variability, and of the various degrees of firmness of the several factors. Others, better informed, succeed in fitting the variations of one factor to another, but fail with the third and fourth, when they have recourse to arbitrary assumptions.*

The search for adjustments and rules.

Its failure for want of reference to all factors.

---

* The most notable example of this kind is furnished in a publication on the Bank Act, lately issued by one of the most prominent of our economists. The following passages occur therein :—

"It is so manifestly desirable that the variations of the rate of interest should proceed, if possible, upon some well-defined and simple basis, that many minds have been directed towards the discovery of a rule. Mr. Tooke always advocated most strongly the maintenance

In the course of this book sufficient information may have been given for the clear appreciation of the constituents of our monetary system, and their reduction to the adjusting points. When these are reached, there ought to be no difficulty about the rule to be

of a large bullion reserve, and in order to prevent undue depletion of the reserve he suggested that the Bank should never follow a falling discount market lower than 4 per cent.—that is to say, that for ordinary discount business the Bank should cease to compete at 4 per cent. As a matter of fact, the Bank would lose very little by such a rule, for when the rates in the open market are really falling, they always keep so far below the Bank minimum as to divert nearly all discount business from it. The effect of the Bank stopping at 4 per cent. would be, of course, that a certain part of the bills held would mature and be collected, and the cash reserve proportionately increased ; such accession of strength being available to moderate the extent of the rebound in the rate of interest when the money market again became active and rising.

" Proceeding further in the development of this principle, it has been suggested by some eminent persons, well entitled to be considered as practical authorities, that a sound and simple rule might be found by having it understood, not in obedience to any positive enactment of the Legislature, but as a general principle :—

" (1.) That the minimum rate of discount at the Bank of England should be regulated by the rise and fall in the total amount of bullion reserve stated in the weekly published return.

" (2.) That, by way of example, as regards the application of this rule, it might be laid down that when the total bullion is, say 15 millions, the rate shall be 5 per cent. per annum ; that the rate shall fall half per cent. for every rise of 1 million in the total bullion, being therefore $3\frac{1}{2}$ per cent. when the bullion was 18 millions, and never descending below $3\frac{1}{4}$ per cent., whatever elevation the bullion might attain. On the other hand, that the rate should rise half per cent. for every fall of half a million in the bullion below 15 millions ; the rate rising, therefore, to 7 per cent. when the bullion had fallen to 13 millions : and if the bullion still continued to diminish, the rate to rise 1 per cent. for every loss of half a million below 13 millions ; so that with $11\frac{1}{2}$ millions of bullion the rate would be 10 per cent., and with 10 millions of bullion it would be 13 per cent. per annum.

" These figures are given as illustrations of the possible applica-

observed. The factors which must be borne in mind are :—

1. The amount of money required for the business of the country itself — *i.e.* the circulation.

2. The increase in our commerce and population.

3. The circulation of the Bank of England note as the supernatant portion of the general circulation.

4. The amount of bullion requisite in due proportion of such circulation.

5. The rates of interest to be effective for the maintenance or completion of such bullion.

6. The amount and character of the Reserve necessary for certain contingences.

---

tion of the rule. The sum of 15 millions as the nominal point, and as representing 5 per cent. per annum, might, perhaps, on full investigation, be found to be too small an amount, but upon that point of detail no positive opinion need at present be expressed. The merits of the suggestion are great. It sets forth a rule of management simple, obvious, intelligible and practical, and it rests upon the solid scientific truth that in the highly-developed banking and credit system of the United Kingdom at the present time, the ultimate and almost the sole regulation of the money market—that is, the market for investments, for dealings in property, and adventures in commodities—is the rate of interest, and the pressure placed on credit by elevations of that rate.

"All notions about 'regulating the currency' (whatever that obscure phrase may really mean) in any other way are delusive, and entirely destitute of support from experience."

In the paragraph marked (2) the attempt is made to regulate the rate of interest by bullion; the two factors are brought into some kind of mutual play by a kind of fixed sliding scale more stiff and arbitrary than the present limit of 15 millions. This is all the more singular, because the author himself pleads a reform chiefly on the ground that the "altered circumstances" demand it. The plan proposed by him takes no notice of further increase of trade, of consequent increase in circulation, and this alone would be

Of these factors the first two, viz., the general circulation in accord with our trade and population, stand *prima facie* in direct relationship without reference to the other four more immediately concerning the Bank of England. The circulation, *i.e.* the coin which it has absorbed, and which it holds, has nothing to do with the Bank; it is only through the note issue that it becomes connected therewith. It happens to supply itself with sovereigns through the agency of the Bank, because that institution manages this business in accord with a truly practical and econonomical method. The circulation never lacks

The free scope given to the demands of circulation.

---

sufficient to destroy the value of the arrangement. But the most extraordinary part of the suggestion concerns the factor interest. He coolly assumes the rate of 5 per cent., without the least suspicion as to the existence of an *international* rate of interest, or the universal value of money, as I have described it on pages 91 to 105. And Mr. Tooke, who suggested that the Bank should never follow a falling discount market below 4 per cent., that the Bank for ordinary discount should cease to compete at 4 per cent., in spite of his high standing, laid himself open to the charge of unmitigated financial alchemy. The confusion as to Bullion Reserve (when such bullion is in circulation by way of Bank notes) is obvious. The author is seemingly unaware of the existence of the "fiduciary" portion of the issue, or the meaning of that word, else he would find that under "the effect of the Bank stopping at 4 per cent.," the accession of strength would not consist of a cash Reserve, but a fiduciary or mixed one. He would find that such a Reserve is utterly beyond the requirements of circulation and banking accommodation, that its *only* effect is that of *driving away* bullion. The reading of the paragraphs shows that their author is compelled to have recourse to arbitrary figures, assertions and declamation. He overlooks the existence of the variations in other factors beyond bullion and interest, and, although admitting that interest must regulate the whole system, he makes the rate of interest solely dependent on the rise and fall of bullion. He does not seem to be aware that this would engender the same system of *post facto* action under which we now suffer, and that another factor is required to secure the independence of the force of interest.

gold coin. The Bank always holds a stock, and pre-

The encouragement of the circulation by continual offer for real equivalents.
pares in time; and not only is the demand instantly responded to, but the *offer of supply* is continually in operation. And this offer of supply, to the extent of one or two millions, is one of the most valuable matters in our system. For whoever has worked for, or purchased, an equivalent, realisable according to the rights of commerce, is instantly able to obtain the legal metallic value for it. He need not wait for money because money is not there, on the contrary, it is offered to him beforehand. All who understand the true operation of the rules of supply and demand, the vivifying effects of the former upon the latter, will admit that upon the premises as to real equivalent, the gold circulation is not only done justice to, but that every expanse is encouraged by such a system, in accord with

The folly of demanding money without equivalents.
the true principles of valuation. The schemers for the various forms of bank note issues—whether they represent wild democracy or Scotch banks, whether they have no equivalent at all, but desire to enjoy its fruits nevertheless, or are desirous of keeping unsatisfactory matters in the hope that they will become equivalents—all overlook this plain fact, as well as the injustice and the folly of all attempts to acquire the right of incorporating "issue" so obtained with the circulation at large.

The independent concurrence between general circulation and commerce.
The freedom with which gold is thus obtainable in this country has often been extolled as one of the valuable features of our system, and with justice, although this does not exclude the fact, that certain other nations are quite as forward in this respect as we are here.* Nor is the supply of gold to the circulation

---

* See " Seignorage and the Charge for Coining."—Effingham Wilson, Royal Exchange.

necessarily dependent upon institutions like the Bank of England. In every country that has a balance of trade in its favour and receives precious metals, the importers, before undertaking the charges of shipping it elsewhere, will first endeavour to give it to the Mint for coinage, and thus keep up the principle of the "offer" at home. The Bank of England, like those of France, Prussia, Belgium, Holland, and others, can do so with less delay, and with greater economy, *pro bono publico*, because they can at once give out Bank Notes, whereas the coining process involves some delay. As I have before said, the increase in gold coin in circulation, concurrent with the increase of our general trade and population, rests upon a perfectly easy process, and results in a positive accession to the money current, when the proper proportion of the increase has been absorbed by our Banking and Clearing system.

The Bank of England note issue not absolutely required for this purpose.

We can, therefore, dismiss from consideration both the general circulation and the increase of commerce and population, for they are independent of the Bank of England. The proportion of the total amount of circulation—viz., 161 millions (see page 108) to about 25 millions of Bank of England Issue (out of which the holders can claim, say 20 millions of bullion deposited by them)—indicates the proportion of possible connection between general circulation, commerce, and the Bank. We need not bear this in mind as far as exact numbers are concerned; the inexorable demand for a fairly regular amount of Bank of England Notes indicates that the general circulation holds sway over, and commands the Bank. It follows that the *circulation* of its notes is *one of the factors* by which the Bank must be guided.

We may dismiss these first two factors as concentrated in the Bank of England note circulation.

The four factors (see page 236) now remaining are—

1. The circulation of the Bank of England Note.

2. The due proportion of Bullion.

3. The rate of interest.

4. The Reserve.

From these we may temporarily set aside the Reserve. It may strike many that the very idea of Reserve suggests an independence for this factor, that it cannot be called a true Reserve, unless it has an independent, if not inviolable existence, especially provided for. Postponing, then, this provision until we have disposed of the three factors preceding it, we find that they concern the duty of the Bank to maintain to the amount of *notes in circulation* a proper *proportion of Bullion*, by means of the *rate of Interest*. That is *prima facie*, the simple aim involving the adjustment of proportions through a lever which is perfectly automaton in its action, but which the Bank is unable to manage, although it alone has the fullest power to apply it.

It is obvious that when there arises the question of keeping due proportion, the factor to which these proportions must be held becomes the indicator. Hence *the circulation of the Bank note* is the guiding factor, and only by keeping it in view can we arrive at a combination which will secure *the proper proportion of bullion*, and so much margin by way of Reserve as will secure the situation. All attempts, therefore, to make interest act upon bullion only, are tantamount to shutting the door when the steed is stolen. If bullion is at, say, 16 millions at one time, and the circulation at 20 (assuming for a moment that such to be fair proportions), it is evident that for a circulation of 25 millions there ought to be 20 millions of bullion, and in the maintenance of proportions which can thus be made to balance by a self-acting process, and which

The factor reserve is also a separate one.

The guiding factor now becomes the amount of circulation of notes.

Bullion must be maintained in proportion thereto.

may result in a higher average or not, there lies the true Proportion of circulation to bullion the true guide. connection between our rate of interest and the international rate, the accord in the mutual system of valuation in which, through our better developed industry and commercial supremacy, we can always hold a balance in our favour. The majority of our economists quite overlook this important guide (see the notable example in foot note to page 234), unaware that the sound trade of the country manifests itself in the refusal to use the excess of issue now offered, but demands the regular maintenance of a proportion of bullion within the ranges of the active Bank of England issue.

The circulation, then, is the guide °alongside of which a level of bullion must be kept, by the simple The simple office of the rate of interest to keep bullion at a level. means of raising or lowering the rate of interest. Knowing, as we do, from experience as well as theory, that the operation of the rate of interest is inexorable and infallible, nothing would appear more simple than that a rule should be found by which its automaton action could be determined. And there are three ways in which we might arrive at this rule.

1. Presuming that we had no previous experience whatever as to its operation, we might The finding of its level. at haphazard lay down a scheme of raising the rate, in order to test it. We might commence by putting the rate rather high, and increasing it progressively. By so *overdoing* the test, the only mistake to which we might be liable would be the attraction of too much bullion—to that few would object—and we might modify our rates afterwards.

2. Having already had ample experience with the Bank of England system, we might en- The test by practice. deavour to trace the errors which we know have been committed, because they failed in keeping

16

bullion. Or, inasmuch as, on the whole, the Bank of England has finally succeeded in again obtaining bullion, and as periods occur in which the extremes are balanced, we might trace a system of average from the practice of the extremes which we find "will do." The mathematician will understand this.

Its proof by theory.

3. We might endeavour to find principles either by independent logical reasoning, subject to comparison with practice, or rules deduced from experience to be also brought back to comparison with practice, and when good reasoning thus seems to agree with practical matters, there is every chance of rendering the search successful.

In the next chapter I shall lay before you certain principles which may possibly answer this purpose, and show their combination with Reserve later on.

THE PRINCIPLES OF COMPENSATING INTEREST IN THE COMBINATION BETWEEN BULLION AND FIDUCIARY BANK NOTES.

It is necessary, firstly, that a minimum, medium, or maximum rate of interest should be established, from which the variations must be led off. The danger of fixing such a rate arbitrarily is one with which many economists are unable to cope. Most of them make 5 per cent. their favourite; others fix upon 3 per cent., as that which the State pays on Consols, because when money is *retiring* from business, it has recourse to this kind of investment. The late proposals in Parliament fixed upon 12 per cent. and 10 per cent. as standards for certain contingences. All these attempts are fallacious, and have but little or no connection

Arbitrary assumption for standard rates are fallacious.

with abstract truths. They are more or less " outside " of the matter.

The true guide for arriving at such standard rate must be taken from the working of the system itself, and the abstract ground therein contained is clearly definable as part of the whole process of valuation. The problem before us suggests it. We are called upon to maintain a given amount of Bank of England note circulation, by adjusting proportions between issue on bullion and on securities. When bullion diminishes, more fiduciary issue must go out, and interest rises, the object of the rise in interest being that of reattracting bullion. When bullion increases, less fiduciary issue is required, and interest declines. It is upon this plea of usefulness as money that fiduciary issues are made, and justifiable. But, whenever the *amount of Bullion* is *equal* to the *amount of notes in circulation*, the need for fiduciary issue for the purposes of the *circulation* (not Reserve) no longer exists.

The true abstract ground for such rates lies in the valuation itself.

If thus at any time there are 25 millions of bank notes in the hands of the public, and but 14 millions of bullion on hand, 11 millions of fiduciary issue must be used, and on 20 millions of bullion, 5 millions of such issue ; but when there are 25 millions of bullion, the fiduciary issue might be set aside for the time without any disturbance whatever to the *circulation*. This is a cardinal point in the controversy which has nothing to do with the question of Reserve, but which represents the great principle in our valuation of a perfect rest in the demand for bullion, and the absence of necessity for fiduciary issue. At such times (if the country bankers' issues are set aside), the whole business of the country is conducted on the pure unmixed metallic basis, at £3 17s 10½d per ounce of standard gold, and so there exists, for the time being, what, from the bullion point of view, may be called a " normal " state.

The point of agreement between amount of bullion and amount of circulation

The truly normal character of such a position of the issue will be more evident to you when you reflect upon an increase of bullion beyond the circulation. If 30 millions of bullion were at the Bank, but only 25 millions of notes current, the position would not be tenable. The 5 millions of bullion over and above the 25 covering the notes would be absolutely idle—*i.e.* they would resemble hoarded money, not unlike the bullion locked up in the Prussian war treasury. No bank, no private firm, nor a combination of them, would or could maintain such an idle stock of money. It would almost immediately disappear, to seek employment abroad, and serve as a means of investment. Without such outlet, a plethora of gold of this kind would prove almost as embarrassing to us as a scarcity, and the inexorable laws of the valuation could not suffer its existence. Throughout the whole history of the Bank of England, such a surplus of bullion occurred only in June and July 1871 (up to 2 millions), but this was due simply to the French, who, during the terror of the war, hoarded gold at the Bank of England. Between this extreme of plethora, with the absolute necessity to export it, and the contrary—the absolute necessity for attracting bullion—lies the state of rest arrived at when the amount of bullion covers the issue in circulation, when there is no call for either export or import of gold.

It is requisite that this should be clearly and distinctly appreciated as the abstract or neutral ground to which the matter must be led back. That it is abstract in its nature so far (as a proposition that can be made without using figures), may be admitted, for it is immaterial whether these figures refer to 10, 20, 25 or 30 millions, the principle of the agreement between bullion and circulation stands forth clearly as a " neutral " one.

The practice of the Bank of England system now shows, that in several instances, this neutral point was reached to within a variation of one-half a million.

The frequent occurence of this agreement at the Ban of England

In 1851, 1858, 1859, 1867, 1868, 1870 and 1871, the Bank of England Reserve of notes frequently equalled the amount of the fiduciary limits allowed by law, showing that the stock of bullion was equal to the amount in circulation ; and if the special Reserves of coin are taken into consideration, these instances become much more numerous. Out of the 1,409 weeks from 1845 to 1871, there were—

36 where there was such agreement, and

68 where there was a margin between 1 and 2 millions ; whilst, when the Reserve of coin is added thereto, there were

101 where the agreement was within half a million.

It follows that at such times of perfect neutrality and peace in the bullion stock of the Bank, an independent and neutral rate of interest should arise in perfect accord with our valuation. It follows also that such a rate, if not *unduly* influenced by some such overweight of Reserve as is then unnecessarily kept at the Bank under the present system, can be held at a figure which is nevertheless the lowest practicable rate, and as such it is subject only to the effect of changes in the international rate. The Bank of England, whenever such phases occur in its issue, goes down with interest to 2 per cent., and has even done business at $1\frac{3}{4}$ per cent. If the Reserve had not existed, its rates might then have been 3 or 4 per cent., or higher, subject to the test of greater accumulation of bullion. The setting aside, or partial abolition of the Reserve, whenever such a phase of agreement between bullion and circulation occurs again, would accordingly enable the Bank to hold for a higher (though moderate)

The deduction of the rate from this normal state of the valuation.

rate than hitherto, and to await the result, so that the right rate can be found by a self-acting process requiring but little discretion. (The suggestion that the Bank's lowest rates, say $1\frac{3}{4}$ per cent., should be taken as the lowest point is evidently wrong, for we know that this extremely low rate is due to the abnormal pressure of the present useless Reserves, which deteriorate our valuation much below its natural level.)

From the broad practice of the Bank.

By another method this true neutral lowest rate can be deduced from the *whole broad practice of the Bank*, after balancing excesses in one direction against excesses in the other. Logicians will admit that, between the variations taking place, there must be a central pivot of absolute steadiness for each occasion, though more or less steady for all occasions; and when, through a series of occasions, a result has been obtained which answers the purpose, the method by which this has been done, and the extreme faults thereby committed, rather confirm the existence and tenacity of the normal point. This is just the case with the Bank of England; it has succeeded by gigantic struggles, which bear the impress and absolute proof of excesses in either direction, in recovering its stock of bullion, and it follows that the true turning point can be traced by testing the extent of the excesses.

By testing the excesses.

The test of these excesses can be made in various ways. Starting from the ground that the agreement between bullion and circulation gives the " neutral" or "normal" or "lowest practical" (which ever term may be deemed suitable) rate of interest, it is then necessary to determine the ratio of increase in accordance with what the Bank has been in the practice of doing. This must be done for special periods, for years, and for the whole term, so as to prove the agreement of the rule for each term with the whole. The

amount of active circulation and the respective
amounts of bullion must be compared with the rate of
interest, so as to show what proportion of fiduciary
circulation the Bank permitted. The extreme ranges
which are brought about can be led back to the normal
state, *i.e.* when bullion is equal to circulation, viz., to
lower normal rates, of which that is the correct one,
from which the excesses in either direction are
equal in extent. It will then be found that between
the rates of 2, 2½ and 3 per cent., the first gives a
nominal excess according to which the Bank has made
too little issue, the rate of 3 per cent. shows a surplus
of actual issue made, whilst 2½ per cent. stands
just between the excesses. Now, inasmuch as
the regularity of the circulation does not admit of
actual over or under issues, the excesses committed
concern unduly low rates of interest, unjustifiable in
presence of the amount of circulation *versus* stock of
bullion, leading to extreme high rates afterwards.
The author has made this test in elaborate tables,
printed in one of his publications, and to these tables
he will later on refer again. The description here
given of this test will show that nothing arbitrary has
been attempted, for the whole proceeding rests again
on abstract proposition, and the deduction of the
normal rate is made from the whole result itself. It
will be found that neither deposits nor other matters
interfere with this rate, the only influence is that of
the international rate. It will hereafter be shown
how, by a proper system of Reserve, it can guide all
necessary variations for increase of circulation at home,
and demand for bullion for coinage, as well as international purposes.

The ratio of increase of interest must next be
determined. If the circulation is at 25 millions, bul-

The practical
test results
in the rate
of 2½ per
cent.

As that on
which the
excesses
below
are
committed.

The
deduction
is abstract
and not
arbitrary.

The ratio of increase of interest to protect bullion. lion at the same amount, and interest 2½ per cent., what rates of interest must be adopted when bullion falls to say 20, 15 or 10 millions, either so as to recover the proper level or for its maintenance ? The inference that some distinct—if not mathematically correct—rule must prevail is natural, a decline of 10 millions of bullion evidently requires a definitely greater proportion of force than one of 5 millions only, for the Determinable by experience within the known ranges of interest. recovery of bullion. If, like in the previous case of normal interest, we were quite ignorant of experience, and chose to apply, at haphazard, the known range of interest from 2½ to 10 per cent., within which absurd extravagances are not likely to arise, selecting 5, or 6, or 8 per cent. for any comparatively moderate reduction of bullion, we could not do wrong on the mere score of obtaining more bullion. For the wholesome and natural corrective, here acting in accord with interest, is *time*. If interest at 8 per cent. is too high, Subject to the natural control of duration of time of each change. it will act more quickly, too quickly perhaps, and 6 per cent., with more extension of time, might have the same effect. Duration of time, involving perhaps days only, can therefore proportionately expedite or modify the violence of attraction of bullion, and this is a most important matter, not only as the ready and natural corrective in any reasonably regular, or even strictly mathematical scheme for the ratio of increase in interest, but as guiding the whole case for the prevention of extremes in either direction.

But, as we have already made sufficient experience The practice of the Bank affords a distinct available guide. with what the Bank of England does, in order to recover bullion from certain stages of deterioration in the stock of bullion, and can trace the proportions to the rates of interest adopted in these special periods, as well as for the purpose of general agreement between them, we can take advantage of the experience already gained. It will be found that the Bank's practice does result in an agreement between periods, and gives a definite average which, under the corrective of time, may be pronounced as operative, and, when free from the overweight of Reserve, will become unfailing far within the present extreme divergences of interest.

Before showing this, I propose herewith to demonstrate a theoretical rule, and to show its general agreement with the practice of the Bank when shorn of its extremes. In all matters requiring the restoration of an equilibrium between two opposing but connected elements, the one element from which the action proceeds must initiate the same with *double* force, so that it may obtain the level by the equal division of the effect. The most commonplace and familiar illustration of this rule is afforded by buying and selling; if the seller asks 101 for his article, and the buyer offers 99, all being clear of interference, the compromise takes place at 100. In physical science, the law of level as represented, say by two upright tubes, connected at the base, demands that when the level of liquid in one tube is to rise 1 inch, 2 inches of addition are required. Most marked is this rule in all that concerns exchanges, if in one country the rate stands at say 25, and in another at 24, and either begin to operate, the final adjustment is 24½. Investigate all other matters of supply and demand, in their connection with prices and offers, and you will find, that when left to themselves, the approach will be made simultaneously from either side, until they meet for settlement half way within the force originally put into activity.

The application of this rule of the double bid to the case of attracting bullion can now best be illustrated to you when you imagine the following situation :—

Supposing there were 15 millions of bullion, interest being at 5 per cent., but for some reason or another 18 millions of bullion, or $\frac{1}{5}$th more were required, a rise of $\frac{1}{5}$th in the rate of interest, from 5 to 6 per cent., would not suffice to produce it. Against the demand, enhanced by $\frac{1}{5}$th, the supply would resist in an equal measure, and instead of 3 millions of bullion, only $1\frac{1}{2}$ would be drawn over. Accordingly, the rate must rise by $\frac{2}{5}$ths, from 5 to 7 per cent., in order to produce the *one-half* which is wanted as a whole. Of the mathematically paramount and absolute force of this rule, as it daily and hourly demonstrates itself, not the least doubt need be entertained. It reigns supreme through all difficulties and contingences, unless these are of a nature to constitute a third element ranged in support of one of the original two, but the power of such third element can never be anything more than a transitory and inferior one, the original forces of supply and demand are the powerful magnets approaching each other. Any disturbance or hindrance caused by such third element is counteracted by a fourth consideration, viz., the greater or lesser duration of time, and consequent greater tension at the disposal of the demand. Between these equalising forces the action of the double bid must become unfailing and almost truly automaton.

The true automaton action of the double bid.

Referring back now to the state of the issue when bullion is at the same amount as circulation, say 24 millions, and interest rules at $2\frac{1}{2}$ per cent., if 4 millions were withdrawn, the minimum rate would have to rise at once to $3\frac{1}{2}$ per cent. (or as much higher as the state of the international interest, to be hereafter referred to with the subject of Reserve, would justify). Or, if with a state of bullion and circulation at 25 millions, the latter were to increase suddenly to 30 millions, a rise of interest to $3\frac{1}{2}$ per cent. would at once be required. If there were, say, 20 millions of bullion, upon a circulation of 24, and interest at $3\frac{1}{2}$, if 4 more

Examples of its working.

bullion were withdrawn, or if the circulation increased (without withdrawal of bullion) to 30 millions, the rate of interest must at once be raised to 5 per cent. If upon the same circulation bullion were to fall to 12 millions, the rate would be $7\frac{1}{2}$ per cent.; if, as it did in 1857, bullion fell to 6 millions, upon a circulation of 21, interest would have to rise to 15 per cent.

The rule would simply involve this—that for every $\frac{1}{2}$ per cent. rise on the rate of $2\frac{1}{2}$ per cent., which accordingly is equal to 20 per cent., a proportion of fiduciary issue may be made equal to 10 per cent. on the existing stock of bullion until the level of the circulation is reached. Accordingly, the lower the bullion falls, the more intense becomes the pressure, because for every 10 per cent. allowable for fiduciary issue $\frac{1}{2}$ per cent. increase of interest is requisite, and the lower the bullion falls, the smaller and the more frequent become the 10 per cent. upon its amount, required to fill up the gap to circulation. Upon this system the following table may be constructed, showing : *The simple rule.*

> 1. The extreme ranges of the Bank of England circulation from 18 to 28 millions. (N.B.—It must be distinctly borne in mind that these are not spasmodic ranges, but gradual increase since 1844—1845=21 millions—1873=25 millions). *Construction of a table to show its working.*

> 2. The amount of bullion from 6 millions to 27 millions (referring only to bullion in the issue and excluding coin in the Banking Department).

> 3. The corresponding rate of interest.

In laying this table before you, I must ask you now, ere you try conclusions upon it, to let me show you how it agrees with the *average* practice of the Bank of England when that practice is cleared of its extremes.

Table 16.—Showing amount of Circulation and Bullion, with rates of Interest to correspond.

		Circulation (Millions).										
		18	19	20	21	22	23	24	25	26	27	28
		Rates of Interest.										
Bullion (Millions).	6	12½	13½	14½	15							
	7	10½	11½	13	13½	14						
	8	9	9½	10	10½	11½	12					
	9	7½	8	9	9½	10	10½	11				
	10	6½	7	7½	8	8½	9	9½	10	10½		
	11	6	6½	7	7½	7½	8	8½	9	9½	10	10½
	12	5	5½	6	6½	7	7½	7½	8	8½	9	9½
	13	4½	5	5½	6	6	6½	7	7½	7½	8	8½
Millions of Bullion.	14	4	4½	5	5	5½	6	6	6½	7	7½	8
	15	3½	4	4½	4½	5	5½	5½	6	6½	7	7½
	16	3½	3½	4	4½	4½	5	5	5½	6	6	6½
	17	3	3½	3½	4	4	4½	4½	5	5½	5½	6
	18	2½	3	3½	3½	4	4	4½	4½	5	5½	5½
	19		2½	3	3½	3½	4	4	4½	4½	5	5
	20			2½	3	3	3½	3½	3½	4	4	4½
	21				2½	3	3	3½	3½	3½	4	4
	22					2½	3	3	3½	3½	3½	4
	23						2½	3	3	3½	3½	3½
	24							2½	3	3	3½	3½
	25								2½	3	3	3½
	26									2½	3	3
	27										2½	3
	28											2½

It is not necessary to carry interest higher in this table, but any higher rates might be added.

The degree of agreement between the rates of interest in the above table, and the practice of the Bank of England, can be traced by comparing with it the circulation, bullion, and rate of interest at the Bank at any time; and this will clearly show how, at certain crisis points, or when otherwise the situation was intelligible, the theory here adopted agrees with the practice. Of these I select as notable examples—

Millions and Decimals.

		Circulation.	Bullion.	Bank Rate.	'Actual fiduciary circulation.	Theoretical fiduciary circulation.
1857.						
31 Oct.	...	20·3	8·1	8 °/₀	12·2	12·1
11 Nov.	...	20·1	6·6	10 °/₀	13·5	13·2
1866.						
18 April	...	22·1	13·0	5 °/₀	9·1	9·1
30 May	...	25·9	11·4	10 °/₀	17·5	17·0
26 Sept.	...	23·0	15·6	5 °/₀	7·4	7·8
1870.						
22 June	...	22·4	20·5	3 °/	1·9	2·0
1871.						
31 May	...	24·1	24·1	2 °/	nil	nil

The exact agreement of the rule at the very dates when the crises of 1857 and 1866 were at their height, confirms its truth ; whilst the periods quoted in 1870 and 1871 show its validity in the direction of plethora. Numerous other instances may be shown wherein the practice agrees. It is of course understood that at other times there is complete disagreement, the Bank going far too low in most of them, and frequently, by way of rebound, too high.

A complete analysis of the practice of the Bank, taking the respective changes of interest, and that at the end of each year with the corresponding status of circulation and bullion as manageable instances, has been made by the author, in tables published in " Reform of the Bank of England."* To these tables attention has already been made on page 247 of this chapter. They are constructed so as to demonstrate at the same time that the neutral rate lies at $2\frac{1}{2}$ per cent., and not at 2 or 3 per cent.

Of the 198 instances of changes in the rate of interest from 1845 to 1871, so investigated, and placed in comparison with systems based on 2, $2\frac{1}{2}$, and 3 per cent., the following results appear :—

* These are too extensive for republication here. Readers who desire to investigate these tables can have copies of the above-mentioned publication by applying to the author, at No. 1A, Princes Street, Mansion House, City.

TABLE 17.—Degrees of Agreement and Excesses between the practice of the Bank of England from 1845 to 1871, and the rule enunciated, compared with basis of 2, 2½, and 3 per cent. as lowest rates on 198 instances of changes.

	Excess of low Interest by too small a proportion of bullion in circulation by															Agreements within one million.	Excess of high Interest by too small a proportion of fiduciary circulation by													
	15	14	13	12	11	10	9	8	7	6	5	4	3	2	1		1	2	3	4	5	6	7	8	9	10	11	12	13 millions.	
At 2 per Cent.																														
Instances.										1	2	4	15	12	16	43	20	15	18	9	9	55	3	5	4	3	6	3		Instances.
At 2½ per Cent.																														
Do.									6	5	11	18	14	30	31	36	13	6	6	6	6	6								Do.
At 3 per Cent.																														
Do.	1	1	2	1	1	5	4	12	17	25	26	19	27	16		21	6	7	5	2										Do.

This Table clearly shows that, whereas at 2 per cent. as the presumed normal rate, the excesses range from 6 on one side to 13 on the other: at 3 per cent., the reverse, from 15 to 5, takes place: whilst, at 2½ per cent., they stand as 7 to 7. If, when bullion was equal to circulation, the rate of 2 per cent. had been the *naturally lowest* rate, the whole issue system would have resulted in an average of too *much* bullion, whereas at 3 per cent., the contrary, an average of too little bullion would have prevailed. Both cases are refuted by the fact that bullion is now at present in fair proportion, proving that the rate of 2½ per cent. is that from which the excesses in either direction are equal in extent, and make this rate the central point as the *lowest normal rate.*

Assuming now that in accordance with what has been said on page 113, the Bank of England circulation, as independent of bullion, may vary of itself within two millions either way, stretching the points of agreement, on the rate of 2½ per cent., to that extent, the following results would appear, as compared with the numbers of weeks of the respective rates of interest from 1845 to 1871 inclusive :—

	Excesses of low Interest by millions.						Instances of Agreement within 2 millions.								Excesses of high Interest by millions.					
	7	6	5	4	3	2									2	3	4	5	6	7
Instances	6	5	11	18	14	30			80						6	6	6	4	6	7
Rates of Interest per cent.			2	2½	3		3½	4	4½	5 •	5½	6	6½		7	8	9	10		
Duration of each rate by weeks			122	195	306		115	143	61	138	72	72	5		39	37	11	20		

And what you must decide is :—*firstly*, whether the extremely low rates of interest below 3 per cent. are due to the heavy idle Reserve of notes, and cause the consequent rebound above 6¼ per cent.; and *secondly*, whether, if these low rates were avoided, and the instances and weeks of their duration were in future comprised within the range from 3½ to 6¼ per cent., we should keep bullion at a more regular level.

I may have succeeded before this in showing to you that when the heavy Reserve of the Bank is set aside for the time, the Bank regains full liberty to hold whatever rate it likes, subject only to possible variations in the market rate upon changes in the international rate. The international rate, as far as the participation in it of States like America, Russia, Turkey, Austria, and other borrowers are concerned, must necessarily be above ours. The participation of States like France and Germany, financially independent as we are, need not go below our rate; and, as a matter of fact, it has been higher than ours. In Prussia it was maintained at 4 per cent., even during the great supply of money in the early times of Californian and Australian gold shipments; but if they should go lower than ourselves, their surplus will find employment in borrowing states, the same as our own would under similar circumstances.

The rate of $2\frac{1}{2}$ per cent., as deduced from the abstract reasoning and the practical results laid before you, may therefore be regarded as the lowest admissible; but it must now be shown to you that the *conditions of the Issue* and the interests of the *Bank in connection therewith*, demand, as the lowest limit, a rate by so much higher as will pay for the expenditure of the issue. The rate of $2\frac{1}{2}$ per cent. is the result of our investigation as to what I have called the normal state of agreement between bullion and circulation, and represents the principle of the valuation then in force. But as we have before ascertained, the nature of an issue does not require this full measure of bullion, for it would then virtually be a bullion issue, and the issuer would be unable to recover the expenses which are now discharged from the fiduciary issue.

The technical expenses of the Bank of England Issue now amount to £185,000 per annum (see page

The liberty of the Bank to keep interest at a suitable level to international rates.

The practically lowest rate for the maintenance of the issue.

Sufficient to cover the technical costs of the issue.

181). Reducing this (by excluding matters not necessarily appertaining to the issue itself) to £150,000 per
annum, the interest earned on fiduciary issue of 4 to 5
millions might be regarded as sufficient to cover them, The fair rate resulting from the moderate issue.
and to leave a small margin. According to what is shown
by the table on page 252, upon a circulation of, say 25
millions, consisting of 20 millions of bullion and 5
millions of fiduciary issue, the rate would be $3\frac{1}{2}$ per
cent.—that is to say, whether the circulation be 23 or
25, or 28 millions, or any other practicable amount,
with bullion in corresponding proportions, the rate to
be maintained as the lowest, need not be less than
$3\frac{1}{2}$ per cent.

The Bank, therefore, need never go below that Its accord with inter-national rates.
rate, because—

> (1) There is *no need to go below the*
> *international rate*, and unless a very sudden
> supply of fresh gold were to come into the
> world's market, this international rate will
> never be below ours.

> (2) Because it is in the interest of the
> Bank, at least as far as the mere recouping Its fair level for the issue itself.
> of the expenses is concerned, to uphold 4 or 5
> millions of fiduciary issue, and for this purpose
> to maintain the rate of interest at a fair level.

It cannot be sufficiently impressed upon you that
the market rate can exercise no direct commanding Its agree-ment with the market rate.
influence upon the Bank rate, unless through the
international rate. No additional supply of gold can
come to this country without being first incorporated
with the Bank of England issue. The Bankers
(excepting the country Bankers authorised to issue)
cannot create notes or actual currency. They cannot
make any addition to the stock of money. If, occasionally, they have larger temporary reserves of actual
money, such larger reserves come from the country

and industrial districts, and flow back again. These phases I have described on pages 152 to 163. It is evident when, with the daily divergencies of a few hundred thousand pounds, the Bank of England stands there with 9, 12, or 15 millions of Reserve, seeking use for it, that Bankers can forestall the Bank itself in going lower, and (as already said on pages 165 to 167) this explains the whole enigma of the seemingly independent influence of the market. Remove this idle Reserve, and both the Bank and the market need not run this ruinous race; they can hold to fair, moderate rates without going lower than the international rate or universal valuation.

On the removal of idle Reserve.

From this point we require nothing more than the consideration of higher rates. The variations in international rates (*universally* dearer money), tell us to keep a watchful eye on the rise and fall of the exchanges. The Bank might watch these, but it is under no obligation to do so, for it is our market rate which will tell the tale first. This in its turn will cause demand at the Bank, and the Bank need but follow the rise. In doing so, any discrepancy of $\frac{1}{2}$ per cent. or more, for a short time, would not make much difference; nay, even if the whole average of our rates were, say $\frac{1}{4}$ to $\frac{1}{2}$ per cent. under the international rate (instead of the present frequent 2 or 3 per cent.), it would not do much harm. On the contrary, being a wealthy nation, and continually amassing gold, we must necessarily part with a regular surplus, and this would be safely, equitably, and profitably done by a rate *slightly* below the rates of other nations.

Higher rates of interest.

Our average level may be slightly below others.

This fair rate, the result of our supremacy, will also be that which gives to our industry and commerce the naturally more advantageous contract basis, now so frequently disorganised and destroyed by the violent

The legitimate advantage of our position.

movements of from 2 to 10 per cent., producing an average much higher than what ought to be. Variations will, of course, occur, as the regulating force of interest must be brought to bear upon the maintenance of bullion; but besides the comparative peace established by the proposed system, the average rate of interest will be below the present one, and tend to encourage our industry and commerce in a more regular manner.

The proportion of bullion suitable to such rate of interest, or that near to it, as the actual operation of the *system will settle by itself*, would, therefore, be

The proper proportion of bullion to notes in circulation.

> With 25 millions of circulation,
> 20 millions of bullion,
> Giving 5 millions of fiduciary notes for expenses,
> Or, with 30 millions of circulation,
> 25 or 24 millions of bullion,
> Giving 5 or 6 millions of fiduciary issue for expenses;

and, in accordance with other changes (rise or fall) of circulation, corresponding proportions of bullion should be maintained.*

The main cause of the low rates through idle heavy Reserve being removed (a fair minimum rate being the

---

* At the moment of this going to press the author's eye alights upon an article in one of our principal papers, wherein the prospects of the money market are discussed. It so happens that the "Reserve" of the Bank is 13 millions, and that the Bank rate is 3 per cent. The writer of the article says, "The Bank is now strong, and money is cheap; but should one of the seemingly inexplicable foreign drains of bullion again occur, we must expect the rate to rise to 6 or 7 per cent." It is most extraordinary that the would-be wise men who write articles of this kind, although they are aware that, when we force interest high, we attract bullion (*i.e.* drain the foreigner), are unable to perceive that when we unduly lower the rate we perform the contrary, and send bullion

result of the natural features of the whole issue), all that the Bank would be required to do is that it should poise the rate at suitable levels, so as to maintain the proportion of bullion once reached, as sufficient to answer the purpose. Now, if you investigate the principles upon which this matter is laid before you, and compare it to schemes which try to establish some absolutely distinct or arbitrary rate of interest, or some definite amount of bullion, utterly at variance with practice, you will see that this system provides for a complete self-adjustment, as far as circulation, bullion, fiduciary issue, and rates of interest are concerned. The only starting point here taken by way of figures (indispensible when figures are concerned), is based upon the principle that it is deducible by practice from that state of the issue, when the *amount of circulation is equal to the amount of Bullion,* a perfectly intelligible matter to which the expression "normally lowest rate of interest" seems thoroughly suitable. This starting point itself, as you will perceive, dissolves again in the system, so that the rates and figures with which I have dealt here, appear only as illustrating the working of the principle.

You must decide whether the statements laid before you bear out the more or less scientific nature of the proposed scheme of regulating interest. If you should think that it will give order and certainty upon self-acting principles, that, with seemingly hard figures, it appears too strict, bear in mind that one of the great

Marginal notes:
The plain principles here made evident as self-acting.

The starting point of lowest interest dissolves again in the system itself.

The order and certainty resulting therefrom and its corrective.

---

away. They then charge the foreigner with causing "a foreign drain"—the unhappy foreigner being all the while innocent of any intention to drain our market. I hope that I have made this matter clear to you—that the *drain does not arise,* but that it is *deliberately caused by our own unduly low rates,* which send away, as if by main force, the small proportion of bullion which the Bank of England need but guard as *status quo.*

correctives alongside of such figures, as already pointed out to you, is the pliable subject of *time*—viz., the greater or lesser length of periods for each rate, determinable by the results as they are made manifest. But there is yet another corrective, overlying the self-acting process and its regulator as an extra force, giving additional certainty to the system against all possible contingencies. This corrective is afforded by the " Reserve " of the system, explained in the next chapter.

The corrective. of time and reserve.

THE RESERVE OF THE COMPENSATING SYSTEM OF BANK NOTE ISSUE.

There can be no doubt that, according to every rule in Banking and matters of commercial intercourse generally, a " Reserve " must be kept, but the object, extent, character and influence of such a Reserve must be clearly definable and must not, as by the present system, be subject to mere rough guesswork, or the almost unmanageable haphazard which defies all efforts.

The necessity of reserve and its clear purpose.

The character of the Reserve of the system proposed by me, and its material difference from that with which the Bank now works, will be made at once apparent to you on reference to the table of composition between circulation, bullion and interest, given on page 252. In that table the first guiding point is the *circulation of the Bank note.* If, by means of the rate of interest, the system aims at keeping the level of *bullion in proportion* to total amounts of the *circulation,* the same automatic action is available to keep the level up to total amounts of *circulation and Reserve combined* in one sum, the proportion of Reserve thus to be kept and protected being entirely at our option. The rates of interest given in that table are deduced from the practice of the Bank, as far as it has

If Bullion can be secured in due proportion to circulation, the same force can secure the addition of Reserve.

succeeded in keeping bullion within the range of the extremes. But inasmuch as the rates in that table will not fall so low as the Bank allows them to fall now, no extreme for the recovery of bullion thus wantonly lost need take place. The practice, in accordance with these rates, will consequently tend to keep bullion at a proportionate level with the circulation. If, then, we succeed fairly in keeping, say 20 millions of bullion with 25 millions of circulation, because we point interest in the proportion of 25 to 20 (see the double bid system explained on pages 249 and 250), it follows that if beyond the 25 millions of circulation we desire a Reserve of 5, 10, or 15 millions, we must point interest in the respective proportions of 30, 35, or 40 to 20 of bullion—*i.e.* raise it successively· so as to secure such Reserves.

By proportionate increase in rates of Interest.

According to the table on page 252, and selecting 25 millions as the circulation at one time, let us assume that Reserves running from 1 to 15 millions were required in addition to the circulation, giving totals of from 25 to 40 millions of notes for the due proportion of bullion, commencing with 25 millions of bullion downwards. The operation is shown in the following table. In the second column, under the head Reserve 0, the rates correspond with the table on page 252. For 1 million of Reserve above 25 millions in circulation the rates would be $\frac{1}{2}$ per cent. higher; for 4 millions from 1 to $1\frac{1}{2}$ higher, and so on, until for 15 millions of Reserve they would rise higher by from $3\frac{1}{2}$ to 6 per cent. It is scarcely necessary to say that when bullion is in due proportion, and the fiduciary Reserve available, that we can have no need for 15 millions of idle bullion above them. The proper balance will lie between 1 and 15 millions, and the table is carried so far only in order to show the strength of the principle which it involves.

Illustrating its operation.

Table 18, showing the Rates of Interest required to secure Reserves from 0 to 15 millions upon a circulation of 25 millions, commencing with 25 millions down to 10 millions of Bullion. (Millions, 00,000 omitted.)

Reserves required from 0 to 15 Millions upon 25 Millions of Circulation.																
Reserves	0	1	2	3	4	5	6	7	8	9	10	11	12	13	14	15
Giving total Issues.	25	26	27	28	29	30	31	32	33	34	35	36	37	38	39	40
Bullion.	Rates of Interest required.															
25	2½	3	3	3½	3½	3½	4	4	4	4½	4½	5	5	5½	5½	
24	3	3	3½	3½	3½	4	4	4	4½	4½	5	5	5½	5½	6	6
23	3	3½	3½	4	4	4	4½	4½	4½	5	5	5½	5½	6	6	6½
22	3½	3½	3½	4	4	4½	4½	5	5	5½	5½	5½	6	6	6½	6½
21	3½	3½	4	4	4½	4½	5	5	5½	5½	6	6	6½	6½	7	7
20	3½	4	4	4½	5	5	5½	5½	6	6	6½	6½	7	7	7½	7½
19	4½	4½	5	5½	5½	5½	5½	6	6	6½	7	7	7	7½	7½	8
18	4½	5	5½	5½	5½	6	6	6½	6½	7	7½	7½	7½	8	8	8
17	5	5½	5½	6	6	6½	6½	7	7½	7½	8	8½	8½	9	9	9½
16	5½	6	6	6½	6½	7	7	7½	8	8½	8½	9	9½	9½	10	10
15	6	6½	7	7½	7½	7½	8	8½	8½	9	9½	9½	10	10½	10½	11
14	6½	7	7½	8	8	8½	8½	9	9½	9½	10	10½	10½	11	11½	12
13	7½	7½	8	8½	8½	9	9½	9½	10	10½	11	11½	11½	12	12½	13
12	8	8½	9	9½	9½	10	10½	11	11½	12	12½	12½	13			
11	9	9½	10	10½	11	11½	12	12½	12½							
10	10	10½	11	11½	12	12½	13				&c.		&c.			

You will see by this, that as more Reserve is required, or as more bullion goes away, so interest rises in proportion, the action of the latter necessity being confirmed, or "double-locked," by the former. The proportionate increase or decrease.

Every other state of the circulation below or above the 25 millions, here assumed for illustration, can be so arranged under one general table. Thus, if the rates Suitable to all amounts of circulation.

given on page 252, deducted from present practice, bring a fair average result, we need only add such

And desirable Reserve. amounts of Reserve as we may deem expedient to keep in addition to circulation, in order to determine the correspondingly higher rates under whose infallibility this Reserve must be attracted and collected with ease.

Illustration in another form. To make the matter more clear to you as far as the rate of interest is concerned, I submit a short table, similarly constructed, placing bullion at the top, upon a supposed circulation of 25 millions, with from 25 to 15 millions of bullion and respective Reserves of 2, 5, 7, 10 and 15 millions.

Table 19, showing the Effect on Rise in Rate of Interest by Successive Reserves of 2, 5, 7, 10 and 15 millions on Circulation of 25 millions.

Millions of Bullion upon Circulation of 25 Millions.										
25	24	23	22	21	20	19	18	17	16	15
Bullion. Rates of Interest required.										
Without Reserve 2½	3	3	3½	3½	3½	4½	4½	5	5½	6
With 2 millions 3	3½	3½	3½	4	4	5	5½	5½	6	7
„ 5 „ 3½	4	4	4½	4½	5	5½	6	6½	7	7½
„ 7 „ 4	4	4½	5	5	5½	6	6½	7	7½	8
„ 10 „ 4½	5	5	5½	6	6½	7	7½	8	8½	9½
„ 15 „ 6	6	6½	6½	7	7½	8	8½	9½	10	11

That is to say : As a usual thing the rates of interest to be adopted " without Reserve " will suffice to keep bullion at the proper level, such rates ranging from

Ranges of interest dependent on Reserve chosen. 2½ to 6 per cent. ; but if 2 millions of Reserve be required they will range from 3 to 7 per cent. *Five Millions* of Reserve require a minimum of 3½ per cent., and so, with every additional million of Reserve wanted, interest must rise until with 15 millions it would range from 6 to 11 per cent.

The characteristics which distinguish the Reserve so arising from that of the present system are the following :— The essential difference

1. The *present Reserve* not only competes with bullion and drives it away from the country, but when, after having done so, it is called upon to act as Reserve to show its supposed practical utility, it causes, by its disappearance, the most violent commotions in the rate of interest. Between th present Reserve

2. The *Reserve here proposed* takes precisely the contrary course. Its creation is dependent on the rate of interest, which, at whatever amount the sum in Reserve is held, assists in attracting bullion continuously, and when the rate of interest rises, the Reserve *increases* in proportion with the danger. And the proposed Reserve.

This is the true office to be performed by a fiduciary note Reserve, and all the suggestions as to our keeping " larger Reserves," ("a regular Reserve of 15 or 16 millions " as the author of "Lombard Street" wishes it) are utterly idle and futile in face of the direct " negative " implied in the present Reserve, but will at once meet with realisation, if the course is taken of rendering the Reserve a real "positive." The true us of fiduciary issue.

Whenever the present Reserve diminishes and extreme danger threatens on that account—people are apt to wonder why we in England, with perhaps, £1,000 million of claims on abroad, should be unable to keep up our stock of gold. They naturally suggest " why should we not sell or recall a few millions of such claims," for these investments appear to be the true Reserve power of the country, and actually increase our stock of money, even to a positive surplus of bullion, whenever we make sudden and violent calls on them. The *sudden* realisation of such claims cannot take place without great efforts and great loss, but if we established this positive Reserve, we The decline of present Reserve and enforced realisation of claims.

should *keep a continual hold* upon such portion
of the investments which we may require to realise
into gold—it being then entirely at our option to lower
the rate of interest and the Reserve, if we find gold
come in too fast, and to keep them at such level as
will suit us. And the tension which would thus be
continually maintained need but a slight effort, in order
to give us an actual bullion Reserve, even over and
above our requirements. For, as those who can duly
appreciate the system will easily perceive, the deliberate
increase of fiduciary Reserve, concurrent with increase
of interest, means nothing less than supplying the
extra force for attracting bullion and holding it in
abeyance, subject only to almost instantaneous action.
Every increase in this Reserve must consequently
bring bullion to a level, from which the next higher
step turns the scale instantly in our favour.

The present Reserve increases when interest falls,
both factors operate against each other with double
violence, whereas by the common-sense view of the
matter, they ought to act in unison, as they will do
by the system here proposed. Our economists must
try to appreciate this simple matter before they will
cease to make wild guesses as to " what proportion of
Reserve must be kept at the Bank," and steer clear of
all the irrelevant matters that now strew the road.
That this is a simple matter nobody will deny ; it
involves a plain change in arithmetic—the substitution
of *subtraction* for *addition, i.e.* instead of *adding* the
present Reserve to the stock of money (falsely calculating interest thereon, causing the simultaneous destruction of both bullion and Reserve), we ought to
deduct the Reserve from the stock of money and poise the
rate of interest, not only so as if that Reserve did not
exist, but as *if it required guarding first of all*. No great
stretch of intellect is required to perceive that this is

Margin notes:
The continual hold by the proposed Reserve upon such claims.

Subject to instantaneous action.

The dis-union or union of the factors.

The simplicity of the matter.

The substitution of sub-traction for addition.

neither a complicated nor an ingenious matter, that its discovery and application resembles many events in daily and in household life, where precisely the same plain principles of common sense act with unfailing certainty. To the mathematician, and to the plainest logician, this problem ought to offer no difficulty whatever. It is absolutely true in its principle, for the timely and precautionary regulation of the rate of interest, is the main point in the controversy, and the upholding of the circulation, with its concurrent regularity of bullion, is that of primary importance. You will now understand what I have said in previous parts of this book as regards the fallacy under which we labour with the present Reserve, and the *total change of policy required* (see page 152, line 9). This total change of policy lies in the turn from *addition* to *subtraction;* both will give us Reserves of equal amounts, but the *added* Reserve brings *ruin and confusion;* the *subtracted* Reserve, *regularity and absolute safety.*

The common sense and plain logic involved.

The reversal of present practice and the safety resulting therefrom.

Of the degree of safety which the system gives you may be able to judge if you bear in mind the following facts :—

The degree of safety.

1. That it does away with the unduly low rates of interest, and thereby removes the chief causes of withdrawals of bullion, and the consequent future unduly high rates.

Abolition of undue low rates.

2. That it provides rise and fall in the rate of interest for the maintenance of bullion in due proportion to circulation by a proven pro rata principle, to be compared with the Bank of England's own successful efforts.

Provision of proven pro rata action.

3. That "time" is the first extra corrective element for any possible extra effort required, by greater or lesser duration of tension.

Its first corrective of time.

4. That *above this, the system of Reserve* supplies a third check or regulator, and this is of especial

importance to what I have said on *international interest.*

If that international interest should at any time rise higher, the Bank of England need but increase its Reserve in order to fully meet such a case, as it is shown in the table on page 263.

For if, in ordinary times, the upholding of the rates against the 25 millions of circulation without special Reserve will already exercise the necessary

balancing effect, the successive additions of Reserve will, with still greater firmness, enhance their power. If international interest rose 2 per cent., 5 millions *more* Reserve will meet the case. At the present time, for instance, the German demands cause a general rise in the bid for gold, and other changes in the valuations are in prospect, which may make gold universally dearer. In order to meet all these contingencies, the Bank *need but determine, at its own option,* to create more Reserve by *simply raising the rate,* and the natural concurrence between the occasion and the proper remedy will here strike you.

For all and every other possible cause or contingency, the Reserve system so established will act as the positive regulating force, remaining in existence and progressively increasing in power, not only leaving the circulation and all other matters undisturbed, but protecting and guarding them in their integrity.

The Reserve so arising will not be actually used— on the contrary, it will be kept sacred, and go down on its own accord when the occasion disappears. Although, as we know, the circulation will not absorb a large sum of Reserve, nevertheless, if on any sudden emer-gency 1 or 2 millions of it were required to temporarily

supply home use, it would be granted without the slightest disturbance to the rate of interest. *The strength and security of the defensive attitude would enable us to do so.* (Our present nervousness on the withdrawal of a few £100,000 for home use appears so very ludicrous in comparison with this.)

What amount of such Reserve shall the Bank hold? Must it be 20 millions, 15 millions, 10, 5, or less, or more? We are so much accustomed to the cry of large Reserves, that the question in this extreme form is by no means surprising. It may strike you that when we have succeeded in maintaining bullion in due proportion to circulation, and thereby have done all that concerns Bullion and *Banking Reserve* (for the circulation means Banking accommodation), there is no great need for 20, 15, or 10 millions of Reserve, even if, as suggested by this scheme, the Reserve costs the Bank nothing and does not appear in the accounts. It will be obvious to you that if the circulation is at 25 millions, and bullion at 20, and the Bank holds interest, on 5 millions of Reserve, at 5 per cent., (see Table at p 263), international interest being at the same rate, the Bank would be foolish to go as high as 7½ per cent., in order to secure an unnecessary Reserve of 15 millions. Not only would the market counteract this, by competition, but this high rate would speedily attract a surplus of bullion to be got rid of by a correspondingly quick reduction in the rate. Those who have no predjudice in favour of a large idle Reserve, will have recognised, long ago, that the system proposed here principally aims at the determination of the suitable rates of interest, which in reality is all that is required.

The amount of Reserve must therefore be balanced on more reasonable considerations, *in fact,* such is the self-acting nature of the whole arrangement that *Circulation, Bullion, Interest* and *Reserve* will find their natural level by a self-acting process, and the proper indicator which gives the initiative to this

The presumed amount of such Reserve.

Will be determined by natural indications.

In reality by rates of Interest.

The balancing of this Reserve

process will ultimately be the legitimate business offering itself at the Bank! Under such conditions

it may then often suit the Bank to keep but 5 millions or less Reserve, at another time to keep 10, for *recollect* this, if any other *emergency* should turn up, the Bank can at *any time* enlarge *the Reserve*. The power to do so lies yet behind all the regulators provided for. And in the due management of this raising and lowering of the Reserve, thus supernatant

on firm active factors, *the discretion of the directors of the Bank of England* finds its proper sphere. It will *engender that superior view of international and general matters of commerce*, which alone should guide the policy of the Bank, freeing us from all the petty expe-

dients to which we are now compelled to have recourse. The scheme submitted, *without reserve*, will cover all these, and secure us against errors ; *with the supernatant reserve*, it will absolutely secure us over and above this according to the degrees of Reserve chosen.

Of other sudden and indefinite contingencies,

revolution and terrible war alone could upset the financial strength of this country. But should these occur (which God forbid), the *very system* here suggested would be applicable to maintain order and regularity. Instead of making the wild at random issues which States like Austria, America

and others have done, and setting aside bullion, the principles of the system here submitted need only be stretched upon some definite and perfectly intelligible plan, which would hold together all the factors, as if by a series of threads which only require drawing in again in order to restore the original solidity of our valuation. Political financial economists of all countries might be willing to understand this, and to derive a lesson from the hint.

THE AMENDMENT OF CLAUSES 2 AND 8 OF THE PRESENT ACT, IN ACCORDANCE WITH THE PROPOSED SYSTEM.

On pages 217 to 224 I have shown you that the amendment of Clause 8 of the Act, would give to the Bank the liberty of carrying out the evident intention of Clause 2; and, if this were done, the principle of reduction and increase of the issue would find its natural application. No great error could be committed that would not at once show its effect and point at the remedy; nevertheless it might be advisable to start at once with some such orderly and well-digested plan as I have ventured to propose. The Bank might take it as a guide of practice, and would undoubtedly confirm its validity. <small>The desirability of prescribing orderly action.</small>

Indeed, the question might here be raised, " Why should there be any alteration at all in the Act, for if this system concerns principally the better, timely and precautionary rates of interest, the Bank need but practise it, and bullion will remain at the level." This is undoubtedly true, and as regards the mere £195,000 per annum which the State exacts, the Bank itself would not only be sufficiently liberal-minded to bear this charge, but the improvement in matters generally would be a counterpoise; nevertheless, no prudent and honest-minded statesman would recommend this course. The present gross profit of the issue of 15 millions must first go towards expenses, for which less than 5 millions are scarcely admissible, and with a proper levelling of bullion, the fiduciary issue above this may not always be insufficient to yield the State's share, whatever future increase might do. That share is derived from the assumption of the full use of the fixed 15 millions, and a serious conflict would arise if it <small>The Bank might " practise " it without reform of the Act.</small> <small>Impropriety of this suggestion.</small>

were not modified in accordance with reduced issue.
More serious than this would be the conflict between
the two kinds of Reserve,—the present as a declining,
the proposed as a rising one. It would be perfectly
impossible to reconcile these two principles without
annulling both, for they cannot act simultaneously.
The legal tender character of the supply thus created is
too directly powerful a lever to admit of so incomplete
an adjustment; the very least thing to be done, on all
pleas of justice and true economy, would be the amendment of Clause 8.

The
necessity
for reform
in Clause 8.

On the other hand, the positive incorporation of
this system into Clause 2 of the Act itself, is deserving
of attention, for the reason that, in this country, we
are justly inclined to settle matters in an orderly
manner, without leaving more scope for discretion
than absolutely necessary, and all our endeavours as
regards the valuation and money matters generally
proceed upon a basis of practical refinement, which has
done so much real good in many directions.

The sense
of order
and refine-
ment
prevalent in
England.

The introduction of this system into Clause 2 offers
no difficulty. If the Government is willing to convert
its State Debt to the Bank into Consols, or if the Bank
will take that Debt into the Banking department, and
put "Government and other securities" into the
issue as occasion may arise, a few words will suffice to
establish the system. The full wording of Clause 2
is given on page 215, the special passage to be
amended being :

Incorpora-
tion of the
system in
Clause 2.

"That it shall be lawful for the said Governor of the Bank of
England to diminish the amount of such securities, and again to
increase the same to any sum not exceeding in the whole the sum
of 15 millions, *as they may see occasion, &c.*"

Involving
but removal
of 5 words.

Instead of using the words, "as they may see
occasion," the clause might continue instead :

"In the manner following, to wit: whenever the minimum rate of interest charged by the Bank of England is 2½ per cent., the issue of notes shall not exceed the amount of bullion held in the Issue Department; but for every ½ per cent. rise above the rate of 2½ per cent. the issue may lawfully be increased in proportion of 10 per cent. on the amount of such bullion." *(And substitution of a short sentence.)*

This sentence, in proper form, would accomplish all, and yet leave the Bank with much discretion. It provides that upon every ½ per cent. rise the Bank *may* make the issue, *yet is not bound to do so.* It may either hold interest as high as it likes, or, what is the same thing, keep *such Reserve* of the issue as it may deem suitable. All charge of unduly high interest must therefore fall away, for it is this system *of Reserve*, as explained to you in the last chapter, *which becomes the intelligible acting force.* At the same time it will be seen that the Bank cannot go down to 2½ per cent. without losing the means of recovering the expenses of the issue. Under ordinary circumstances the rate need not go below 3½ per cent, although, as before said, we may, now and then, find occasion to lower our rates slightly below the international rate.* *(Leaving the discretion in Reserve.)*

No objection can be made to the incorporation of this sentence in Clause 2 on the score of legislative practice. The late Government and Parliament, through the proposals made by Mr. Lowe and Sir John Lubbock, in 1873, have themselves established the introduction of a rate of interest in the Act. They based the action *(The principle of rates of interest. Admitted by Parliament.)*

---

* As I have said before, any sudden discovery of fresh gold fields might lower the international rate generally, but the discovery of California and Australia are *historical events*, which do not repeat themselves in centuries, and the earth is sufficiently explored. Fresh gold fields can only be in the inaccessible ice-bound or the unhealthy tropical countries.

of their amendment on the rate of 10 and 12½ per cent., contingent upon events stated in the most arbitrary and assumptive manner.

As regards the rate of interest of 2½ per cent., here proposed as the "normal" one (see pages 246 to 256), you must admit at least that it is deducted from abstract proposals in financial science and confirmed by practice; and if I have demonstrated to you the self-acting powers of the whole arrangement, you may prefer the *precautionary* method to that based on 10 and 12½ per cent., which begins its action *after the mischief is done*. And here I come again to the point which marks the reduction of the whole of this controversy to within narrow limits, for the relationship between these proposals of Mr. Lowe and Sir John Lubbock and that here made is evident; all that is now required is the slight turn in favour of the recognition of the principle that the regulation of our issue system should *begin with the beginning and not with the end*.

It will be noticed also that this proposal does not necessarily involve the abolition of the limit of 15 millions, although its abolition might just as well take place. With the regulating system prescribed (the true effect of which is nothing less than the maintenance, at almost absolute level, of bullion, prepared for, carried out and strengthened by several additional means), it is not at all likely that the sum of bullion of 20 millions, or thereabouts, will ever again vary by 15 millions, as it has done, so as to call into use all the fiduciary issue which caused the withdrawal. The level will be maintained, so that the utmost possible divergence will not require more than a portion of the 15 millions. On the other hand, this very fact proves that there is no need for fixing any limit, and it may therefore as well be abolished.

THE ADVANTAGES OF THIS REFORM TO THE BANK OF ENGLAND AND THE PUBLIC.

The Bank of England, if thus freed of its present false and ruinous Reserves, and giving preference to true and rising Reserves, would be enabled to recover the full use of its capital, rest and deposits.

The freedom of its Resources secured.

On referring to pages 191 and 192, I have shown you how, when the present Reserve stands at 12 or 15 millions, or indeed at any less amount, so much of the Bank's other Reserves—viz., capital, rest and deposits —are kept idle. It might possibly strike you that if, by the adoption of the increasing issue, the Bank can always create a Reserve, there is no necessity for any specific sum being kept standing in the accounts. The Issue Department need but state the amount of notes in circulation, and the bullion and securities held against it. The item of idle, profitless Reserve in the Banking Department would therefore disappear, to be replaced by active, interest-bearing securities, and the accounts on a presumed circulation of say 25 millions and 18 of bullion *might be rendered* as follows :—

Disappearance of the idle Reserve

Plainer statement of the accounts.

ISSUE DEPARTMENT.

LIABILITIES.	ASSETS.
Notes in circulation . 25 millions	Bullion . . . . . 18 millions
	Securities . . . . 7 ,,
25 millions	25 millions

Example without specific Reserve.

BANKING DEPARTMENT.

Capital . . . . . $14\frac{1}{2}$ millions	Gov'ment Securities. 15 millions
Rest . . . . . $3\frac{1}{3}$,,	Other Securities . . $28\frac{1}{2}$,,
Public Deposits . . 7 ,,	Coin . . . . $\frac{1}{2}$,,
Other ,, . $18\frac{1}{2}$,,	
Seven Days' Bills . $\frac{1}{2}$,,	
44 millions	44 millions

Thus showing all the real resources of the Bank fully employed.

The systems of the Banks of France and Prussia do not involve any specific Reserve* But inasmuch as we here are so closely wedded to a stated Reserve, *and inasmuch, as explained in the chapter before last, the amount of express Reserve created by this system is the supernatant and really corrective factor, the amount of which gives the extra tension,* upon perfectly intelligible grounds, we may act quite wise by maintaining such an amount of extra Reserve. Assuming, then, that such temporary express Reserve need not be of the extreme amounts of 12, 15, or 18 millions, but, for argument's sake, say 5 millions, how should the accounts stand?

Why should we not in the Issue Department state "Notes in circulation," and " Notes in reserve," as representing the real meaning of the active issue? You will admit that this can easily be done, that the present method of lumping the whole issue is a meaningless *hocus-pocus*, and that a more intelligible statement is preferable. If this were done, and supposing there were 25 millions of circulation and 25 millions of bullion, with 5 millions of such " first temporary " Reserve in the Banking Department, the accounts might appear as follows :—

ISSUE DEPARTMENT.

LIABILITIES.		ASSETS.	
Notes in circulation .	25 millions	Bullion	25 millions
,, in Reserve in Banking Departmt. }	5 ,,	Securities	5 ,,
	30 millions		30 millions

Interest 3½ per cent.

---

* It might here be suggested that the two accounts should be joined into one, as it is done by the Banks of France and Prussia, who hold no special Reserves ; and many people scoff at the present separation of accounts. I have already explained before (see page 43) that I am in favour of the two accounts, and I consider their separation a valuable and scientifically true matter, provided it is done in an intelligible manner.

BANKING DEPARTMENT.

LIABILITIES.		ASSETS.	
Capital	14½ millions	Reserve of notes .	5 millions
Rest	3½ ,,	Gov'ment. Securities 13	,,
Public Deposits . .	7 ,,	Other Securities . .	25½ ,,
Other ,, .	18½ ,,	Gold and silver coin .	½ ,,
Seven Days' Bills .	½ ,,		
	44 millions		44 millions

In looking at this situation, bearing in mind that there is a full measure of bullion and everything "safe," you must first decide whether 5 millions of Banking Reserve are sufficient for accommodation to the public. If you have regard to the fact that the circulation means the extent of the accommodation, you may think it ample, if not superfluous. If, in spite of the fact that the deposits increase in times of pressure, you desire to create some Reserve against their sudden withdrawals, you may deem this sufficient for the present, *because at any time the Bank may increase it by raising the rate of interest.*

The balance over "first Reserve" still available.

In the meantime, the Bank, by placing 5 millions of securities into the Issue Department, would, by the interest these produce, cover the technical expenses of the issue, and acquire the Reserve of 5 millions in exchange, enabling it, as a set-off, to fully invest the greater portion of capital, rest and deposits. I need not point out to you that in the matter of safety of account to the stockholders, you would have at any time not only the "Reserve of notes in the Banking Department" as assets against the corresponding liability in the Banking Department, but the 5 millions of securities as double assets. If the Reserve were increased from 5 to 10 or 15 millions, with rates of interest of 4½ and 6 per cent., or more, you would be in precisely the same position of balance between liabilities and assets.

The expenses covered by first Reserve.

The same liabilities and assets.

The case must now be shown with less bullion than equal to circulation, say 20 millions :—

LIABILITIES.		ASSETS.	
Notes in circulation £25 millions		Bullion . . . . . £20 millions	
Reserve of notes in Banking Departmt. } 5 „		Securities. . . . 10 „	
£30 millions		£30 millions	

Interest 5 per cent.

ISSUE DEPARTMENT.

LIABILITIES.		ASSETS.	
Capital . . £14½ millions		Reserve of notes . . £5 millions	
Rest . . . . . 3½ „		Gov'ment. Securities 13 „	
Public Deposits . 8 „		Other Securities . . 25½ „	
Other „ . 18½ „		Coin . . . . ½ „	
Seven Days' Bills . ½ „			
£44 millions		£44 millions	

You see that although 10 millions of securities, instead of 5, have passed from the banking to the issue, this would make no difference in the amount of Banking Department investments, and on these the interest earned on "other securities" would be 5 per cent. On the 10 millions of fiduciary issue the gross profit per annum would be £500,000, from which the expenses of £150,000 deducted, there would remain a profit at the rate of £350,000 per annum for division between the State and Bank.

We may further resolve to increase the Reserve, say to 10 millions, 5 millions more of securities passing to the issue. In this case the profit on the fiduciary issue, made at 6¼ per cent., would be at the rate of £975,000 per annum, leaving £825,000 for division between the State and Bank.

If there were but 15 millions of bullion the account might be—

ISSUE DEPARTMENT.

LIABILITIES.		ASSETS.	
Notes in circulation	£25 millions	Bullion	£15 millions
,, in Reserve	10 ,,	Securities . . .	20 ,,
	£35 millions		£35 millions

Interest 9½ per cent.

Example with small stock of bullion.

and the Government profit would increase accordingly.

In all these cases, the transfer of securities from Banking to issue will give room for the same amount in the former, and this would be " naturally " filled, for the Bank would receive either notes or securities in exchange for bullion. For the time being, the total in both departments will thus be in accord with the rise of interest, *i.e.* serve as another natural guide for determining rates.

Now if you can possibly be brought to recognise that the large Reserves which we hold at present in spite of ourselves are not proper, that the constant cry for more is foolish, and if you admit that, by the use of the system here proposed, we can create Reserve as we like, on a perfectly solid and the most conservative basis, you will also perceive that although we may go to any amount, yet there is a wholesome check against extremes. The larger the issue is made, in divergence from bullion, the quicker will bullion come in, but *the larger* becomes also the State's share of profit. Hence the Bank of England practice by this system, founded on the proven effective rule of the poising of interest as shown by table on page 262 ; made absolute by the respective durations of rates, and finally held in superior control by the power of Reserve, must engender a judiciously balanced use of the latter.

The check on unduly large issues.

The whole action will accordingly result in a network of compensation, in which *all* the factors concerned must remain at averages as near as they can

The compensating action of the whole system.

possibly become, with fullest liberty for mutual increase.

I assert, without hesitation, that within a short time after the introduction of this system

The Bank of England

1. Will acquire a stock of bullion of an average sufficient to serve all purposes. The movements in this stock of bullion will be more controllable, and not exceed one-third of the ups and downs to which we are now accustomed.

2. The rates of interest, now varying between extremes of 2 and 12 at the Bank (and $1\frac{1}{2}$ to 15 in the open market), will be more regular, varying, say between 3 and 6 per cent. as utmost extremes. The changes will be less frequent.

3. The Bank will be able to satisfy all the demands of circulation, and legitimate accommodation to the public without inflation of the circulation.

4. The Bank will be in a position to maintain *intact* a regular Reserve, required or supposed to be required for certain contingencies, and by means of raising this Reserve and interest it will be able to guard against all possible contingencies that may occur.

5. The Bank will be enabled to discount bills entirely on the *merits of the bills or securities* themselves, and of the 200 millions of bills in the London Market, it will obtain a regular share of much larger dimensions than it has ever held. The Bank will thus be enabled to take a much more active and steady part in the great business of the country, and give to the nation the real benefit of its immense resources, and make better profits at the same time.

6. The deposits and other business of the Bank are likely to increase considerably.

7. Larger dividends will be paid even without any sensible increase in the deposits. *Larger dividends.*

Bankers and Discount Brokers

8. will be able to carry on a more steady and satisfactory discount business. The larger business to be done by the Bank will not come into competition with them, on the contrary it will expand and regulate the entire field of discounts. The supposition that a larger discount business to be done by the Bank will come into competition with Bankers is a great mischievous fallacy, that which the Bank would do more, can only be a per centage on the whole and would leave ample space. Moreover, the majority of bills taken by the Bank will pass first through the hands of Bankers and Discounters. Still more abominably false is the supposition that Bankers and Brokers now profit from the extreme variations in the rates of interest, and do not care to see them modified. It can be shown not only that they suffer more from the unduly low rates than they profit by higher rates, but that they are compelled to follow the vagaries of the present issue in all that concerns its effects on overtrading, speculation and insecurity. *Advantages to bankers.* *Less competition with Bank.* *A better average of interest.*

9. The discount brokers will be able to obtain legitimate advances from the Bank on first-class paper in a more regular manner, but in most cases it will suit both Bank and brokers at once to discount the bills. *Advantage to discount brokers.*

The General Public

in its turn will profit from this better state of things, the crises and panics will cease, and the power of taxation for the benefit of the nation and its Government, will be enhanced. *Advantages to general public.*

Allegations and promises like these may appear venturesome to those who are hopelessly involved in

Scepticism
for want
of con-
temporary
comparison.
the petty expedients and the scepticism prevalent
under the present system. We are so much accustomed
to the practice of the day, and have such unbounded
faith in the Bank of England and our great prosperity,
that many of us would look upon the strangest
anomalies as matters dictated by providence. But if
there were two Englands, running the same contemporary course, in every way identical, but the one with
the present, the other with this improved bank note
system, the latter would gain a greater advance in
prosperity.

In fact we do not *know what a better* state
of things *would* mean, and those only who fully
realise the bad construction of the present system,
Realisation
of the
strong facts
shown in
this book.
can form an estimate of the harm done by it,
which, were it not for our prosperity generally,
would have ruined the country long ago. In
the beginning of this book I have shown you
. the want of progress of the Bank, and that
since 1844 there has been but a slight increase,
(apparently 15 per cent.), whilst every other institution
in the country, and the commerce in home and international trade has four-folded, or increased by 300
per cent. Here is some standard to judge by, which
Demon-
strating the
grave fault.
does not necessarily compel us to say that the Bank
should also have four-folded its business, but which
certainly entitles us to expect that, for argument sake,
the Bank might have partaken of one-half of this
increase. The difference which this would make in
the accounts of the Bank would be considered a wonderful thing, yet there is nothing to stop the Bank's
progress in that direction but the spirit of blind, if not
criminal, obstinacy, which refuses to give way to patient
investigation. If a proper reform is carried out, a
change will occur in the status of the Bank, in the
interests of our trading community, and the prosperity

of the country of the most agreeable kind. *The history of the development and legislation of this country teems with examples showing that reforms have almost always exceeded sanguine expectations.* Many of our most valuable arrangements, of which, in the field of monetary matters, the Clearing House system is an example, owe their origin to comparatively trifling bits of truth, and are found fraught with unheard-of benefit. The same thing may take place in reference to the matter here considered. England, in adopting this true regulating system, would not only be able to extend its legitimate influence all over the world, but would thereby secure its own legitimate supremacy.

The history of this country teems with the surprisingly beneficial results of reform.

THE COUNTRY BANKERS' ISSUES.*

The proposed reform of the Bank of England note issue can take place without any pressing necessity for immediate reform in the provincial issues. Nevertheless, at some time or another, the country Bankers' issues

Reform of country issues not absolutely required.

---

* In the next Parliamentary enquiry upon the subject of the currency the advocates of the issue of £1 notes will be strongly represented. They may be divided into three classes.

Class 1 wants an issue of £1 notes for the sake of their convenience, and not for the sake of the credit. They say, "Let the Bank of England issue 20 or 30 millions of £1 notes against sovereigns, the bullion Reserve of the Bank will then be stronger!" The fallacy of such a suggestion is obvious, the sovereigns would belong to the note holders, and if the Bank, now unable to keep its stock of bullion at a level, were to rely upon this extra 20 or 30 millions, the confusion would become all the greater. "But," say the advocates of this plan, "the use of paper in lieu of sovereigns is cheaper, the latter, if deposited at the Bank, will be saved from loss by abrasion and wear, they will remain at full weight!"

Here a striking example of the bold ignorance with which financial schemers come forward, will be made manifest to you. *The*

must be dealt with, as an anomaly which, at the present time of more refined ideas as to money, requires correction. The quasi-legitimate plea advanced in favour of these issues is, that they furnish the convenient £1 note to the districts where they are current. It has been alleged even that the Scotch people think the notes of their banks safer than sovereigns. Idiosyncrasies of

---

technical expenses attending the manufacture and administration of Bank note issues *far exceed the loss* per annum by *abrasion of coin.*

Professor Jevons has calculated that on the average a sovereign in circulation becomes light in eighteen years, *i.e.*, that by that time it loses the legal three-quarters grain and the right of tender. This calculation I have verified by researches as to the sums coined by the Mint since 1816, the light coin taken in at the Bank, the exports and imports, and the proportion of light coins remaining in circulation. Substantially I agree with Mr. Jevons although I would extend the period to twenty years. But I will go further than he does. Instead of assuming that on the 123·274 grains 0·750 grain is lost, I will take a whole grain, and allow one-quarter grain for costs of recoinage, so that, within twenty years 1·232 grain, or, say, 1 per cent. are absorbed. This would show that the annual wear and tear on coin costs *one-twentieth per cent.* The issue of our Bank notes cost £180,000 (exclusive of the £195,000 paid to the State) on a circulation taken as high as 30 million pounds. Let us reduce this, by economies, to £150,000, the annual cost of the issue would accordingly be equal to *one-half per cent.*

The annual technical cost of the Bank of England note, the lowest description of which is £5, is accordingly *ten times as high* as that occasioned by *the wear of gold coin.* The use of 30 millions of sovereigns would cost £15,000 a year, and the commonest description of plain machine-made Bank note paper (not water marked) for 30 millions of notes would cost that ; machine-made water mark paper would cost more than double, and hand-made paper five times as much. The engraving and printing must all be carefully done, and when actively used, the notes would require renewing on the average at least every two years. Above this comes the administration necessarily connected with such an issue, and if anything like fair order is to be maintained, far from the great care and attention now paid by the Bank to its notes, the administration on so large a mass of £1 notes would cost much more than the

that kind must not be listened to, but *the convenience of £1 notes may be recognised* apart from them. It has indeed been proposed that the Bank of England should issue £1 notes, but there is no valid reason why this should now be done; the communities in and around London are so much accustomed to the more healthy system of £5 notes and upwards, that the

present issue. The doings of the country and Scotch Bankers, with their small individual issues (the expenses of which also exceed wear on coin considerably), cannot guide us in this great national issue. It is only through the admirable attention bestowed by the proper departments in the Bank, and the fair expenditure incurred, that we hear so little of forgeries. The technical expenses of the Bank of France and the American issues are higher even than those of the Bank of England, and the veriest *rag-issue* costs much more in paper, printing and administration than the annual abrasion of coin.

It is to be hoped that these facts, easily verified, will dispose of the idea above-mentioned. In any reform of the Bank of England issue provision might be made for a few millions of £1 notes, it being distinctly recognised that this is not done for the purpose of credit, or on account of cheapness, but the use of such notes would be confined to *convenient remittance* by letter (in lieu of post office orders). That is all that can be said in their favour, their heavy cost, and the danger of letter stealing far outweigh even this plea. For all and for every other purpose of the circulation the actual sovereign remains the most natural, and for its maintenance the most economical of the mediums of exchange of the value of £1 each.

Class 2 of the advocates of £1 notes, represented by several English, and chiefly Scotch Bankers, want to issue 20 or 30 millions (or more or less) of credit notes, or notes backed by the State debt. In the course of this book I have several times alluded to these schemers, but so persistent are their demands, that you may well listen to stronger special arguments against them. As you have learned, our circulation now amounts to 161½ millions—with which the business of the country is done. Now if 30 millions of credit notes forced their way *into this circulation*, either of the following must happen :—

introduction of a £1 note would be a novelty of no particular merit.

Suggestion to satisfy this plea. For the country districts, habituated to the use of these notes, the plea of the convenience of the £1 note remains valid, and, in order to satisfy this, it stands to reason that the issuing Bankers cannot do so at their own expense, viz., by issuing notes only against

---

(1.) Our circulation must either remain at 161½ millions (for the moment), when, in order to give room for 30 millions of notes, 30 millions of gold must be exported, or

(2.) Our circulation must increase from 161½ to 191½ millions? What will be the consequence in this case? Do you suppose that this will give an impulse to our external trade? Can our production rise in the same proportions? Certainly not. The only effect then which such an illegitimate addition to our currency would have, is that of *raising our internal prices artificially!* producing what is termed "inflation." Nobody would be the better for it, but we should certainly lose our power to compete with other nations in manufacturing; our exports would cease, our imports increase, the foreigner would take payment in gold. It is for this reason that Austria, with its fine manufactures, is no international trader; it is for this reason that the United States (see foot note on pages 85, 86 and 87) are in the mire, and that in spite of their splendid resources, the curse of pauperism invades the land! Think what this means, in a country where the over abundance of soil need but be scratched to produce a crop; where mechanical ingenuity is at the highest pitch of development. The American Government seems to have recognised now to what is due the drain on the national resources, and that (although it has always held a fair metallic reserve) the issue of notes, based on Government security, must now be contracted. By no other means can the present extravagant level of prices be reduced so as to moderate imports of foreign goods, and promote the export of home produce. That this makes trade flat, especially the import business, is obvious, and the ordeal in the lowering of prices of American goods must also be gone through, until, from this lower level, the industry and ingenuity again increase, when the chance of mitigating against the present minus balance, and that of ultimately liquidating it, will arise. So far the United States have not much contracted the issue, they have only refused to issue more than 400 millions of legal tender notes, dollars, and an equal amount of "national currency"

sovereigns; some allowance must be made to them for credit issue sufficient to cover the expenses. The whole of these credit issues amount to £15,800,000, a sum which, at 4 per cent., would yield upwards of £600,000 per annum profit to the Bankers; the technical cost of printing and administering the issues (conducted on a much cheaper plan than the Bank of

---

notes (the latter under some combination with "deposits" which have no relation to the question of currency at all), yet this limitation has already produced crisis and seemingly bad trade. For it is in the nature of such issues to crave for more and more notes and more inflation, the mere standstill already produces violent reaction and conflict. Hence there are many people in the United States who harass the Government to make more issue, and according to latest accounts free Banking is likely to be introduced. The ultimate unavoidable reaction will now become far more violent, in geometrical degrees of progression, without taking into account the delay of the settlement, during which the present state of things would have continued and become intensified. The cry for more issue in the United States, as well as in other countries, naturally proceeds from those who would have to make or to receive them in the first instance. No true equivalent is at the bottom of such notes, even if made by the State for State-payments. The first issuers or recipients make the first large undue profit ; the second and third participate in lesser degrees, until, finally, the circulation is forced to accept them at par and to bear their influence on prices. That this suits the book of issuing banks, contractors, financiers and others, is evident, and the immense fortunes made thereby are proofs of this suitability. So in other over-issuing States, there are large individual fortunes made through the original and the subsequent play of prices. But, and all the evidence shows this, although in America and elsewhere these large accumulations take place, the drain on the resources of a country goes on (see foot-note, on pages 85 to 87), until at last the goose with the golden eggs can lay no longer, and the fortunes themselves lose their vantage ground. The general principle here shown, holds good in all degrees, whether the premium on gold be 10 or 50 per cent., whether in America, Russia, Austria, Turkey or Hayti (where 500 paper dollars are worth 1 dollar silver). The "return to specie payments" becomes more and more difficult. England, after her successful wars in 1816, received large cash payments

England issue) may not exceed £50,000 or £60,000. Now, if these Bankers were authorised to issue on credit, say, one-third of the present sum, or 5 millions —yielding £200,000 per annum—they would not only cover their costs, but gain a profit large enough* to induce them to continue the present issues, under the

* Or temporary Reserve.

from France, her immense acquisitions and political superiority enabled the fullest development to take place. Nevertheless, without the spirit of abnegation, without that refined "respectability" in household matters which yet distinguishes so large a portion of English society, the recovery would have been scarcely possible. So may French thriftiness soon recover the losses of the late war. But neither the Americans nor other nations seem to be aware of the great moral lesson which this matter involves, they continue in extravagant imports and prices, neither the people nor their leaders possess the healthy instinct which bound Englishmen in their aims to balance the account, and then led to England's "international wealth." In the coming struggle for "returning to specie payments" of all the over-issuing States, the advantage of England's position will become all the clearer.

In this country the recommendations to issue these notes come chiefly from Scotland. They are profitable to Bankers, and with the wholesome restrictions imposed by the law, these issues *so far appear* to have done much good to the issuers. Fortunately, the *authorised* issue of Scotch Banks is but 2¾ millions, or about 1⅔ per cent. on the mass of 161½ millions in circulation. This small portion does not affect us much, and it is even possible that, floating on the strength of our whole national wealth, the system may present a false appearance of superiority. Many people are of the opinion that the thriftiness of the Scotch, the careful and refined methods of banking in Scotland, and not its currency system, are the cause of the fair appearance of matters. It is also said that a Scotchman prefers a bank note to a sovereign; but Scotch idiosyncrasies are not those of the world at large, and give no reliable foundation. Indeed it is just possible that any mishap in the Scotch system will make the sovereign *the favourite for ever*. Such rapid changes in popular conceptions frequently occur when matters, slightly tainted with delusion, break down once. And if the Scotch system were let out of its bounds, or became the standard for England, we might

proviso that, for the balances issued by them above the 5 millions, *they ought to hold gold coin.* The plea of having 16 millions of £1 notes would thus be satisfied. On issues on gold coin.

The true meaning of this must be clearly understood, for should this matter come under discussion in Parliament, the great cry of the defenders of this system will be the plea of convenience of the £1 note The true meaning of this improvement and the margin for expenses.

---

experience this much quicker than we now think possible. It has been alleged that the Scotch demand for a £1 note issue is owing to the pressing needs of Bankers. There is no necessity to go this length for reasons to combat the fallacies which the system involves, for these culminate in—

Class 3, also Scotch, which actually starts the proposition *to do away with gold,* and to adopt pure credit notes of £1, "backed by the government debt." There are many specimens of Scotch views on this matter. I have now before me a publication on "The Bank of England, the Bank Acts and the Currency," by "Cosmopolite," most ingeniously and forcibly written, analysing the Bank accounts—giving figures and schemes—but all is treated from one stand-point, expressed in the following sentences, casually occurring :

"A metallic currency for internal purposes is one of the fallacies which will disappear before long."

"The true basis of credit is the National Debt," "let the Government Debt be the primary basis of the circulation ! ! "

"What objection is there to the use of such £1 notes ? " the writer asks, and answers himself—"There are none."

The above remarks, which I have made on Class 1 and Class 2, may state some of the objections as worthy of consideration—but to opinions such as held by " Cosmopolite " they appear, no doubt, trumpery.

"Cosmopolite" must be told that his suggestions are not new. The literature of all countries teems with precisely the same thing, and has done so for many generations. Metallic currency has been condemned, as only fit for fools, by thousands of writers before him, and the world has not yet recognised " such truth." Yet there can be but *one* truth, it is either Gold or Paper—one must be supreme by the laws of nature. The assertion of a truth does not merely depend on human resistance by way of human folly—where such a truth is

to the population, to farmers, and others, in the ranges of the respective Banks—a cry which may overwhelm the interests concerning the valuation. The mere convenience part of the matter can be met by an allowance of 5 millions of issue (or less), and for the purpose of satisfying this plea, in preference to a total abolition of issue systems which have a

---

absolute (and nothing but absoluteness will do in this case), it *asserts itself with unerring* mathematical *force*, in spite of all endeavours to prevent it,—and so such issues would have asserted themselves and their superiority, even if they had never been tried before. To this plain broad idea of truth as a natural principle, "Cosmopolite" must first rise, before he is fit to descend again to practical trial. Descending to such practice, "Cosmopolite" will find that the thing has been tried, over and over again, in many countries, with the direst results, and surely, after the many chances the system has thus had, its truth ought to have asserted itself; men are not such outrageous fools as to refuse so cheap and comfortable a method of conducting monetary matters.

The proposition to make the National Debt the basis is also very old. The Government of a country is nothing else but ourselves, and all schemes of currency attempted on the sole " credit " of " ourselves " differ in so far from Mr. Micawber's I. O. U.'s as they lead ultimately to bloody revolutions and social ruin. The worst of the present issues admit at least that metallic money must be in the mixture, and the proportion of fiduciary issue determines the degree of the inferiority of the whole. "Cosmopolite" mistakes the force of the one for that of the other (like many others have done before him), and the limited field of Scotch experience he takes for the great international world. Social democrats and young economists, before they have learned the first elements of financial science, are very prolific in similar ideas, and the proposals made by "Cosmopolite," and many others, differ from the "young" ones in so far only as they are accompanied by more or less ingenious attempts at putting down and arguing with figures derived from a practice with a small per centage, and the cobbling up of larger figures based on the great practice of the whole, the very foundation of which is to be utterly reversed. "Cosmopolite" attempts to lay down figures for the circulation. How are these to be kept? Will the notes have the same par value as gold? "Cosmopolite,"

remnant of vested right, this course suggests a compromise to which country Bankers must yield, whilst the allowance of 5 millions of credit notes is not so serious an element of disturbance in our valuation as the present 16 millions (15.8).

In all other respects the authorised credit issue of these 15.8 millions is a blot upon our

The Act of 1856 an insult to Peel.

---

himself, no doubt, will be as pleased as Punch with them, take them at par, and expect others to do so. But, alas for human folly,—for many people may still prefer gold,—namely the *unconditional currency* (independent of Government Debt, and valuable abroad), called "sovereigns;" hence they will ask higher prices in paper so as to guard themselves against the changing condition of Government. This is, unfortunately perhaps, an element which "Cosmopolite" must take into account. More notes must accordingly be issued, in order to meet the rights of these unbelievers in paper money, and inflation will set in at once. But should the light of "Cosmopolite" dawn upon these heathens, and all agree upon its brightness, inflation would nevertheless take place. The natural neutral indicator of gold, upon whose action depends the equalisation of trade between ourselves and other nations, and the ultimate determination and accord of prices by increase or decrease of our own numerical store for internal business, being lost, what is to be the guide for the requirements of the circulation? Shall Government refuse to grant more issue, or what shall guide it for the contingencies arising? The Government could not refuse the cry for more notes, and the neutral standard being lost, other loose indications must be adopted. What shall these indications be? Increase of population, increase of trade, of prices, occurrence of accidents, or what? Shall the Chancellor of the Exchequer or bankers determine it? Or shall the *demand* have its rights? Any miscalculation would produce inflation, and if the demand had its way, what a demand there would be!! When inflation has once commenced the craving for more cannot be arrested by natural laws of supply and demand, on goes the absorption and the accumulation. Whereas $161\frac{1}{2}$ millions of money now circulate in the country, of which 145 are metallic money, there would be 200, 300, 400 or more of paper money. The rise in prices would not only not benefit us internally, but would destroy our commerce outwards; and ultimately the system would break down to revert again to metal. Of all these

legislation, and contrary to the spirit of the Act of 1844. The virtual repeal of the clauses concerning their liquidation, by the Act of June 1856, is an insult to the memory of Sir Robert Peel. Having (see pages 108 to 112) in circulation in this country 161 millions of money, it stands to reason that the 16 millions of country issue force their way into it so as to drive 16

---

matters—plain in theory, confirmed in practical history, visible in their due measure in the American and other issues at this day—the proposers of schemes of this sort have not the slightest notion, nor would they be likely to gain it, until we had gratified them with the adoption of their happy conceptions, and the whole result was before them. The game is not worth so large a candle, and the British public may prefer to leave Cosmopolite and kindred spirits to lament over its blindness.

In the Parliamentary enquiries it is to be hoped that the sound, simple, English common sense, will not allow itself to be long hampered with these very old, yet ever recurring, ideas, and in justice to many Scotch economists and bankers, it must be mentioned that they are also opposed to such absurd schemes. It is possible that this book may strengthen the hands of the opponents of such false suggestions by directing attention to the real fault in our otherwise so healthy metallic currency system.

There is yet another set of proposals to be disposed of. Many writers on the subject of issues recommend that the " Mint " should issue notes or certificates or other documents. They make all sorts of clever inventions as to the Mint's proceedings, advocate the establishment of a "note department," and a "treasury department.' Some of them want to convert the Mint into some kind of issuing bank, in total ignorance that no issue can exist without connection with actual current mercantile business, with all its attendant contingencies and risks, and that neither the " Mint " nor " Somerset House " can make issues of notes without becoming *de facto* bankers. Others make some kind of combination between Bank and the Mint as to "promises," "certificates" and *hocus pocus* generally.

All these absurd proposals originate in the ignorance as to practical facts, and the awe with which the ignorant regard the, to them, mysterious doings and the supposed power at the Mint. Although

millions of bullion out of the country. Nobody has the advantage of this but the country Bankers. The nation, as a whole, loses 16 millions of gold, to regain which it must make struggles in times of pressure. If these issues were once abolished, the regular industry and commerce of the country would soon replace them by gold, for they are but a percentage on the several hundred millions of our business, and a comparatively slight turn in our favour of the Exchanges would give us the gold instead. Vested rights and privileges, granted to the disadvantage of others, do not establish a principle for their maintenance ; on the contrary, modern legislation adopts the principle of

---

certain mints issue mint-certificates against gold sent to them for conversion, which, when the Mint is busy, postpone the delivery of coin for several days, such certificates are nothing more than all ordinary contracts for a certain amount of money on a certain day. In all and every other proceeding, the Mint is but a manufactory, which converts bar gold into coin. It differs from other manufactories inasmuch as it has no capital, no stock, no initiative whatever. Like the country miller, who grinds the farmers' corn into flour for them, so it awaits its customers, but, unlike the flour miller, it has not even the faculty to buy its corn, viz., gold, from the customer.

Its sole aim and purpose is that of using the best mechanical process for making regular coin from irregular quantities of rough gold brought by the owner. The best machinery, the best workmen and superintendent, is all that concerns the action of the Mint. Some portion of our coinage is even made by *private* firms, to whom the State delivers the metal to turn into coin, under proper control. If any hocus pocus as to issue were possible with the public Mint, it ought to be equally possible with the private firms, whose machinery can make coins and medals by way of contract.

It is to be hoped that the many clever inventions and combinations brought forward in connection with the "Mint," will at once be repudiated by the State—they are but the result of gross ignorance of facts coupled with fanciful conceptions—a combination which leads to the most obstinate "authorative" (?) suggestions.

absolute abolition. What can otherwise be more absurd than to give the right of such issues to certain Banks and Bankers, and to withhold it from others? Are Banks and Bankers so distinct from other trades—financial people, merchants, and workers for profit—that the State should grant them privileges, to which any firm or individual may be entitled, because they choose to call themselves Bankers?

Is proof of the need of reform.

The most serious thing connected with these issues is their baneful influence on the valuation. They give false prices, and when, in case of crises, they are supposed to be available, just the contrary happens; the issuing Bankers draw in the notes, and thus increase the embarrassment of the Bank of England. Imagine what would take place if the right of issue were conferred upon other Banks, Bankers, and individuals! How much should they issue? It will be obvious to you that our present 127 millions of gold (gold coin and bullion) would leave the country to be replaced by 200, 300, or 400 millions of notes. What would be their effect on prices? Would any body work the harder for it? would our industry profit? Nothing of the kind. On the contrary, there would be more laziness and more luxury at first, until the smash set in. If the right of issue were confined to Bankers and merchants alone; there are more than 2,000 (including branches) of the former, and upwards of 20,000 wealthy firms of the latter, so that if on the average each one had the privilege of issuing but £6,000 the aggregate would be 132 millions. If Banks and Bankers alone were to issue, they would each put in circulation about £60,000, on which they could certainly earn interest—would this earning of interest by one set of men be a compensation for the inevitable ruin of the whole nation? Although there are many persons who recommend such a course for

The damage to our valuation.

England, there is happily no chance of their being listened to. The principle, however, is maintained in this country by allowing the issue of country Banks to continue. The mischief done by them is only reduced in proportion; its effects are nevertheless visible in the many bitter struggles between our vigorous prosperity and the system of valuation of which these notes form a part.

You may possibly agree with me that the country Bankers' argument in favour of their profits must give way to the improvement in the valuation, whilst their plea for the convenience of the £1 note can be met by permitting them to issue an amount amply sufficient to pay expenses. The recommendations which I have made in this book concern principally the Bank of England itself, and they can be carried out without any sensible disturbance in the present Act. But if the full subject of our banking law be brought forward again, the whole Act might undergo a revision. Enlightened statesmen must deal with this matter.

Enlightened men must deal with the whole subject.

CONCLUSION.

I have received so much encouragement from all quarters that, according to suggestions made to me, I have not hesitated to address this appeal to you—the stockholders of the Bank; and I am in hopes that there are among you gentlemen of high intelligence able to appreciate the views here advanced, and of influence sufficient to cause inquiry into their validity. The stock of the Bank of England is a magnificent property, whose value requires the application of the most refined principles of just economy. Beyond this, the action of the Bank of England is so identified with the interests of the country, the crises and panics now occurring are so injurious, not only to the mercantile

The matter here elucidated a fair subject for inquiry.

classes, but to the industrial classes at large (and consequently injurious to the prosperity of all) that we might for once give up the blind admiration of the Act of 1844, and the reverend contemplation of the Bank of England, and subject the system under which it works, with the results shown to you in facts and figures, to a scrutiny unfettered by the traditions and dogmas of bygone times. And when, as you see, this investigation will lead to amendments which will not upset the Act, but which can actually be reconciled with one of its provisions, there should not be much diffidence in entering upon this investigation.

If you review the whole of the suggestions made since 1847—their extreme divergencies of opinion, from " no issue " to " every body's " issue, their absurdity, &c., and all the useless endeavours made in Parliament—you will find that the principles laid down here give a point of view which has hitherto been overlooked, and you might feel disposed to ask the Government for an investigation of the " fitness " of what I have endeavoured to convey clearly to your minds. You will now also understand that these matters could not be brought out excepting by an exhaustive treatise like this, although the subject may now appear a very simple one, as it so often happens when a deep error has been dug out.

Finally, I must ask you to refer again to the preface of this work, wherein I repudiate all intention to say anything unfavourable as regards the Directors of the Bank of England. The high position which they hold lifts them above undue criticism, as well as above the praise of a writer on the Bank of England system. They frequently suffer the wrong of abuse, whereas in reality the system and its anomalies with which they battle should be blamed. When such system is reformed it is quite obvious that under the charge of the highest mercantile authorities, representing, so to speak, the degree of civilisation at which we have arrived, it will become perfect. This holds good, not only here in England, but in all other countries where the commercial and social financial interests centre in a leading institution, under a council selected from the most prominent men in commerce. Their success with a proper system certain.

In the preface to this book I have also made allusions to previous publications on this subject. Other publications of the author

One of these, " Reform of the Bank of England Note Issue," a Statistical Critique of the Operations of the Bank Act of 1844," is the substance of a paper read before the Statistical Society; the other, " Letter to Mr. Gladstone on the Reform of the Bank Act," embodies the former by way of abstract.

The first publication treats the matter in a way more suitable to a scientific society, where many things are understood by common consent. Many of its readers thought that the want of progress of the Bank of England had not been brought forward sufficiently, and suggested to me to write the book now before you, with the special view of bringing this matter into greater prominence. Nevertheless, the publication above referred to, contains valuable tables, showing the averages of circulation of fiduciary issue—the idle Reserves or idle Deposits. The table of special interest is that which demonstrates the validity of the rule as to the lowest practical interest, spoken of on page 253. In addition to these, complete returns of the Bank's weekly statements from 1844 to 1872 are given, with separate columns for bills discounted, temporary advances, Bankers' balances, &c., and rates of interest, so that the inquirer will find ample and useful material for the confirmation and examination of what has here been advanced. Contain matters in support of this book.

Of these publications 300 copies have been reserved by me, for the purpose of gratis distribution to readers of this book, who wish further to follow up the subject. They may apply to the address at foot, enclosing three stamps for postage. In conclusion, I declare my willingness to answer enquiries and to correspond with parties competent to discuss the subject of the Bank of England issue.

The author willing to correspond with competent parties.

ERNEST SEYD.

1A Princes Street, Mansion House,
London, E.C.

OTHER PUBLICATIONS BY THE AUTHOR.

"California and its Resources." 8vo. 168 pp. Trübner and Co., Paternoster Row, London, 1858.

"On the Establishment of an Anglo-Californian Bank and a Refinery of the Precious Metals in San Francisco." 8vo. 93 pp. (Private Issue.) London, 1861.

"Bullion and Foreign Exchanges Theoretically and Practically Considered." 8vo. 700 pp. Effingham Wilson, Royal Exchange, London, 1868.

"The Question of Seignorage and Charge for Coining." 8vo. 59 pp. Effingham Wilson, Royal Exchange, London, 1868.

"The Depreciation of Labour and Property which would follow the Demonitisation of Silver." 8vo. 109 pp. Effingham Wilson, London, 1869.

"Letters to the *Times*." See the "Gold Coinage Controversy," republished for private circulation by the Bank of England, 1869.

"Universal Coinage and Variations in Foreign Exchanges." Read before the Statistical Society. See *Journal* of the Society for March 1870.

"Enquête sur la Question Monetaire." Séance du 31 Mars 1870. Evidence before the Imperial Commission, published by the French Government.

"On Currency Laws, and their Effects on Pauperism." Read before the Statistical Society. See *Journal* of the Society for March 1871.

"Die Münz-Währungs und Bankfragen in Deutschland." 8vo. 204 pp. Bädeker, Elberfeld (Prussia), 1871.

"Bemerkungen ueber das neue deutsche Münzgesetz. 8vo. 47 pp. Bädeker, Elberfeld (Prussia), 1871.

"Suggestions in reference to the Metallic Currency of the United States of America." 8vo. 253 pp. Trübner and Co., Paternoster Row, London, 1871.

"Improvements in the Process of Coining." Read before the Society of Arts. See *Journal* of the Society for the 26th January 1872.

"The London Banking and Bankers' Clearing House System." 8vo. 68 pp. Cassell, Petter and Galpin, 1872. (Translation in French, E. Guyot, Rue de Pacheco 12, Brussels.)

"Reform of the Bank of England Note Issue." Harrison and Sons, St. Martin's Lane, London, 1873.

"Letter to the Right Hon. W. E. Gladstone, M.P., &c., on Reform of the Bank of England Note Issue." 1873.

www.ingramcontent.com/pod-product-compliance
Lightning Source LLC
Chambersburg PA
CBHW021032030726
47496CB00006B/1500